T0333208

A HISTORY OF
WHITBY

'Girls Skaning Mussels'; a photograph taken in the 1890s near Tate Hill Pier by Frank Sutcliffe. This perennial task had to be performed by the womenfolk, ready for baiting the fishermen's long lines. The collecting, skaning and baiting of mussels were regular and major preoccupations of fishermen's families. Supplies of mussels from the nearby scaurs were quickly exhausted by demand and fishermen often had to buy them from Boston or even the West Coast. Hanging from the wall can be seen a wicker 'skep' used for carrying the coiled long line with its wicked barbed hooks. The Sutcliffe Gallery

A HISTORY OF
WHITBY

Andrew White

Phillimore

First published in 1993 by Phillimore & Co. Ltd
Second edition 2004
This paperback edition published 2019

The History Press
The Mill, Brimscombe Port
Stroud, Gloucestershire, GL5 2QG

© Dr Andrew White, 1993, 2004, 2019

The right of Dr Andrew White to be identified as the Author
of this work has been asserted in accordance with the
Copyright, Designs and Patents Act 1988.

All rights reserved. No part of this book may be reprinted
or reproduced or utilised in any form or by any electronic,
mechanical or other means, now known or hereafter invented,
including photocopying and recording, or in any information
storage or retrieval system, without the permission in writing
from the Publishers.

British Library Cataloguing in Publication Data.
A catalogue record for this book is available from the British
Library.

ISBN 978-0-7509-8987-9

Printed and bound in Great Britain by
TJ International Ltd, Padstow, Cornwall

Contents

LIST OF ILLUSTRATIONS

Frontispiece: 'Girls Skaning Mussels'; a photograph taken in the 1890s

ACKNOWLEDGEMENTS

All the illustrations are by the author or from the author's collection with the following exceptions:

Bodleian Library, Oxford, 63; Hull Maritime Museum, 99; The *Illustrated London News*, 19, 78, 84, 103; Liverpool Museum, 75; Proprietors of *Punch*, 107, 108, 109; Prof. P. A. Rahtz, 56; Frank Meadow Sutcliffe, Hon. F.R.P.S. copyright The Sutcliffe Gallery, 1 Flowergate, Whitby, N.Yorks. (by agreement with Whitby Literary & Philosophical Society), frontispiece and 77; Whitby Literary & Philosophical Society, 36, 39, 40, 41, 72, 74, 76, 89, 93, 94, 95, 116, 117, 118; Whitby Public Library, 53; Redrawn from the 60-inch Ordnance Survey map of 1852, 20, 35.

This book could not have been written without the help and advice of a number of people. My first debt is to those great pioneers of Whitby history, Lionel Charlton, Dr George Young, Richard Weatherill and Canon J. C. Atkinson.

Then there are those friends and relations who have produced sheaves of postcards and press cuttings without which so many small but important facts might have escaped; my late aunt, Miss J.H. Thompson, Mrs V. Ash, and Mr M. Blaylock. My late mother, Mrs Margaret White, read the first draft with a native's critical eye and also lent me many family papers which add an extra dimension to several issues, while my father and brother offered advice on the shipping section.

At the Whitby Literary & Philosophical Society I should like to thank successive librarians for help in locating items in the Kendall Room at Whitby Museum and in particular the courteous and efficient Keeper, Mr W.C. Harrison, and his colleagues the Curator of Maps, Mr H.L. Fleming, and Mr W. Leng for their prompt and helpful responses to my numerous enquiries and requests for copies of material in their care. I am grateful to their successors in 2004 as well, especially the Joint Keepers, Roger L. and J. Graham Pickles, and Christiane Kroebel, Hon. Librarian. In 2018 I offer thanks to their successors as well.

At the Liverpool Museums Myra Brown kindly provided useful reference material, while Steven Tomlinson at the Bodleian Library, Oxford, helped with Stukeley material. Elizabeth Melrose at North Yorkshire County Libraries found me appropriate trade directories, while the superb library of the Society of Antiquaries of London provided access to many obscure and otherwise inaccessible volumes. I have been brought up to date on the latest archaeological discoveries by several people, especially Rachel Newman and Richard Fraser, for which I am very grateful. I owe thanks too for a long and useful correspondence on Whitby pictures with Cliff Thornton. Christine Workman was helpful on Richard Ripley.

Finally, I would like to thank my wife, Janette, and my three children, Susannah, Annabel and Thomas, for allowing me to work relatively undisturbed and for putting up with my preoccupation and writing in every minute of spare time during the latter half of 1991, and the former while I was revising the text in early 2004. I wish to dedicate this third edition to the memory of our elder daughter Susannah, who loved Whitby.

I offer this as my small homage to a town I have known since earliest infancy. I hope it finds favour with an exacting readership.

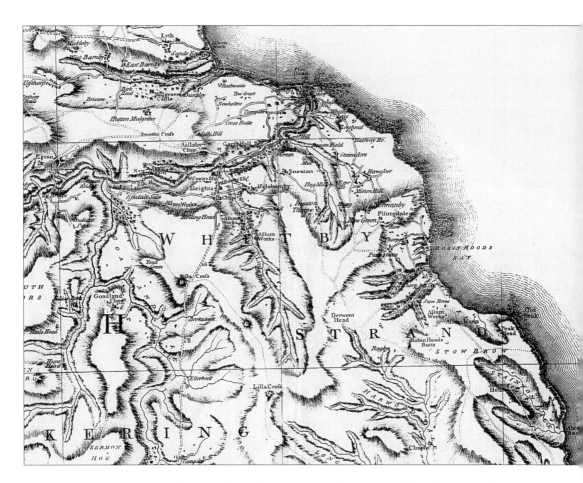

1   *The environs of Whitby, from Jeffrey's map of Yorkshire, 1775. Although this map does not use contours it is still apparent that steep rocky cliffs, high moors and deeply-cut rivers like the Esk and its tributaries all contributed to the isolation of Whitby. The sea was the only practicable access for many centuries. Among man-made features it is the alum-mines, both coastal and inland, which demand attention.*

Introduction

Whitby lies on the North Yorkshire coast between the Tees and the Humber. Here, in the shadow of the ancient abbey, the river Esk empties into the North Sea between high cliffs.

The Esk is tidal still as far as Ruswarp Dam and at low tide presents a narrow channel between sandbanks but at high tide there is a broad expanse of water which has long offered a safe haven to shipping, one of the very few on this coast. The harbour itself and the mouth of the Esk occupy an ancient geological fault. On the east side the cliff is tall and rocky, with alternating layers of shale, sandstone and clay. On the west side of the harbour the cliff is much lower and very largely a capping of boulder clay over sandstone. This has made it very unstable and a number of attempts have been made in recent years to protect the foot of the cliff from erosion. Both cliffs are being eroded quite rapidly and it is thought that several hundred yards of the cliff top have been lost to the sea since the abbey was first established, with a consequent loss of early remains.

Eastwards the cliffs are cut back in a series of notches, fronted by the Scaur, an area of shale and rocks. Saltwick Nab, which closes the view to the east, is a low promontory whose appearance owes much to the activities of the alum-workers, and traces of a small harbour contrived out of blocks of stone still survive on the shore to the east of the Nab. Westwards start the Sands, one of Whitby's most popular features. The cliff is not vertical here; much of it has been cut back to an angle of rest. There are several rocky outcrops such as First and Second Nab, while further to the west are groups of rocks projecting down to low tide level, known as Lector Rocks. The Sands stretch on westwards to Upgang, Newholm Beck, and Sandsend, where the Eastrow and Thordisa Becks enter, and end with the great rocky headlands of Sandsend Ness and Kettleness.

On the east cliff a royal monastery was established in the mid-seventh century, ruled over for many years by the Abbess Hilda, herself a princess of the Northumbrian royal house. This monastery, called Streanaeshalch, was exceedingly powerful and its influence must have spread far beyond the little fishing town that grew up at its feet. Destruction in the ninth or tenth century by Viking raiders, however, left the site in ruins until the visit of a monk of Evesham, called Reinfrid, in the early years after the Norman Conquest. The monastery was refounded and became once more important not only as a religious centre but also as an economic power, owning a fishing-fleet and widespread properties.

After the Dissolution of the monasteries the abbey was pillaged for its stone and the gaunt ruins suffered the winds and storms of a wild coastal position. Today the ruins are consolidated and in the care of English Heritage and form a dramatic backdrop to the town.

Immediately below the abbey, on the edge of the cliff, lies the parish church. Its Norman origins are immediately visible from the outside but nothing can prepare one for the feast within. The whole of the interior is crammed with seats, box-pews lined with red or green baize, and galleries everywhere. The church served a huge parish with numerous small rural townships, each of which had its own pews. Carpenters in the 17th and 18th centuries fitted it out in a purely domestic style, plain and infinitely appealing, with tall clear glazed windows and staircases running hither and thither up to the galleries. It is like no other church and what a miracle it is that no Victorian restorer chose to destroy its unique atmosphere!

Down below on the harbourside we must mentally peel away the accretions of centuries to visualise the original appearance. On the east side there is a large area of sand known as Collier Hope. Further up, where the bridge now crosses, was probably a natural narrowing of the river. Above it the harbour opened out, with two great sandbanks called High and Low Bell. On the west entered the Bagdale Beck, once a considerable stream. Where it joined the harbour was a wide opening between sandbanks called the Slike, which is now marked on a smaller scale by the dock at Dock End.

On the other side of the river, and further up, was the mouth of the Spital Beck, named from the hospital which stood here in the Middle Ages. Both of these becks continue to run, although the Spital Beck is constricted in its course and the Bagdale Beck is culverted and runs unseen below Bagdale and into the dock. Further up still is the bend in the river known as Larpool, beloved of many artists who chose to frame their views of the town from here.

Considerable changes have occurred to this original appearance. At the harbour mouth a succession of piers has been built since the 16th century in order to encourage the Esk to scour a deep channel and to hold back storm surges and gales from the north. In the harbour area itself the sands by the riverside have been colonised by building out on piles, creating a number of new streets and reducing the width of the harbour. From time to time evidence comes to light of these piles and the former marine character of the areas on which they stand. At Larpool the river begins to be affected by the railway viaduct and the diversions created when the Whitby & Pickering Railway arrived here in the 1830s. Ruswarp Dam forms an artificial limit to the tidal range of the river and originally served to create a head of water for the mill here.

Whitby's natural harbour gave it early importance as a port for fishing boats and as a place of refuge. By the early years of the 18th century vast numbers of coal-carrying vessels were passing each day on their passage between the Tyne or Wear and the Thames. When storms threatened, Whitby was one of the few safe places on this generally rocky and inhospitable coast. From 1702 a toll on passing ships paid for harbour improvements and these in turn gave rise to an important shipbuilding trade. Whitby's lack of a hinterland and poor access by road made sure that it could never develop as a manufacturing town and while ship ownership was a significant economic activity in the town very little in the way of locally made goods was ever carried in those ships. Prosperity during the late 17th and 18th centuries has left Whitby with a very distinctive legacy of buildings and, indeed, much of its atmosphere.

Despite some features of its geographical position and because of others, Whitby developed a very large share of the nation's ship-owning, especially among transports for the navy and colliers, and a proud name for shipbuilding. Moreover the associated port trades and the inshore fishing industry, together with the very large number of deep-sea mariners, meant that Whitby's prosperity hinged to a very marked degree on things maritime.

In the 1830s a railway was constructed to overcome some of Whitby's difficulties in communicating inland. This was not like any other railway but one which was until 1847 entirely worked by horses, with an inclined plane at Beckhole to carry it up to the higher levels of the moors above Goathland. Indeed, it was these wild moors which cut Whitby off from inland towns and determined its history.

The railway brought with it a new commodity – visitors – especially after the line was altered for steam traction and was joined to the growing national network. Up on the West Cliff, hitherto a series of grassy fields, a complex of smart new terraces and a crescent began to take shape, under the influence of the railway baron George Hudson. These new houses were specifically designed to accommodate visitors, generally of the more well to do sort, since Whitby was becoming a resort for the middle classes who were attracted by the beautiful scenery, the atmosphere, the comings and goings in the harbour and the fossil hunting, newly fashionable. Royal Crescent was never completed and the grandiose schemes left unfinished by George Hudson's financial collapse, but the visitors kept on coming.

Another accident of fortune which brought vast employment and some prosperity to Whitby in the mid-Victorian period was the fashion for Whitby jet as jewellery, encouraged by the queen's penchant for mourning. At a time when a number of traditional trades were feeling the pinch, scores of small jet-workshops were set up in yards and behind houses all over Whitby.

The 20th century has seen the decline of several of Whitby's staple industries. Shipbuilding has gone. The port trade, while still significant, is only a shadow of its former self. Like most seaside resorts Whitby has seen a considerable change in its visitors, with the competition of cheap continental resorts and package holidays. Now many of the town's visitors appear at the weekend or come only for the day. Nonetheless, the town can still become uncomfortably full in summer. Its atmosphere still provides the greatest draw and amusements are on a relatively small scale and contained within one area. Most people come for the beach, to wander through the narrow streets of the east side, to watch the harbour activities, to sample the local cuisine, or to visit the abbey and the splendid and eccentric parish church.

Many people, however, know Whitby only in summer. In winter it presents a very different appearance, the streets bare and windswept, many shops closed and holiday cottages empty. Employment is in short supply and alternatives to tourism few. This is part of the price it pays for its location and is the inevitable consequence of houses and cottages rising beyond the means of local people, leading to out-of-season depopulation. Despite all this Whitby has managed against all the odds to avoid the worst effects of decline which beset so many seaside resorts. It still has a life of its own and retains many old established families on both sides of the river. Events such as the Regatta, which takes place each August, appear on the surface to be intended as visitor attractions, but the rowing races offer us a roll call of fine old Whitby names and many of the events bring out local people of all ages to watch.

I have taken the opportunity in the second and third editions to update a number of areas where changes have occurred or new evidence has come to light. This is particularly significant in cases such as the Anglian monastery, where recent excavations have radically altered the picture, but a host of small advances have also been made in other fields; it is quite a surprise to me to find how much needed rewriting after only 11 years and again after another 14.

One

THE TOWN

Whitby is a very distinctive town. Its shape and layout are determined by the river Esk, which runs out into the North Sea between high rocky cliffs. On the cliff-top to the east lies the unmistakable shape of the Abbey ruins and of the parish church, while that to the west is crowned by Victorian hotels and boarding houses. Down below, red-roofed houses cling to the relatively small areas of level ground on both sides of the river and creep up the lower slopes wherever the cliffs make it possible. At a narrowing in the river a swing bridge links the two halves of the town, while further upriver a modern high-level bridge strides across the river just below the woods of Larpool. To seaward project two stone piers with concrete and timber extensions, while other, shorter piers control the swell within the harbour. Everything is very compact. Yet Whitby has a longer and richer history than most larger towns. The emphasis has changed over the centuries: site of a royal monastery in the Anglian period, then medieval abbey, a herring port and shipbuilding town, the base for colliers, military transports, Greenland whalers and manufacturers of alum, the home of jet workshops, a seaside resort … the list goes on. Whitby has kept reinventing itself.

The town seems to have grown organically, with very little planning until the Georgian period, and rather more, but only in distinct areas such as the West Cliff, during the Victorian era. It suffers much the same isolation today as it has always done. In fact it is probably more cut off by sea than at any time before, and the railway link is slower and offers less choice than in the 19th century. However, the success of the North Yorkshire Moors Railway and its extension to Whitby itself have been of great benefit to the town in recent years. Even the road, by which most visitors arrive today, negotiates twenty miles of moorland from Scarborough, Pickering or Guisborough, and the weather can be highly unpredictable, with deep snow in winter and thick sea mists that can roll in very rapidly at almost any time.

Although we know quite a lot about the Anglian monastery, and everything points to a settlement of sorts, perhaps village rather than town, below the cliff, it is not until after the Norman Conquest that we start to find any physical records of what was to become the town of Whitby. The Anglian monastery and the medieval Abbey are so important that I have given them a chapter each (Chapters 3 and 4), which removes them from the chronological account contained in this chapter.

DOMESDAY

Other than the information which we have on the Anglian monastery, our earliest evidence of the countryside around Whitby is given by the record called Domesday, compiled under the orders of William I in 1086. Domesday's purpose was to be a record of the extent and value of the new territories which had fallen to the king as a result of his conquest of England. The basis on which it was created and the detail in which land is recorded vary from area to area.

Since the purposes for which Domesday was compiled differ from those for which historians wish to use it, the information is often tantalisingly brief or vague. However, reading between the lines as well as on them we can see that the area round Whitby had before 1066 belonged to Earl Siward and had then been valued at £112. This amount is fairly meaningless and any attempt to translate it into modern values tends to ignore a host of relevant factors.

What is significant is that by 1086 this value had sunk to a mere 60 shillings, or little more than one-fortieth of its previous value. A laconic entry reads 'almost all waste' and further that while in the group of subordinate townships there is capacity for 24 ploughs only six are in fact working, two belonging to the lord, one to eight freemen and three to 30 villagers. Whitby itself could support 15 ploughs but only three are at work. Such decay of agricultural land can only be due to the state of unrest that had been endemic in the region for the past few years and in particular to the savage punitive measures which William had meted out following the massacre of his York garrison in 1070, the so-called 'harrying of the north'.

By 1086 the land of Whitby and Sneaton, technically a 'berewick', 15 carucates or ploughlands in total, was in the ownership of Hugh Lupus, Earl of Chester, but the actual tenant was William de Percy, who was to be a generous benefactor to the abbey. There were 10 villagers and three smallholders. No sign here of the town which was to develop; many minor Domesday settlements listed as belonging to the manor as 'sokeland' are ones which we would now regard as integral parts of Whitby. The list enumerates Fyling and North Fyling with one and five carucates – or 'ploughlands' – respectively, Gnipe [Hawsker] with three, Prestby with two, Ugglebarnby with three, Sowerby with four, Breck with one, Baldeby with one, 'Flore' with two, Stakesby with two and six bovates, and Newholm with four. Many of these names can still be recognised in their modern forms. Within the boundaries of modern Whitby are Prestby, the site of the former abbey, Sowerby, between Mayfield Road and Ruswarp, according to Kendall, Breck, which is lost, and Baldeby, which is probably in the Mayfield Road area (Wood's Map of 1828 shows 'Baldaby Lane' for the modern Mayfield Road). 'Flore' is placed by most authorities in the upper Flowergate area (Flowergate probably means 'the road to Flore'), and Stakesby is still with us.

The similarity of names and indeed their survival over the last nine centuries, remarkable as it is, should not blind us to the fact that the Whitby of those days was a very different place. On the cliff-top stood the extensive ruins of the former monastery, now in process of recolonisation by the monk Reinfrid and his companions, though the area was still lawless and the monks were forced to retreat to their cell at Hackness at about this time.

Below the cliff was the tiny harbour of Whitby, probably even then lying on both sides of the river. The houses were of timber and thatch and, even allowing for large families and a high level of omission, we must envisage a tiny community, and one that has suffered greatly in the recent years of strife and bloodshed as Angles, Danes and Normans fought for power. A small fishing fleet would sail in search of herring or dry its nets on the beaches.

Further afield there were separate hamlets in what is now Flowergate, Stakesby and out towards Ruswarp, where there was a water-mill. A long narrow strip of coastline also belonged to the manor, stretching eastwards to Hawsker and Peak and westwards to Kettleness, but little of it was cultivated. The moors behind were bare and used for little but grazing. Here were few villages but instead farmsteads of Viking Age origin occupied the tops of the dales in ones or twos, scraping a precarious living from the land.

THE BOROUGH

Whitby was not a self-governing borough until the early 19th century. In the Middle Ages the abbots of Whitby were unwilling to allow their tenants even a measure of independence and Whitby's adventure with borough status was short-lived.

In many towns and villages in the Middle Ages the landowners decided to exchange their relationship of respectively power and service with their tenants for a cash relationship. The former tenants effectively would buy out the landlord's right to services and to tolls and would pay instead a fixed rent, which they collected themselves. In this way a corporate body would be created, to look after the interests of the community, or at least of the small number who had the necessary qualifications of property or a trade. The community was able to diversify its interests and could become collectively prosperous on the proceeds of trade, tolls or markets.

This process generally involved a charter, important enough to be guarded at all costs by its holders against legal attack by the landlord's descendants or by the crown. Its effect on town-planning was that a new borough would often develop a distinct market place and more particularly a series of standardised long narrow plots for building houses or outbuildings upon, which are usually called 'burgage plots'.

Such plots are not exclusive to chartered boroughs and seem to have developed independently in many places in the Middle Ages, perhaps because they satisfied the needs of the age. The name burgage came to mean a plot of land, and not necessarily the tenure by which it was held. This is important when we look at some of the early evidence for Whitby.

In about 1128 a charter of Henry I granted to the abbey such a burgage in Whitby. This does not imply that the town at that date was a free borough. The story of this is more complex.

Between 1177 and 1189 – the exact date is unknown – Richard, abbot of Whitby, granted the rights of free burgage to the inhabitants of Whitby. Presumably this was either of his own free will or at the instigation of the townspeople, and in either case in return for some cash benefit. However, this state of affairs was not long allowed to continue and in 1201 a charter of King John was obtained disallowing Abbot Richard's charter on the grounds that it was inconsistent with the dignity of the abbey. The matter went again to arbitration soon afterwards but with the same result and the conclusion that the abbot had not had any power to grant it.

So ended the short-lived borough of Whitby. Thenceforth until the political reforms of the 1830s the town was a chattel of the abbey and of succeeding lay landlords, as long as they chose to enjoy it. It seems likely that Abbot Richard's successor thought better of his arrangements and escaped from them via a legal loophole. Despite this a number of the more respectable townspeople continued to be called burgesses and several plots in the town were known as burgages. One result of Whitby's humble beginnings and later urban growth has been the fact that much of modern Whitby is not in Whitby at all, but in Ruswarp, Hawsker or Stainsacre townships, into which it has overflowed. This can cause unexpected problems in using the census and other official documents.

PARLIAMENTARY REPRESENTATION

Medieval Whitby was represented in parliament by its abbots, or rather they represented their own interests there. The townsfolk had seen their town receive borough status and lose it again within a few years, and with that went their voting rights. Whitby was again represented in parliament during the Commonwealth, but at the Restoration the privilege was again lost.

It was not until 1832 that Whitby was given a chance to send an M.P. to Parliament; even then the town was not at first listed among the new boroughs created by the Reform Act, but the efforts of Richard Moorsom to have it included were eventually crowned with success. It is somewhat ironic, then, that he was not chosen as the first M.P. for the new borough, being too liberal for the electorate, which consisted of only some four hundred people. This honour went instead to Aaron Chapman, a Conservative. In celebration a huge outdoor feast was held for 2,000 people in a field at Bagdale. One hundred and seventy-six plum puddings each of 10 pounds in weight, together with 40 gallons of sauce, were brought to the field in a wagon from the *Angel Inn*. In addition 5,000 pounds of meat, over 4,000 loaves, and 1,700 gallons of ale were provided. If all of this was eaten it must have provided indigestion and hangovers for days to come. Recently a naïve painting of this so-called 'Pink Dinner' – pink was then the Conservative colour – has been given to the Museum by members of the Chapman family.

In 1847 Chapman was succeeded by Robert Stephenson, son of George, both of them being key figures in the development of the railway system. When he died in 1859 a Liberal, H.S. Thompson, chairman of the North East Railway

Company, got in by a small majority, largely as a result of a split in Conservative ranks when George Hudson was taken out of the running at the insistence of his creditors. Since then the seat, with a largely rural community as its electorate, generally returned a Conservative candidate, until the landslide of 1997 unexpectedly produced a Labour member, Lawrie Quinn. Normality returned in 2005 with the election of Robert Goodwill for the Conservatives, and he retained his seat in the three subsequent elections of 2010, 2015 and 2017.

DEVELOPMENT OF THE STREET PATTERN

The pattern of streets developed early and our evidence for their early history is heavily dependant upon the abbey cartulary. Many years ago, Hugh Kendall established the date of first mention of most of these central streets, but we should beware of assuming that this can be equated with the date that they came into existence. In most cases the streets are likely to antedate their first documentary mention by many years.

Starting on the east side Henrietta Street appears quite late; it is an 18th-century addition to the town, named after the second wife of Nathaniel Cholmley. Before this it was an undeveloped ledge of the cliff, known as 'the Haggerlythe' as far back as 1270. The far northern end of this ledge still retains its original name. It lies along an area of unstable undercliff, with dire geological consequences on several occasions.

At the foot of the Church Stairs Henrietta Street joins Church Street, the name for the whole length nowadays as far south as Spital Bridge. Originally it was Kirkgate, but only so far as the Market Place where it became High Gate. Where it joined Bridge Street it became Crossgate, then from the end of Grape Lane was Southgate, impassable at high tide beyond Boulby Bank. It changes considerably in elevation, from some 40 ft. (12m.) above OD at the *Duke of York Inn* to 24 ft. (7m.) north of Grape Lane and down to 14 ft. (4m.) south of that point. An alternative road from Spital Bridge to the town at high tide can be traced in Weselden Bank, which rises up behind the old gas works, and runs parallel to the site of the ancient ropery on the cliff-top.

2 *Nos 159-64 Church Street, south of the former Friends' Meeting House, show clear evidence of their 17th-century timber-framed origin with a jettied upper storey and stucco facades.*

3 *The doorway of 10 Brunswick Street, a typical 18th-century brick-built house in Flemish Bond (alternate headers and stretchers in every course). The 'honeysuckle' fanlight is especially fine and to accommodate it the entablature is broken. Such a design could be found in many mid-18th-century pattern books.*

Geological investigations have shown that the existence of Church Street is quite fortuitous. It is founded on a bank of sand at the bend of the river which was protected from erosion by a cliff fall in antiquity, covering the cliffward side some two metres deep in rocky debris and tailing off towards the harbourside. This gave Church Street a small but significant elevation above floods and a slightly firmer footing than it might otherwise have had. This event is undated but we might hazard a guess that it was before the 10th century; in other words before any substantial human settlement took place.

Bridge Street, once Wayneman Street (named after a family who kept an inn here), is unlikely to be older than the bridge it serves; as we shall see, that may still place it quite early in the medieval period. On either side of it are streets which give every appearance of being built out on harbourside sandbanks. Sandgate runs in a curve northwards, as far as the Market Place, dating back to 1640, with its 18th-century town hall, while Grape Lane follows a matching curve to the south, rejoining Church Street beyond the former Friends' Meeting House. These were at one time known as 'the Low Streets'. Both of them present a solid wall of buildings to the harbourside, originally punctuated by 'ghauts' giving access to shipping. If the properties in these streets were to be excavated it is likely we should find a complex pattern of development and gradual consolidation of the sands by means of piles and progressive timber staiths, such as those found on the ancient waterfronts at Chapel Lane Staith in Hull and at Blands Cliff, Scarborough.

On the other side of the river the street pattern has changed considerably over the last few years. At the west end of the bridge was once the Old Market Place, where Baxtergate, Golden Lion Bank and St Ann's Staith all met. The buildings on the harbour side of St Ann's Staith survived well into the 19th century while matching buildings on the other corner where New Quay Road now meets the bridge (known as 'Boots Corner') were only demolished in 1974. All of these at one time made the bridge end much more enclosed and it was this rectangle which formed the Old Market Place. Golden Lion Bank is named after the public house of that name and leads to Flowergate, which is one of the oldest streets, named as the road leading to 'Flore', a place mentioned in Domesday. Flore itself was perhaps in the vicinity of Flowergate Cross and no doubt the road to it had at one time a semi-rural aspect. North of Flowergate is an area developed in the 18th century, which we shall come across later.

To the south is Brunswick Street, once called Scate Lane, which gives access to the south end of Baxtergate. Another link, a little further to the west, is formed by Union Steps joining Bagdale to the upper end of Flowergate and the former Union Mill. Like the Donkey Road which runs parallel to the Church Stairs, Union Steps is a combination of a steep setted road for horses and a flight of steps for their drivers.

Baxtergate is another ancient street, containing, in *Angel Yard*, the main coaching inn of the 18th and 19th centuries. Many yards link it to New Quay Road and Dock End, though formerly there was no road on this side and the yards gave access to staiths on the harbour. Baxtergate gives way to Bagdale; the Bagdale Beck is now culverted but the road follows its little valley and the raised footpath on the north side still represents a panniermen's track. At the back of Broomfield Terrace is a small building with a conical roof, all that is left of the once popular Broomfield Spa, where Victorian ladies and gentlemen came to take the waters. On the other side of the street is the Friends' Burial Ground, a plot of land bought by the Friends from Nicholas Sneton, a shoemaker, in 1659. In this plain and unassuming area of turf with a mere scatter of gravestones, reached via an

4 *Pre-Georgian cottages in Brunswick Street, bearing a date of 1690. There is no single dominant building tradition in Whitby, timber, brick and stone all being used equally until the 19th century.*

anonymous gate, many of the former merchants and leading townspeople of 18th century Whitby lie buried.

Turning the other way now from the bridge we see first St Ann's Staith and then Haggersgate, which runs around behind the buildings of Marine Parade (Haggersgate is the older street). Pier Lane dives steeply down from Cliff Street to join Haggersgate at its end. North of this is Pier Road, now the main area for amusements, with the Fish Quay on its east side by the harbour. All this area is reclaimed from the harbour and dates from the early years of the 19th century. Before that the quay ceased at Tyreman's Coffee House and the harbour at that time backed directly on to the houses in the Cragg. The Cragg itself, once a rookery of yards and cottages, was turned around at this time, so that the former backs of houses now faced on to Pier Road. The Cragg lies considerably above the level of the Fish Quay and has to be approached by steps.

The road ran originally only to the West Pier or the sands, below the cliff, but in the mid-19th century a new road, the Khyber Pass, was cut, linking the harbour to the new buildings of the West Cliff.

BUILDINGS OF THE OLD TOWN

If there is any single building type which predominates in Whitby it is the modest Georgian cottage or terrace house of brick with gauged brick relieving arches over the windows but, with the exception of the West Cliff and Fishburn Park, the older parts of the town are a delightful mixture of all periods and styles. This is due to continuous rebuilding and refacing of property on the same sites.

Excluding for the moment the abbey and the parish church, there are no surviving medieval buildings in the town, though there may be re-used timbers from earlier buildings incorporated in those of later date. Indeed there is little earlier than the late 16th or early 17th centuries. The *Olde Smugglers* in Baxtergate, formerly the *Old Ship Launch* inn, claims a very precise date of 1401, but on no obvious evidence. White Cottages, near the top of Salt Pan Well Steps, similarly claim to date from 1595, though they appear to be at least a century later. What may be part of a mid-15th-century merchant's house was found at 159 Church Street in 1993, so Whitby may have further surprises up her sleeve.

In the town itself the oldest surviving houses, of 16th-century date, seem to be 9-10 Sandgate and the rear part of the Marine Café, backing on to Haggersgate. Both of these are timber-framed behind cladding and modest in scale. Recently, medieval timbers have been exposed in a shop near the former Friends' Meeting House. Abbey House also contains 16th-century work, and re-used medieval details which have led to claims that it substantially represents the Abbot's House. It is more likely that we owe it to early Cholmleys who robbed the ruins for what material was to their taste. Bagdale Old Hall also has 16th-century origins but was so heavily restored in the late 19th century after sinking to the level of tenements that it has little to show of the original home of the Conyers family.

5 *Houses in the Cragg, once a rookery of intricate yards and home to many of the fishermen. It is now dominated by holiday cottages. The Cragg is raised several feet above the roadway of Pier Road while its western side abuts the cliff, scarred with the marks of many former buildings, such as those of Barry's Square.*

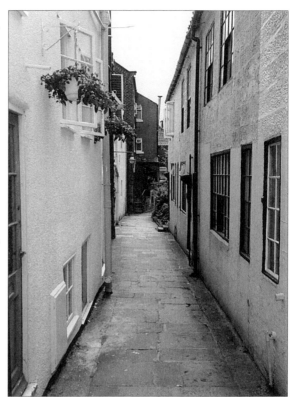

6 *A view of Whitby from Coffee House End in about 1750, from a reprint by King in the* Whitby Repository *of 1867. A painting of this same view is in Whitby Museum. Tyreman's Coffee House stood roughly where the Marine Café now stands. In the background is a small jetty marking the end of Haggersgate, beyond which there was no direct access to the river front. Rows of privies attached to the backs of these houses discharged straight into the harbour!*

7 *The north front of the Cholmleys' great Banqueting Hall at the Abbey House, built between 1676 and 1682. It had a short life, being severely damaged in a gale in the late 18th century. The Cholmleys had by now moved to Howsham in the East Riding and so never bothered to repair the hall. The building has recently been restored as part of the adaptation to form a visitor centre.*

8 *The Baths, Library and Museum building as it was, brand new in 1827. It can still be recognised today but has had oriel windows added to the upper corners.*

On the corner of the Market Place and Church Street is a group of shops constructed on the site of the pre-Reformation chapel and possibly re-using some of its materials. These date from the 17th century and of similar date is a row of jettied houses (nos. 159-64 Church Street) between the end of Grape Lane and the Friends' Meeting House. A stone doorway possibly relating to the chapel was found in the former Dyson's shop to the south of the Market Place in 1994.

Dates start to appear on houses late in the 17th century and although they cannot always be taken at their face value they do give some useful indications. In Rose and Crown Yard, off Flowergate, for instance, is a datestone to Thomas and Elizabeth Walker, 1703. On the house in Grape Lane where James Cook stayed when he was apprenticed to John Walker are the initials of Moses and Susannah Dring, dated 1688, while a house at the foot of the Church Stairs has a stone on its façade, now very worn, inscribed 'Leonard and Isable Hart Hous Built in the Year of our Lord 1705'. In Brunswick Street is a range of stone-built cottages bearing a date of 1690.

We will examine in more detail the Georgian developments because they were the first elements of urban planning in Whitby. However, there are one or two individual buildings which call for attention here. In the Market Place is the town hall, built in 1788 in the classical style by Jonathan Pickernell, Harbour Engineer and builder of the West Pier, for Mr Nathaniel Cholmley as lord of the manor. It is a very simple but effective building, with a single large room on the first floor, carried on Tuscan tetrastyle colonnades surrounding a central drum containing a spiral stair. A cupola on the roof carries the clock and bell. Another prominent public building which now no longer serves its original purpose is the former baths, museum and library building, completed in 1827. We will look at its function later. It stands in Pier Road and is a plain but well-proportioned structure of three storeys and seven bays – the oriel at either end is a later addition.

The Whitby Commercial Newsroom, built in 1813, is a charming little building on Marine Parade and now the home of 'The Dracula Experience'. Graham Leach has entertainingly disentangled the Articles of Agreement for its construction to reveal how it was built and what it looked like when new.

Georgian Growth

During the relative prosperity of the 18th century Whitby hardly grew at all in extent, though its population grew markedly. A considerable amount of rebuilding took place on existing street frontages and even more infilling took place on back land. Houses there were usually for rental and housed many of the poorer families. We will examine these yards and courts later.

On the main streets we can see many grand houses of the period, occupying older plots. A few examples will suffice. At 23 Baxtergate, a large stone house set back behind iron railings on the south-east side belonged to Mr Coates the shipbuilder. Esk House, a large house near the railway station, lost as a result of bombing in the last war, was the home of another shipbuilder, Thomas Fishburn, and later of Thomas Brodrick. Another shipbuilding family, the Barrys, occupied a house built by Thomas

9 *Tin Ghaut, one of the picturesque areas of Whitby which was demolished in 1959. The Ghaut gave access to the harbour side from the end of Grape Lane and was typical of many such passages now gone which gave the harbour some of its essential character. 'Ghaut' is a specifically Whitby word for a narrow passage but it may be related to the dialect word 'gowt' sometimes used for a narrow watercourse.*

Hutchinson soon after 1763 which was much later demolished to make way for the bus station. On the corner of Flowergate and Skinner Street is a very grand stone house, now unfortunately defaced by later extensions, built for John Addison and later occupied by the Campion family. It was successively Flowergate House, the *Crown Hotel*, and a working men's club. Finally, just off Haggersgate is the Missions to Seamen building, a fine brick house built for John Yeoman, a shipowner, in about 1760.

Outside the town area were a number of gentlemen's houses such as Airy Hill, built in 1790 for Richard Moorsom, Field House, just off what is now Upgang Lane, High and Low Stakesby, and Meadowfield, belonging to the Simpsons. Most of these have since been swallowed up in the suburban growth of Whitby. The gentry houses of most influence on Whitby were the Abbey House, home of the Cholmley family from the 17th century, and Mulgrave Castle, seat of successive Lords Mulgrave. The Cholmleys were old-established, living initially in the Abbey gatehouse, but spent much time away from Whitby, abandoning it altogether for their new principal seat at Howsham in 1743, although as lords of the manor they retained considerable interests in the town. A painting of the Steward's Room at the Abbey House in 1840 by Mary Ellen Best reveals a house that was essentially mothballed, awaiting occasional use by the family for seaside visits.

Sir William Burrell gives a telling description of both the Abbey House and of Mulgrave Castle in 1758:

> At Whitby Mr Cholmondly [Cholmley] has built a large house [Abbey House] close to Whitby Abbey. It is situated upon a high hill which might command a noble and extensive prospect (having the sea in front, on the other side Whitby river adorned with high banks covered with wood, and beyond a great range of cultivated country; at the foot of the hill is Whitby town) had not the stupidity of its owner contrived to shut out the view of the town by stables, dog kennels etc, the sea by high walls. The

most pleasant room in the house is very judiciously converted to a kitchen. The abbey is a terrible prospect of the Gothick disposition of its former owner who, when he built the dwelling house, gutted this noble aedifice and it now stands almost subdued by time, the arches and roofing being entirely fallen in and the whole place, once the asylum of religion, is now become an habitation for rabbits …

From Whitby to Mulgrave is 4 miles to Mr Phipps, who has a very pretty hunting seat [Mulgrave Castle] built by the Duke of Buckingham, but has received great improvements from the present owners, Mr Phipps and Lady Lepel. It is situated on the top of a hill about half a mile from the sea. On the back front is a spatious grass walk planted on each side with evergreens and ash trees, from which there is a beautyfull prospect of the sea. In front they look over a tolerable country entirely bare of wood, except a vale belonging to Mr Phipps with the hills on both sides of it, at the top of which is the ruins of [Old] Mulgrave Castle, now a heap of rubbish. At the bottom of the hills runs a small stream quite through the vale, which might be made extremely pretty, as well as the woods, if the absurdity of the country would permit it. But their claim of turning beasts into the woods to browze renders all intentions of the owner to beautify it ineffectual.

In most towns there were moves in the 18th century not merely to rebuild individual houses but to create planned streets, often to certain standards. Whitby was no exception. The first new area to be developed was Henrietta Street, set at the upper end of Church Street and on a ledge in the cliff. Building began here in 1761 and it soon became a fashionable area, which seems odd to those of us who can remember it as a very dingy and poor place. The reason is not far to seek. In 1787 a serious landslip occurred here, destroying a number of new houses. The fine octagonal Methodist Chapel was another casualty. Further landslips have occurred since, most particularly in 1870, and it must have been manifestly clear that the subsoil was unsuitable for building. At all events the fashionable people moved elsewhere, leaving it to poorer families. The cliff above has continued to give trouble, with many small landslips from the churchyard.

In 1762 building began on Farndale Fields, leading from Flowergate up on to the West Cliff. A new street called Skinner Street developed here, and to

10   Timber-framed houses of the early 18th century forming the northern side of the Market Place. The nearest building carries a date of 1704 while other buildings on the opposite corner, beyond the Town Hall, are even earlier. This market place was first laid out in 1640 by Sir Hugh Cholmley.

11 & 12   *'The Landslip at Whitby' from* The Graphic *of 21 January 1871. A large piece of cliff, several graves in the churchyard and a number of houses including Mr Harland's pipe manufactory, fell away because of the effect of rain and frost on the boulder clay beneath. It was virtually a repeat of the events of nearly a century before.*

the west in what is now Well Close Square other houses sprang up, though in neither area have the 18th-century buildings survived in any number. A fine terrace known as Poplar Row survives just off Skinner Street.

One of Whitby's largest planned developments of the century was built on fields at the top of Flowergate. This was to become St Hilda's Terrace, but was known then as New Buildings. This row of 25 houses did not have a single overall design and so there is a considerable variety in size and layout. There is even a mixture of stone and brick, brick being most common, but despite this the overall feeling is of quality and there is an impressive frontage to the south, high above the valley of the Bagdale Beck. Behind the houses is a service road giving access to stables and coach-houses, some of which are now in separate ownership from the original houses.

Immediately to the south of these houses and at a lower level is Whitby's other planned 18th-century row, which forms the north side of Bagdale. The houses here are again mainly of brick and set back up long front gardens, with service access to the rear. Nos. 12–14 are of stone and form a terrace within a terrace, dating from 1816, but Bagdale, like St Hilda's Terrace, was originally let out in lots for individuals to build their own houses within very general specifications. St Hilda's Terrace belongs to about 1779 (no. 14 has a datestone on its rear wall) and the Bagdale houses to the 1780s, with the exception of Nos. 12–14.

On the other side of the harbour, off the lower end of Church Street, stands Prospect Place. Because of the position of the cliff edge, this is approached by steep steps. Two rows of solid stone houses set one above the other stand athwart the steps, erected by Gideon Smales, shipowner, shipbuilder and raff merchant, in 1816, according to the plaque on the front.

13 *The eastern side of Henrietta Street. A surprising degree of uniformity exists in this group of houses, built of brick with prominent string courses, and many in the street have relieving arches over the windows and doors. They date from soon after 1761, and the street became unfashionable after the northern end collapsed in 1787. They are once again highly desirable, this time as holiday cottages.*

14 *St Hilda's Terrace, originally known as New Buildings, contains some of the best houses in Whitby. The Stone House, so called for obvious reasons, is the grandest both inside and out. Some of its brick neighbours, particularly towards the west end, are quite modest. A number have suffered the later addition of another storey above their original parapets, often in a contrasting brick.*

15 *Engraving from a drawing by John Bird, used in Young's* Picture of Whitby, *1824. It shows the new Bagdale Terrace and above it St Hilda's Terrace, with the flagged path of Downdinner Hill entering from the right. The horse in the left of the view is a strange-looking animal, with legs in all the wrong places!*

THE WEST CLIFF

After the development of Farndale Fields the West Cliff remained unchanged for half a century. Wood's map of 1828 marks virtually the whole area between the Mount and Upgang Lane as the property of Mrs Rudyerd. Just above Flowergate Cross stood Union Mill, a five-sailed windmill forming a prominent feature in the 19th-century skyline of Whitby.

All this changed in the middle of the century with the building of a substantial number of new streets and terraces containing hotels and boarding houses. Within a few years the face of Whitby was quite altered and serving the needs of visitors became a significant occupation for townspeople.

Although George Hudson, the 'Railway King', is usually held responsible for the development of the West Cliff estate, it would appear that a Whitby Building Company was already in existence in 1843, some time before he took over the Whitby & Pickering Railway. A prospectus was launched in that year to buy land

16 *Poplar Row, behind Skinner Street, is part of the same Farndale Fields development by the Skinner brothers, after 1762. With their lack of cornice and high parapets these houses have a slightly austere appearance.*

17 *Whitby from the sea, in a steel engraving published by Rock & Co. in 1855. The view is dominated already by the new hotels and boarding houses on the West Cliff.*

and build 14 lodging houses to plans by G. Matthew of Whitby. Indeed, there had been some discussion as early as 1827 as to the merits of building lodging houses upon the West Cliff to accommodate visitors.

There is no doubt, however, that Hudson became the driving force behind the project, which he saw as a means to establish himself as a credible candidate for election to Whitby's vacant parliamentary seat. In the event he was offered the vacant seat at Sunderland first. It is also true that Whitby people always gave him credit for his hard work, despite his subsequent bankruptcy and disgrace.

East Crescent and East Terrace, the block including the *Royal Hotel* and what was to become *Kirby's Hotel*, were the first parts of the scheme to be completed. After this came the Esplanade and part of Royal Crescent, all by 1859. Whatever unifying factors there are in the style and layout of these areas is due to architects George Townsend Andrews of York (who worked extensively alongside George Hudson and also designed the town's railway station) and John Dobson of Newcastle, who was already responsible for much of Newcastle's 'Tyneside Classical', built for Richard Grainger. John Street and Hudson Street were ready in the same year, one of the first guests at No. 1 Abbey Terrace in John Street being Mrs Gaskell, here to carry out research for *Sylvia's Lovers*.

The Saloon (now known as the Spa) followed in the 1870s under the leadership of Sir George Elliot, along with other terraces. The impetus behind the scheme had been lost, however, and Royal Crescent remained unfinished. Development on the remainder of the West Cliff estate was much more protracted and to no

18 *The* Royal Hotel *and West Cliff from a drawing by George Weatherill published in about 1850. This block and the East Crescent were the earliest parts of the West Cliff estate to be developed, initially under the direction of George Hudson, the 'Railway King'.*

19 *'Whitby, Yorkshire – with the new improvements' from the* Illustrated London News *for 1852. The view, from the East Cliff, takes in the harbour and former gun battery (centre right) but focuses on the new developments on the West Cliff, built with the intention of providing accommodation for the middle-class visitors now being attracted by the railway link. This 'magnificent pile of buildings' includes a 'splendid hotel, recently built, containing warm baths, and every convenience for the accommodation of visitors'.*

coherent plan. A map of the town in about 1860 shows a proposed square to the west of the Crescent and other streets which remained unbuilt. A promenade, North Promenade, was built along the cliff-top and the areas left vacant by the failed development were later occupied by tennis courts and gardens.

There is an extraordinary house near the junction of Cliff Street and East Crescent called 'Strenshall', originally 'Khyber House'. It was successively the photographic studios of John Stonehouse and of George Wallis. Seen from the west it is a very ordinary two-storey villa of light brick with a spiky turret echoing those on the abbey. From the east, however, it is a building of five storeys, the lower ones disappearing down the cliff towards the Cragg! Rarely do the back and front of a house look so completely different in scale and appearance.

The savagely ugly *Metropole Hotel* of 1897-98, adding its domineering profile with four incongruous corner turrets to the centre of the promenade, does little to enhance the cliff-top prospect.

During the 1930s, another brief period of prosperity, this time for the golfing or tennis holiday, hotels like the *Marvic, Monk's Haven, Morningside* and *White Point* appeared; indeed much of the flavour of this area is of that date, including a number of spacious private houses such as those on the north side of Upgang Road.

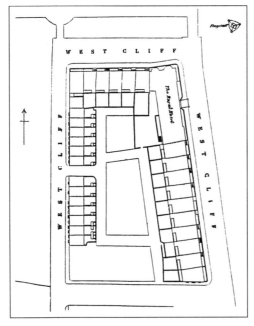

20 *The earliest phase of the West Cliff development, captured on the 60-inch Ordnance Survey map of 1852.*

In Argyle Road and Ocean Road large red-brick houses began to emerge at the very end of the 19th century, serving the growing middle-class population which had hitherto been thinly scattered throughout the town. The area was convenient for the new West Cliff railway station, too. Subsequently there has been much infill, in the grounds of the former Field House and elsewhere. The cliff is too unstable to encourage building very close to its top but new housing has filled up most of the available space as far as the boundary of Whitby on the Sandsend road.

The effect of all this building over such a short space of time was to change the focus of the town. We shall look at the effect of the new hotels in a later chapter, but as far as the houses were concerned a new social order was established in a very few years, encouraging the settlement of families who had little to do with the activities of the harbour below and whose income had little to do with the sea.

Ethel Kidson, in her novel *Herring-fleet* (1912), gives an interesting insight into the attitudes of the new suburbs of a thinly disguised Whitby:

> Her father was doing a better class trade, and wished to forget his connection with the old homely folk of the High Street. For the besetting sin of many people in the New Town was pride and snobbishness. They had as many caste distinctions as the Hindoos. They seemed to change for the worse when they went to live over the Bridge.

POPULATION

Before the 19th century, estimates of the population of Whitby are unreliable. Young gives 1,500 in 1610, 2,500 in 1650, 3,000 in 1700, and 5,000 in 1750, but without any evidence for these figures. Charlton put the figure in 1776 at 12,000, while Francis Gibson claimed that in 1782 there were over 15,000 inhabitants. Both are clearly over-estimates. In 1811 the official census gave a figure of under 8,000, but did not include men away at sea.

Rather more accurate is the private census carried out by Dr Young in 1816, producing a total figure of 10,203. By 1821 the official census placed it at 10,435 and it had actually decreased by six at the next census of 1831. In 1841 the number had risen to approximately 10,975 and by 1851 to around 12,000, the uncertainty again

21 *Royal Crescent from the east, a dignified range of four-storey buildings to the design of John Dobson of Newcastle intended to serve as private hotels and boarding houses. Royal Crescent dates from the 1850s but was never finished; the matching western half remains unbuilt.*

22 *Steel engraving by Rock & Co. of London entitled 'Royal Crescent, Whitby'. It dates from 1852, long before even the left-hand half of the Crescent was completed, and the right-hand half is completely imaginary. It does, however, give a good idea of what the overall effect would have been.*

23 *Miller's Yard, probably the one which ran between Haggersgate and Cliff Street, in about 1900. A typical Whitby yard, with steps allowing access to various ledges in the cliff, this contains some decent Georgian houses, by this time sub-divided. It also contains a maze of inter-connecting rights, such as separate privies, net-stores and drying grounds, which make it such a nightmare for solicitors to separate such formerly-rented property into freeholds.*

being due to the number of seamen away from home. From then on the population rose slowly to a peak of 14,086 in 1881 and has since as slowly declined to a level of about 12,000.

These figures disguise other trends, since the actual area of the town and its influence grew steadily with the amalgamation of townships which formerly had separate population records. A direct comparison of the area regarded as urban in 1816 with the same area today would show a tremendous decline, partly as a result of movement away from the yards and courts at the heart of the town into lower density suburbs.

Another significant conclusion is that a population of around 10,000 in the late 18th century placed Whitby in the second or third rank of towns, behind major cities and industrialised towns and on a level with many county towns. Its population today places it at the lower end of the scale of towns; established urban character, however, and historic development are all important in determining our perception of a settlement. Equally, Whitby's relative size in the 18th and early 19th centuries goes some way to explaining its importance and influence.

YARDS, COURTS AND STEPS

It is a common mistake for those who do not know the town well to refer to the east side as 'the old town' and to think of the west side as new. On the surface this might appear to be so, since the east side of the town contains many former fishermen's cottages and looks rather more quaint due to the steep slopes and romantic roofscapes, while the west side – in particular the West Cliff – has some of the main Victorian developments. The truth is, however, that as far as standing buildings are concerned both sides of the harbour are of equal antiquity and if the west side looks newer this is due to more change and demolition having occurred here. Areas such as the Cragg and the yards off Baxtergate and Flowergate could once match in every way the overcrowding and deprivation of the upper end of Church Street.

Whitby is a town dominated by its geographical position. The narrow ledges of level ground on both sides of the harbour were quickly colonised by streets such as Baxtergate, Haggersgate and Church Street. Long, typically medieval, plots – which are usually called 'burgage plots' even if in Whitby there were in strict legal fact no burgesses to enjoy them – ran back to the cliffs and down to the river. In time the open ground at the rear of these plots became built up, often when frontage owners started to capitalise on their assets. They built and rented out cheap cottages and tenements to the newcomers who were attracted by prosperity, and so we find so-called 'yards' developing behind the main street frontages.

As well as the access to cottages these yards often formed a means of communication between streets, diving down between property boundaries. Lanes and yards such as Ellerby Lane off Church Street and Bakehouse Yard off Haggersgate exemplify this type. Today we tend for legal reasons to formalise differences between 'official' and 'unofficial' thoroughfares, whereas in previous generations there was no such distinction, leading to an unplanned maze. The charm of neighbouring fishing villages such as Robin Hood's Bay and Runswick lies precisely in this informality of street pattern.

Because of the steep cliffs and the pressure of demand for housing many of the yards on the west side were built up against the living rock – to see this, walk along the Cragg and look at the slots and beam holes cut into the cliff for

24 *Tin Ghaut seen from the harbourside. This famous piece of Whitby was demolished in 1959 and its site is now marked by a car park. Drying grounds were in great demand for the cramped cottages in densely packed yards and even the harbour provided some space at low tide; older photographs of Whitby regularly show washing strung out above the mud. The small timber buildings attached to the house on the left were originally privies discharging into the harbour.*

houses which were mostly demolished in the late 1950s. On the east side behind Church Street the cliff slope is more gradual and here houses were built against each other in a crazy climb up the cliff. The most famous houses of this type, the well-known galleried houses of Boulby Bank, were demolished in a monumental piece of town planning folly in 1958. (Cappelman's Yard, also in Church Street, had no less than three levels of wooden galleries across between the houses.) Such galleried houses were almost all tenements, with a household or more per level.

A similar fate befell the picturesque Tin Ghaut, between the Harbour and Church Street, in the following year. This was typical of the many entrances which pierced the solid ranks of buildings fronting the harbour and giving access for loading and unloading. In spite of the destruction there are still many steep and picturesque corners containing inextricably mixed-up houses with their red pantiled roofs, which together demonstrate the quintessence of Whitby. The danger of building on the unstable lower levels of the cliff was dramatically demonstrated at the end of November 2012, a notoriously wet year, when Aelfleda Terrace, set above lower Church Street and built in 1861, began to slip, just like the Haggerlythe at the top end of Henrietta Street in the 18th century. Five brick cottages had eventually to be demolished.

THE PARISH CHURCH

Whitby Parish Church is truly unusual and defies any attempt to categorise it or to dissect its special charm. Pevsner declared: 'It is one of the churches one is fondest of in the whole of England', while Sir Alec Clifton-Taylor was equally complimentary. Its overall appearance and plainness accord well with modern taste but to many Victorians it was anathema. Indeed, one Victorian parson, the Rev. W. Keane, described it as: '… now perhaps the most depraved sacred building in the kingdom …'.

What really upset such people was that it was, and is, shamelessly a preaching church, an auditorium designed to fit in the greatest number of people with a view of the pulpit. Two and a half thousand people, it is said, could be accommodated. The chancel, in contrast, and hence the sacrament of the communion, was lost in Stygian gloom beneath the white barley-sugar columned Cholmley pew. To Georgians this hardly mattered but when the ritual of the following century made the activities of the priest in the chancel the centre of attention the church proved quite unsuitable. However, with commendable if unusual restraint the Victorians did not sweep away the interior, or even the offending pew. It was not until 1905 that a very discreet and tasteful reordering of the chancel took place under the distinguished architect W.D. Caroë, a fact for which we should give thanks.

Most of the charm of the building springs from its entirely original interior; the exterior does not give much of a hint of what is to be seen inside, apart from the large 'domestic' Georgian windows or the external steps to the multitude of galleries. A walk around the outside helps to give some feeling of date and sequence since once inside one is seduced by the furnishings and sees little of the architecture.

The nave is essentially Norman; an ornate doorway, now disused, stands to the east of the present porch. Perhaps one of the early abbots was responsible for

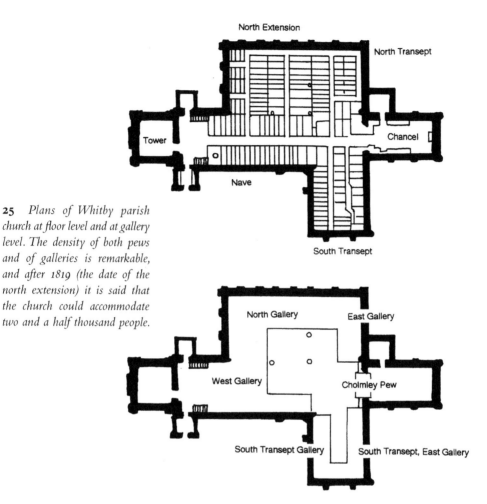

North Extension

North Transept

Tower

Chancel

Nave

South Transept

25 *Plans of Whitby parish church at floor level and at gallery level. The density of both pews and of galleries is remarkable, and after 1819 (the date of the north extension) it is said that the church could accommodate two and a half thousand people.*

North Gallery

East Gallery

West Gallery

Cholmley Pew

South Transept Gallery

South Transept, East Gallery

its building, in order to avoid public use of the abbey nave. Of the same date is the chancel as well, so the Norman church was as long as the church is today. Whether or not it had transepts is uncertain. That to the north was certainly rebuilt or added in about 1225, concurrently with the new work at the abbey, while its counterpart to the south was added in 1380 to contain a series of chapels.

It was also in the 13th century that the west tower was added and it was through this that the main access to the church was gained. No doubt the exposed and windy position here led to the door being moved to the south side in due course, and the tower was reduced in height in the 17th century, perhaps for the same reasons.

Charlton states that the church, 'nearly preserved its ancient form till about the year 1744, when the north wall growing very bad, and being in danger of falling, it was taken down and rebuilt, with the windows in somewhat a more modern taste …'.

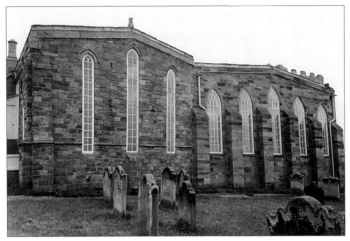

26 *Whitby parish church from the north, showing the medieval transept (left), its lancet windows filled with plain Georgian glass, and the extended north aisle of 1819 with intersecting tracery in its glazing bars. Despite its lack of pretention there is some attempt in this extension to match the symmetry and proportions of the medieval work.*

27 *Whitby parish church from the south-east. On the right is the Norman chancel, restored by W.D. Caroë in 1905, while to the left is the medieval south transept. On the eastern face of the tower is the chasing for an earlier, higher, roofline. Note the domestic-type windows and rooflights and the external stairs giving access to galleries.*

It was not only the north wall of the nave that was altered. It is a truism that churches reflect in their fabric the changing economic situation of the communities they serve and in Whitby's case that community was growing steadily in wealth and sophistication from the end of the 17th century. The church could not contain the growing population, nor yet the parishioners from its outlying townships who walked here every Sunday. Something had to be done, and it was.

The thing that was done was the building of galleries around the inside; not just three as in many Georgian churches, providing a close parallel to contemporary theatres, but a whole succession of them. The first was added in 1697, along the south wall of the nave, followed by no fewer than two at the west end in 1700 and 1709. In 1757 the south transept gained its gallery and the north transept in 1764. In 1819 a large new extension was added to the north side of the church, between the nave and the north transept. To do this the north nave wall, according to Charlton only built in 1744, was demolished. This work was carried out with the support of the Incorporated Church Building Society; the plans indicate that the design was by John Bolton, architect. Across the west and north sides of this space new galleries took their place.

It is the galleries which give the church its feel and proportion. The low pitched roof with sky lights is supported by thin columns and the general constriction of space overcome by compact solutions gives it the feeling

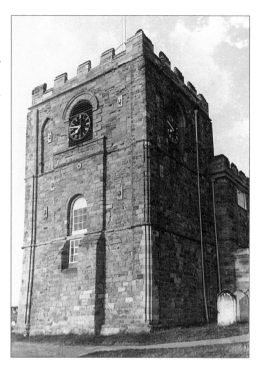

28 *The massive Norman west tower of the parish church, seen from the south-west. The evidence of a blocked west door and blocked or blank upper lancets hints at an unusually complicated history, which may have included the loss of the uppermost storey in the 17th century.*

29 *The parish church from the north, from a steel engraving by Rock & Co., dated 1855. Much of the cliff in the foreground has fallen or become unstable in recent years.*

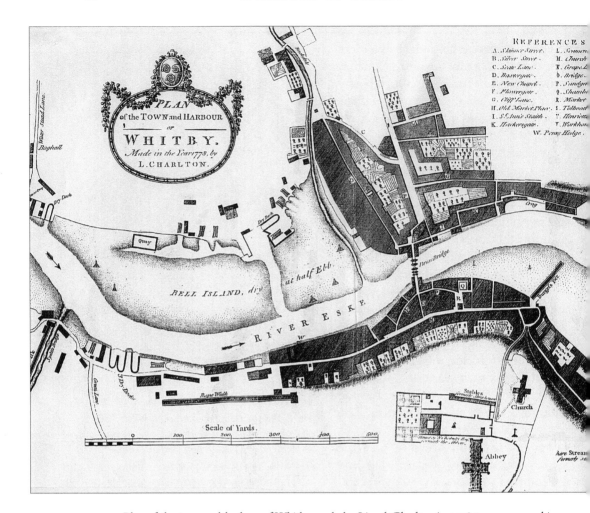

30 *Plan of the town and harbour of Whitby made by Lionel Charlton in 1778 to accompany his history. Useful as it is in some respects it is spoilt by the 'block planning' of the built-up areas and does not compare in quality with Wood's Map of 1828 or Pickernell's of 1841.*

of being between decks in a contemporary ship. The similarity does not bear close examination but there may be real links between the two since no craftsman in wood in Whitby could fail to be influenced by the shipbuilding trade and would tend to use its style and proportions.

Both the galleries and the body of the church are filled with box pews. These are of many different designs according to the taste and purse of their owner, since the majority of them were private property which could be bought, sold or left by will. The oldest are those in the south transept, used by parishioners from the townships of Eskdaleside, Ugglebarnby and Hawsker-cum-Stainsacre. In one of the Eskdaleside pews are two carved dates, 1641 and 1655, so the pews are presumably older still.

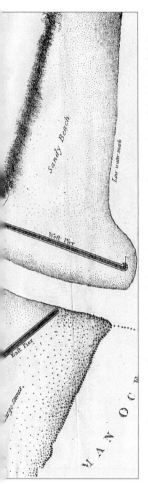

Over on the other side of the church the pews are hard and narrow, dating from after 1819 and apparently free. Elsewhere and especially in the galleries there are some very distinctive pews lined with red or green baize held in place by rows of brass tacks, with seats facing in both directions. Those pews without such lining contain many graffiti including over forty of ships alone, carved during sermon time, which we will see in more detail in chapter five.

The great white Cholmley pew, built across the chancel in about 1600-25, illustrates the breathtaking assurance of the early members of the family to do just whatever they pleased.

As this is not a guide to the church I will not attempt to detail all the fittings. However, some are well worthy of mention. The pulpit dates from 1778 and was made at the expense of John Huntrods. It originally stood in a highly precarious position suspended across between pews but was moved to its present position in 1847. The two curious objects made of leather tubing attached to it are identified as ear trumpets used by Mrs Andrew, the deaf wife of a rector in 1809-43! Why she needed two is not explained. The attractive brass candelabrum dates from 1769.

A small wooden rack, kept in the churchwardens' pew, held the 'Galilee bread', a bequest dating from 1847 when Mrs Alice Galilee left the income of a cottage in Jackson's Yard, Church Street, to provide bread on Sundays for poor people. This custom is now more or less discontinued but matches the traditional bread dole and bread cupboard at places such as Cartmel Priory and Kirkby Stephen, both in Cumbria.

In the tower are 10 glorious bells, one of the finest peals in the country, the sound of which is enhanced by the lofty position of the church. They were recast and augmented from earlier bells by Percy Shaw Jeffrey and his wife of Bagdale Old Hall in 1950. The belfry contains many boards recording gifts to Whitby Public Schools, the Lancasterian School for Girls, the Dorcas Society and other charities.

Surrounding the church is the equally distinctive churchyard. The wind and salt air have etched the gravestones and centuries of coal smoke have blackened them to the point that many inscriptions are no longer legible. Most are of sandstone from local deposits and weather very easily. Areas of the churchyard to the north and east have also fallen over the cliff as a result of the very marked erosion. The churchyard is now closed because of the density of burials; one of the last people to be buried here was Chancellor Austen of York, a former rector and notable figure at the turn of the century. His grave is near the top of the church stairs. Nearby stands the Caedmon memorial, set up in the form of an Anglo-Saxon cross in 1898 and unveiled by the then poet laureate, Alfred Austin, to commemorate Whitby's most famous poet.

31 *An atmospheric corner of Whitby churchyard, the sandstone gravestones etched by the hand of time and the fierce gales. A high proportion are now illegible but those inscriptions which can be read have now been recorded while it can still be done. Those gravestones that survive are plentiful enough but they are a mere fraction of the number of burials made over the centuries in this ground. This churchyard was closed in 1858.*

OTHER CHURCHES

For many centuries the parish church stood alone in Whitby, its privileges jealously guarded. Its parish was very large, serving many isolated townships in the moors and the moorland dales, and the parishioners walked or rode to Whitby each Sunday, whatever the weather, no doubt despite many a loud complaint.

A number of these townships achieved their own chapels of ease in time, but still owed allegiance to their mother church, to which parishioners still had to come to be baptised, married or buried. Growing population in the late medieval period made some changes necessary and so did the rise of nonconformity.

In Whitby itself there were two early chapels whose status is not quite clear. At the corner of the Market Place with Church Street is a group of old houses which Young claims had replaced a pre-Reformation chapel. On the other side of the harbour, in Baxtergate, was the old St Ninian's Chapel, latterly used as Messrs. Hayes' and Falkingbridge's wine vaults and demolished as late as 1927. This plain stone building is thought by some to have been a bridge chapel, if indeed the medieval bridge end lay as far south-west as this, which I doubt. In the 18th century it was known as the Callice-House, which has been taken to be a variant of 'Chalice-House'. However, this seems an unlikely derivation, so other possibilities should be considered. The former was known in 1595 as 'a howse called a chappell' and I cannot resist the suggestion that it may not have been a chapel at all, but rather a house for chantry priests engaged in one of the chantry chapels in the parish church.

Next in order of date were the Friends' Meeting House, established in 1676, and the old Presbyterian Chapel (later Unitarian) in a yard at the foot of Flowergate, its first building dating from 1715, though its congregation was founded some twenty years earlier. The Presbyterian Chapel was largely founded and supported by the benefactions of Leonard Wilde, a sailmaker. Both places of worship were enlarged in the early 19th century but still retain some of their charm.

The Society of Friends was to exert a powerful influence on Whitby in the 18th century. From a position of persecution in their early days, partly as a result of the attitude of the established church and partly as a result of their own uncom-promising attitude, the Quakers quickly won themselves respect. They believed in plainness and straight dealing – no Quaker would swear an oath because it was said that a Quaker should be the same all through and honest at all times. Plainness of dress was a virtue also and so the Friends stood out as a clearly marked group. They became the backbone of the merchant community despite the difficulties which they met in time of war – as pacifists they would not arm their ships – nor did they involve themselves in smuggling or handling of smuggled goods, because it defrauded the Revenue. Those that did arm ships were expelled from membership.

The Methodists had an octagonal chapel at the far end of the Haggerlythe from 1761-2. This fell into the sea and was replaced by an huge one set high on steps above Church Street, built in 1788. John Wesley preached here in 1788 before it was quite finished and men were positioned along the edges of the, as yet, unrailed galleries to stop others falling over! Another chapel was built in Brunswick Street, at that date Scate Lane, in 1814. The present Brunswick Methodist Chapel dates from 1891. The Primitive Methodists had a chapel in a yard in Church Street, known somewhat unkindly as Ranters' Meeting Yard, from 1821.

32 *The Church Stairs on a Sunday morning, with returning churchgoers, c.1910. Sir George Head described the sight in 1835 thus: 'These steps may be seen every Sunday covered from top to bottom with old and young, parents at the decline of life, children at its commencement, both together surmounting the arduous ascent, and wending their way to the sacred edifice … I was forcibly reminded, on such an occasion, of Bunyan's beautiful allegory of "The Hill of Difficulty"'.*

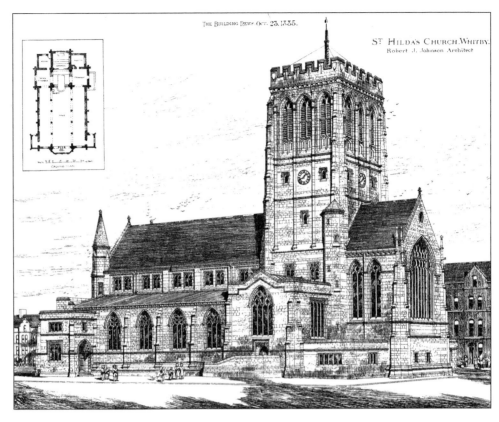

THE BUILDING NEWS OCT. 23. 1885.

ST HILDA'S CHURCH. WHITBY.
Robert J. Johnson Architect

33 *St Hilda's church, illustrated in* The Building News, *23 October 1885. This large and imposing church, designed by R.J. Johnson of Newcastle, was intended to serve the growing middle-class population of the West Cliff. There is perhaps a touch of imitation of the Abbey on the opposite cliff. The tower, however, was not built until 1938, and then to a more modest design. The West Cliff development, mostly Classical in inspiration and detail, becomes Gothic in the area around the church.*

34 *The gallery of St Ninian's church, Baxtergate, much as it was in 1778. The ground floor by contrast was heavily restored in an Anglo-Catholic manner in the 1880s.*

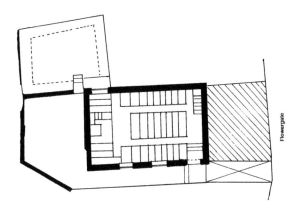

35 *Ground plan of the Independent (Unitarian) Chapel, redrawn from the Ordnance Survey map of 1852. This simple chapel, rebuilt in 1812 on an older site, lies down a yard on the south side of Flowergate and retains much of its original furnishing.*

In 1776 a new St Ninian's chapel was built in Baxtergate, on the opposite side from its predecessor and further to the west. It is unusual in being what is described as a proprietory chapel, that is, one which is owned by its congregation rather than vested in the diocese, as a result of its being built by subscription. A total of 30 subscribers paid £64 each, and became shareholders in it. Until 1863 it was known simply as 'Baxtergate Chapel'. A plain brick structure approached by steps from the outside, it has galleries around three sides of the interior. Its pews were replaced in 1881–82, when it became Anglo-Catholic in ritual, but in the gallery many original pews survive, some with ship graffiti like those in the parish church.

The 19th century saw a great growth in the provision of churches of all kinds. St John's in Baxtergate was added at the middle of the century. St Hilda's Roman Catholic church in Bagdale is a pompous affair of 1867 replacing a more modest structure of 1805; its south-west turret, reduced in height in 1990, appears to be a direct echo of the abbey. Another St Hilda's, this time Anglican, crowns the West Cliff development. Dating from 1884–86 it similarly imitates the abbey, this time with its central tower. This tower was a late addition of 1938, a more modest affair than was originally planned.

This church is very grand and attractive enough from the outside but lacks charm, as do so many of its date. Its size is explained by the need to cater both for a growing West Cliff community and for the large number of visitors lodging in the area. In winter the congregation used the nave but in summer extended into the aisles. The present church was preceded by a temporary structure in 1868 known as the 'Iron Church'.

On the opposite side of the harbour St Michael's church, a simple structure with a bellcote, was inserted on the waterfront near Tin Ghaut in 1847–48, but it is long gone, a car park occupying its site.

Most of the 19th-century churches represent either the realisation that the new suburbs required a convenient place of worship or the general freeing up of attitudes exemplified by Catholic Emancipation. At all events the new situation makes a very great contrast to that of the medieval period where one church ministered exclusively to a vast but sparsely populated parish.

COMMERCE, TRADE AND SERVICES

Whitby's minor trades and industries were heavily influenced by the major ones of shipbuilding and the port trade. A glance at the *Baines' Directory* for 1823, for instance, shows just how many trades were dependent upon shipping, such as sailcloth weaving, ropemaking and block-and-pump-making. However, Whitby was also the natural market centre for a wide area of moorland and dales communities and so served all the usual purposes of a place of exchange of surpluses and a supplier of otherwise unavailable commodities. Among these were services such as the law, banking and medicine.

Whitby was therefore well supplied with lawyers, banks and medical services. Probably most country people did not undertake a visit to Whitby for a single purpose but to buy and sell in the market, to invest their surpluses in shipping, to prosecute a neighbour and to have some uncomfortable medical condition examined. In 1823 there were six partnerships of attornies, five banks and a savings bank, two physicians and nine surgeons in the town.

Thomas Peirson opened a bank in 1778, followed by the Sanders brothers in 1779. Their bank was in Church Street near the Market Place. A house still standing at 51 Church Street was built in 1800 as the bank of Margaret and Robert Campion. The Campions had many other business enterprises, such as sailcloth weaving.

In Grape Lane was the bank established by Wakefield Simpson and Abel Chapman in 1785. They were both Quakers, like the Sanders. Under the name of the Old Bank this continued until it was taken over by the York Union Bank in 1892. To generations of Whitby people it was known more generally as 'the Green Gate' and the house still stands, though much altered. The kindness and humanity shown by the partners in the bank was legendary. As an example, my great-great-grandfather George Willis went to this bank in 1856 with great need of a loan of £100 to pay his share in the brig *Active* and later, in 1865, to buy out a partner for £456. In each case Simpson, Chapman & Co. lent him the money without security, relying on his good name and their own good judgement, in neither of which were they mistaken.

In 1823 the finer things in life were also available – two shops sold musical instruments, while five watch and clockmakers were at work. An umbrella maker could also be found in Baxtergate, as could a clay tobacco pipe maker. By 1851 the list of non-port activities had extended, catering for the needs of visitors and for middle-class residents. Music teachers, dancing masters and artists appear in the census of that year, as well as lodging house keepers, a fossil dealer and a large number of jet miners, dealers and workers who exploited Whitby's natural assets.

Until the opening of the railway, goods came into and out of the town by pannier pony, by carrier's cart or by sea. We shall see more of these in a later chapter. The railway changed the picture considerably by giving access to a new hinterland and ultimately by opening Whitby up to manufactured goods from elsewhere and ending its long isolation.

Whitby must have acted as a market centre a long way back into the Middle Ages but evidence is rather lacking. In the 17th century we have evidence from different sources. Five Whitby merchants and shopkeepers issued halfpenny or farthing tokens in the period 1667-71. William Harrison and John Rymer were mercers, John Hird a vintner, and William Lotherington and Henry Sneaton pursued unrecorded trades, the latter in Flowergate. His token is well known for its arms of three ammonites. Lotherington was a Quaker. At this time it is fairly clear that Whitby was a modest place, serving principally as a market for dairy produce, which was shipped out coastwise, and for cloth which was bought

36 *A £5 note of Sanders' Bank, containing a minute engraved view of the harbour from Larpool. Sanders' Bank was at 93 Church Street, nearly opposite the Town Hall.*

and used locally. We should perhaps not underestimate even these, as Whitby was in 1638 the largest shipper of butter to London, with 6,566 firkins.

By the 19th century several windmills stood in the vicinity of Whitby. The five-sailed Union Mill near Flowergate Cross, established in 1800, provided cheap flour for the poor and also, on occasions, a dividend for its 800 subscribers. Subscribers appear to have held a ticket, which was stamped every time a dividend of flour was paid to them. The idea of a Union Mill was not uncommon. Some fifteen others are recorded in England and Wales. This windmill once formed quite a landmark on the Whitby skyline. Bagdale or Wren's mill was in Factory Fields behind Chubb Hill and Hanover Terrace, and survived until 1862. Anderson's Mill stood near the Scarborough & Whitby railway line from at least 1778 until perhaps 1887. A very ancient site at Ruswarp accommodated successive water mills, the last of which, built in 1752 by Nathaniel Cholmley, burnt out in 1911 and subsequently rebuilt, has only recently ceased to function.

There is not space to write of all the small businesses which once flourished in the town. One, however, that is worthy of note still continues to flourish after over a century and a half. This is Botham's, bakers and confectioners. Mrs Elizabeth Botham, a widow with a large family, began her business perhaps in the late 1870s as a confectioner. Our family tradition credits her with a pie cart, which she took down the Pier. Later she had a shop in Fishburn Park and by the 1880s was in Skinner Street where the firm's main shop and restaurant still stand. She also ran a little beerhouse called the Hole in the Wall down the yard, on which she could keep an eye from her back parlour. Mrs. Botham's reputation was based on the quality of her ingredients, a basis which her successors maintain. Probably the continued success of her business was due to the custom of serving a late afternoon Yorkshire high tea which hotels and guest houses maintained for many years, a legacy of Victorian custom. In recent years the bakehouse has moved up to an industrial estate off the Scarborough Road at Helredale, which also has a shop, making four in all: this one, Skinner Street, Baxtergate and Sleights.

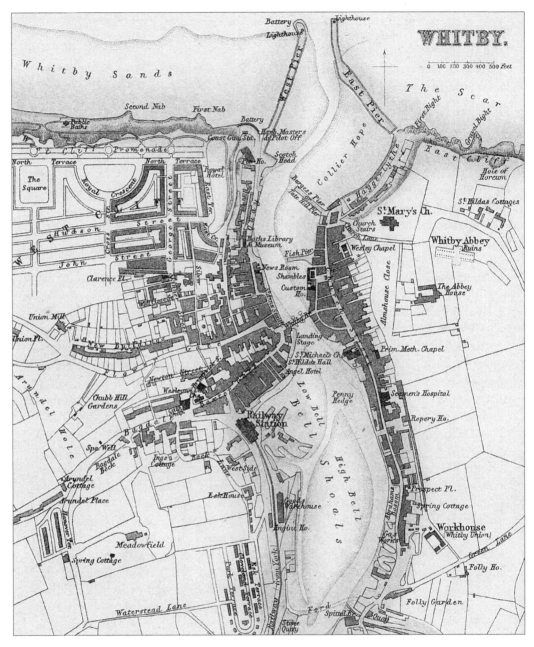

37 *Map of Whitby in about 1860. The railway has arrived and, since its takeover by the York & North Midland, has been converted to steam haulage. The new station has accordingly moved north to the edge of the town, among the shipbuilding yards. On the West Cliff work is underway to build the grand terraces and crescent for the new middle-class visitors, part of George Hudson's speculation to turn Whitby into a seaside resort. To the south of the station Esk Terrace and Cleveland Terrace have been completed. Behind them speculative builders will soon be running up 'superior' working-class housing in the fields between Waterstead Lane and Meadowfield.*

Another success story, though more recent, has been that of Whitby scampi, a product of Whitby Seafoods, which seems to have gained a virtual monopoly in shops and cafes across the country.

EDUCATION

In 1734 the Rev. James Borwick wrote in reply to his new Archbishop's enquiry:

> There is no endow'd School in my Parish – All the Masters and Mistresses (excepting such as be Dissenters) who teach English, Mathematics, or Grammar, – are careful to instruct their Scholars in the Church-Catechism, and to send them to Church …

It is somewhat surprising to find that Whitby did not support an ancient grammar school as so many towns of its size did during the 16th and 17th century. The brief existence of some such school is hinted at by the testimonial signed by 28 Whitby men in support of Christopher Stephenson, schoolmaster, in 1679. The terms of this suggest that he was not a native and that he was under some suspicion of religious non-conformity. The so-called Public Schools for Boys, run on the Lancasterian system, did not begin until 1810 in a room on Church Street. In 1821 it moved to a new building on the Mount, paid for by subscription. Its counterpart for girls was founded in 1814, in Cliff Street.

A number of other schools, run mainly by clergymen, widows and spinsters sprang up after this, and there were also many Sunday schools, which were not quite what the term conjures up today. Although they had a religious purpose they also provided a basic education for very poor children who worked the remainder of the week to live and to support their families and were only free on Sundays.

Lionel Charlton, the historian, came here in about 1748 and taught mathematics at his school in the old tollbooth, as well as pursuing a career as a land-surveyor.

The quality of teaching must have varied enormously. In 1823, for instance, you might have had your education from Mary Lister in Little Angel Yard, Dorothy Lund in Church Street, Sarah Mort in Flowergate, or from Elizabeth and Ann Seamer in Baxtergate or from any of four other ladies. To follow a classical education you might have approached the Rev. Robert Moffatt in Church Street, while for a commercial grounding you might go to Skinner Street where the Rev. James Rutherford kept his establishment.

Although the late 19th century saw many official schools supported by the various churches, St Michael's and St John's, for instance, or by the school board, the private schools remained an important source of education well into the next century. In the 1920s, for instance, there was a boys' school on the site of the present police station. Known as West Hill School or Bulmers, it was run by Mr R.T. Bulmer; later, renamed Caedmon College, it provided a 'day and boarding school for girls, boys and kindergarten' as an advertisement of 1938 states.

It was not until 1912 that the new county school in Mayfield Road was opened. This provided a wider and more general education to what would now be called secondary level. Later it became a grammar school but with the change to comprehensive education it has changed its name again to become Whitby School. The first headmaster was Dr William Aloysius ('Wab' or 'Bill') Bradley, who taught here until 1934.

In addition to all these there was a strong movement during the 19th century for scientific and literary education, especially for those interested in self-help. The Whitby Literary & Philosophical Society, founded in 1823, served both roles (Philosophy included what we would now call natural sciences) much as mechanics' institutes did elsewhere. In Whitby, however, both supporters and users tended to be middle class in origin, not artisans.

A kindred body was the Institute of Popular Science and Literature, established in 1845, which occupied the Friends' Meeting House during a low ebb in that body's fortunes. It contained a large library, scientific equipment and a telescope, and lectures and classes were given in subjects as diverse as French and navigation. Both institutions were fostered by the great interest in popular science and especially the infant science of geology at this period; geology was especially relevant in Whitby because of the rich fossil fauna and the many exposures of different strata in the cliffs and foreshore.

Many of the old schools lay among buildings, tightly hemmed in on all sides, with a playground, perhaps, but no playing field. During the last 20 years the opportunity has been taken to provide new schools on the edge of the town. Airy Hill and Caedmon Schools lie close together at the top of Waterstead Lane in an open position among fields. There is a similar arrangement with the schools on the east side of the town, a move to the outskirts where there is more level space.

HEALTH CARE

Like many other towns, the history of health care in Whitby is patchy because the care itself was patchy.

Probably the earliest evidence is that of the leper hospital built by the abbot, William de Percy, at Spital Bridge for a man named Orm in A.D. 1109. Orm has the doubtful honour of being one of the earliest recorded lepers in Yorkshire. After Orm a monk called Geoffrey de Mansell contracted leprosy and became the inmate of this small house. Later the house was enlarged and took in both sick and healthy – leprosy having fortunately declined during the 14th century. Many former leper hospitals became in effect retirement homes for public servants after the 13th century, because places in them were in the gift of the rich and powerful and particularly the Crown. The inmates of the Whitby hospital were fortunate in obtaining the gift of the old clothes belonging to the monks of Rievaulx every year at Martinmas (11 November). This hospital, dedicated to St John Baptist, probably did not outlive the Dissolution of the monasteries. Some small remains of it survived into the 19th century, just to the south west side of Spital Bridge, which clearly took its name from the institution. Recent survey work on the site of the redundant Whitehall Shipyard of the Old Sail Loft suggests that traces of the medieval hospital may have been incorporated in that.

Although various charities had some bearing on the care of the sick there was until 1786 no actual building to provide a focus for health care, particularly for the poor. The dispensary was established first in Haggersgate, then in Borough Place in Church Street, then finally in 52 Church Street, in a purpose-built structure, with an elaborate code of rules. Public subscriptions supported it and poor people could obtain help and medicine from it if they could obtain the support of a subscriber. This system was of course much better than anything which had gone before, but still left much to be desired.

A seamen's hospital was founded as early as 1676, though in its early years it is referred to as 'Hospital Houses'. 'Forty houses in the town of Whitby, contiguous to each other' are referrred to as having existed in the Charity Commissioners' Report of 1897, and it was more concerned with housing than healthcare, like many such institutions. Its purpose was to support poor seamen, their wives or widows, and the education of their children, the funds being drawn from a levy on ships, masters and seamen of Whitby, as well as from legacies. In 1842 a pompous new façade in the Jacobean style was added to the hospital in Church Street by Scott & Moffatt (Sir Gilbert Scott), but the accommodation behind is much more modest.

In 1870 a cottage hospital was established at 16 York Terrace, moving first to the Old Brewery in Church Street in 1898 and then to the 'Green Gate' in Grape Lane in 1901. This latter building had been the premises first of *The Grapes* public house and then of Simpson, Chapman & Co.'s bank. Even after the hospital function moved on these premises continued to house clinics.

In 1925 a new War Memorial Cottage Hospital was opened in Spring Hill and this with various outstations such as St Hilda's (the former workhouse in Green Lane) continued in use until a new hospital offering more comprehensive services was built nearby in Spring Hill, opening in 1977. The War Memorial Cottage Hospital was demolished in the same year and St Hilda's passed out of use in 1979 and was sold.

BOMBARDMENT!

In the First World War Whitby became one of the few English towns to be subjected to direct enemy action. On 16 December 1914 a wholly unexpected menace loomed suddenly out of the mists of the North Sea. Just before nine o'clock in the morning two large men-of-war were spotted by the look-out at the signal station, heading up the coast from the direction of Scarborough. Shortly afterwards they manoeuvred in unison to bring their stern guns to bear on Whitby and commenced firing. Whitby was enjoying the rare privilege of being fired on by a hostile power, without any means of retaliation.

The two ships were *Derfflinger* and *Von der Tann*, both battle cruisers of the German High Seas Fleet, armed with 12-and 11-inch guns respectively. The aim of the attack was not primarily to inflict damage on British coastal towns, nor to demoralise the civilian population, though the Germans succeeded to a limited

38　*No. 1 Grove Street, the house of Mr Blewett, showing damage caused to the gable and roof by German shelling in December 1914. Postcards showing the results of the bombardment were very popular at the time, reflecting the mood of shock and wonder that the British lion could have its tail pulled in its own den.*

extent in both of these. Instead the assault was intended to draw out elements of the Grand Fleet on a retaliatory strike and catch them on freshly laid minefields between the English coast and the Dogger Bank. Von Ingenohl's fleet of six ships split into detachments to bombard Scarborough, Whitby and Hartlepool. Only at the latter were there shore batteries capable of responding.

Whitby was by no means a strategic target; it had no industries significant to the war effort, other than perhaps the fishing, and it had no military installations. The only target of importance was the signal station, capable of reporting the presence of the raiders. With their customary accurate gunnery the German ships knocked this out within the first few salvoes. Other shots fell far and wide, perhaps due to the rolling of the ships. Most fell in the area of Fishburn Park, causing considerable damage to houses. Considering the number of shells fired in the 11 minutes of the bombardment it is extremely lucky that there were so few casualties. Some shells fell far inland, the furthest coming to earth at Woodlands and Thistle Grove in Sleights.

Although the parish church was almost unscathed, the buildings now forming the youth hostel on the East Cliff and the Caedmon Cross were struck by shell splinters. One of the most serious casualties was the west end of the abbey which was seriously damaged. This was not to be an unmitigated disaster since the damage led to the site being taken over and consolidated by the Office of Works, to its ultimate benefit.

To the civilian population the bombardment was a very frightening event, the first taste of total war to have been inflicted on Britain since the Napoleonic Wars and the raids of John Paul Jones. It made people doubt for the first time the omnipotence of the Grand Fleet, since the raiders escaped. However, six weeks later the balance was somewhat redressed at the battle of the Dogger Bank, where a similar raiding party was caught, the *Blucher* sunk and *Seydlitz* and *Derfflinger* badly damaged. Moreover the raid proved useful as propaganda in recruiting men into the services; it was seen as a chance to hit back, though all too many lives of recruits were simply thrown away in senseless engagements in France.

Two

HARBOUR AND BRIDGE

Whitby harbour occupies the post-glacial estuary of the river Esk and naturally divides into an upper and a lower half. The Upper Harbour, above the bridge which links the east and west sides of the town at a natural narrowing-point, was used as a safer anchorage in storms, for laying up ships over winter and for shipbuilding. Because of the deep swell that could enter the harbour before the present piers were completed the lower harbour was not a safe mooring in the 16th and 17th centuries.

In good weather much shipping would lie off in Whitby Roads, the area to the west of the harbour mouth, waiting for the tide. Especially deep-laden vessels could also lie here awaiting unloading into lighters. There was deep water here but if the wind freshened suddenly from the north or west there was a danger of being driven on to the Scaur, the rocky foreshore to the east, or into the piers. The lower harbour was satisfactory in good weather and was used by many fishing boats. Gradual improvements to the piers, especially the large-scale harbour works which successive harbour engineers such as Jonathan and Francis Pickernell carried out between 1781 and 1861, made a considerable difference to the safety of the harbour.

In the upper harbour two large mud banks, High and Low Bell, were exposed at half ebb. Recent changes in the harbour and the building of new wharves have rearranged the channel of the Esk and moved the mud banks around. At spring tides the harbour all but dried out, leaving vessels aground. A considerable tract of land has been recovered from the harbour over the last two centuries and buildings and car parks now cover the former Walker and Langborne Sands at the end of Bagdale, where shipbuilders once worked.

There was until recent years little need for quays. Fish was landed from fishing boats onto the various staiths. Whitby Stone Company had a wharf near Bog Hall for the convenience of loading its heavy cargoes and there was some quayage on the east bank of the river above the bridge, but otherwise Whitby's shipping acted as a carrier between other ports, putting in at Whitby only for repairs or laying up. Colliers unloaded their coal on the beach into carts; alum vessels made the best approach they could to the awkward alum loading facilities along the coast, often lying on the open foreshore.

Apart from the convenience of loading and unloading, however, quays and staiths by the river's edge became a necessary means of communication along the harbour side. Between 1786 and 1789 a quay was built between the Scotch Head and Haggersgate, continuing the staith allowed for in an Act of Parliament in 1749 from the bridge to Tyreman's Coffee House End. Another quay was to be added in 1828 between Barry's dock and the *Angel Inn* or Horse Mill Ghaut. St Ann's Staith dates from around 1820 and was extended in 1840. The staith at Dock End was completed just before Francis Pickernell's retirement *(see below)*.

In the lower harbour there are four piers; projecting seaward are the East and West Pier, while the Burgess or Tate Hill Pier and to its south the Fish Pier project into the harbour from its east side. Opposite Tate Hill Pier and at the base of the West Pier is the projection known as the Scotch Head. Between the East and Tate Hill Piers is a sandy beach called Collier Hope, presumably from the colliers which lay here to unload coal. Near the Scotch Head is an area known formerly as the Little Sands, though today there is little sand on this side of the harbour.

The West Pier is attached at its base to the Battery Parade, so called from the gun battery which once stood here, with eight guns and a magazine. Parts of this, including the two small round-houses, still remain. The head of the West Pier also carried a six-gun battery, but both batteries were dismantled after the Napoleonic Wars. A further battery had stood at the end of the Haggerlyth on the east side of the harbour, but two men were killed here in 1782 by the bursting of a gun and in 1785 the whole battery slipped into the sea. A battery is still shown in this position, however, overlooking the East Pier, on Pickernell's plan of 1796. The danger came not only from

39 *'A view of the East and West Piers of Whitby Harbour with West Cliff and the Road' by H. Chapman, 1777. This interesting early view shows the West Pier without its lighthouse and before the building of the Battery. A bark sails out into the Roads towing the pilot's tender astern.*

40 *A drawing in Whitby Museum which shows the gun battery at the base of the West Pier in place behind a timber stockade. In the background is a track running steeply down from the East Cliff to the Scaur, believed to have been built by the Cholmley family. Cliff erosion has long since removed any trace. The drawing is by Capt. James Thornhill and dates from 1796.*

41 *Part of Jonathan Pickernell's plan of the harbour, dated 1796. This detail shows the West Pier before its extension, the gun battery, and Scotch Head.*

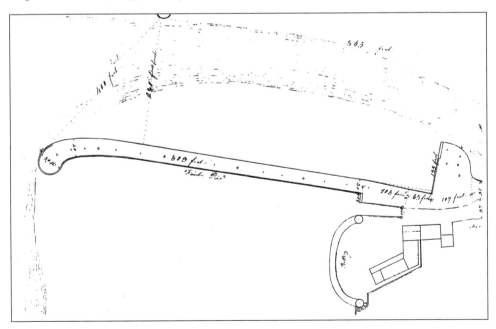

42 *One of the two 18th-century roundhouses which terminate the gun battery. Originally used for ammunition and storage they have somehow survived to the present day.*

the French but also from the American John Paul Jones who actually appeared off Whitby in 1788 and threatened the port. A strategic analysis of Whitby's position and need for defences was produced by Francis Gibson, the multi-talented Collector of Customs, in 1794.

Beyond the West Pier to the north-west are the Sands, and, further out, Whitby Roads, a fair-weather anchorage for shipping. The East Pier has not until recently been connected to the land at its base, partly because of the crumbling nature of the cliff behind it. Instead, access has been gained by a structure called the Spa Ladder, which over the years has needed frequent replacement. A narrow gap between the cliff and the base of the pier gave access to the rocky Scaur beyond it. In the last few years the rapid crumbling of the Haggerlythe, the narrow shelf of land at the northern end of Henrietta Street, has called for a more radical approach. A steeply sloping ramp now gives access to a stone link to the pier, while rock armour protects the foot of the adjoining cliffs to the east. How long this arrangement will last is anyone's guess. The sea tends to have the last laugh.

To the north of the East Pier is the Whitby Rock, a treacherous shelf of shale projecting well out to sea. Through this runs a natural geological fault called the Sledway, providing a narrow channel of deeper water.

Because Whitby was such an important haven for the huge fleets of colliers sailing between the Tyne and the Thames its harbour works were supported by a tax levied on goods landed at Whitby itself and on coal loaded at the port of Newcastle and its members, from 1702 until 1861, when the tax was repealed. This remarkable tax was no doubt achieved because of the very substantial ownership of colliers by Whitby (it was third in order of all collier-owning ports in England in 1702-4). Indeed the terms of a letter to the shipowners of Newcastle by their counterparts in Whitby in 1717 suggest that the latter were very influential in regulating the coal trade.

Work on the Piers is first recorded in wills of the 1530s, where benefactors left money for the purpose. In 1632, at the command of Hugh Cholmley, the West Pier was built or rebuilt in stone (it may have been of timber before). In 1734 and

1749 it was lengthened by 300 ft. and terminated in a five-gun battery. Between 1800 and 1814 Francis Pickernell added to both its length and width. The East Pier, perhaps a creation of the 1702 tax, was extended in a slanting direction to the north-west in 1844-50. One can still easily make out the original half-round end embedded in the later masonry.

Lighthouses appeared at the ends of both piers, on the west in 1831 and on the east in 1854. The final improvement which much reduces the swell in the harbour but adds nothing to the appearance of the piers consists of extensions to both piers in 1912, taking the form of concrete bases carrying timber uprights and decks. These form a delightful promenade for visitors to Whitby and a 'pier ender' is a fine appetiser before a meal. The East Pier 'bridge' has been missing for some years, but there is now talk of reinstating it.

Massive blocks of Aislaby sandstone form both piers. It is still possible to see the joints and lewis-holes used for lifting the blocks on the East Pier but the West Pier has long been rendered over on top. Both piers retain some of their original 19th-century furniture such as capstans, pulleys and mooring posts by which ships were warped into harbour or tied up. Until the end of the 19th century the West Pier had no railings but instead a low wooden rubbing strip to prevent the hawsers from chafing on the stonework.

43 *'West Pier & Lighthouse at Whitby', a lithograph by an anonymous artist soon after the building of the new lighthouse in 1831. On the left is one of the two roundhouses connected with the Battery. The pier is complete with capstans, bollards and a rubbing strip for hawsers. As Dr English points out, this print has an icy cold look about the sky but the figures throw firm shadows suggesting sun!*

Jonathan and Francis Pickernell between them carried out many improvements to the harbour as successive harbour engineers. Jonathan (*c.*1738-1812) probably came from Hampshire. He became Harbour Engineer at Whitby in 1781 and was responsible for the West Pier, the Town Hall and many minor works. His son was an engineer at Sunderland but his grandson, Francis (1796-1871), took over Jonathan's role at Whitby in 1822, succeeding James Peacock who had been engineer from 1812 to 1822. Francis built the East Pier, the lighthouses, the bridge and many of the staiths. When Passing Tolls, the source of money for harbour improvements, were abolished in 1861 he retired with a handsome pension from the Government.

The effect of building the piers was to protect the harbour from north-westerly gales, to reduce the swell and to prevent the blockage of the river mouth by the longshore drift of sand. Even today, however, the harbour needs constant dredging to maintain the deep water channel. The harbour bar is noted as long ago as 1588 in the English version of 'the Mariner's Mirrour'. In 1838 Finden noted that the lighthouses displayed a light at night as long as there was eight feet of water on the bar while a flag on the West Cliff performed the same function by day.

The harbour had a number of natural hazards, some of which have already been enumerated. John Wooler produced a chart of the harbour and its approaches in 1740 which gives instructions on approaching from both north and south. Part of this is quoted below, complete with dialect spellings and traditional leading marks:

44 *'Whitby Pier and Lighthouse' from the* Saturday Magazine, *27 July 1833. Accompanying text records the completion of the 'handsome lighthouse, eighty feet high, in the form of a Greek Doric column … within the short space of eleven weeks'.*

Directions for avoiding Whitby Rock.
When you come from the south ward you must Observe
to keep the north Cheek of Robinhoods Bay open with
High Whitbie about a sailes breadth and when you bring
Larphill house on with the East Pier End or when you
get Limber head on with Stakesby Hall then you are
clear of the Rock and may stand into the Head and may
bring up in 6 to 8 fathoms at Low Water good Ground.

When you come from the northward keep Roe Cliff a sails
breadth open with Kettleness Point and it also carrys
you clear of the Rock all the way betwixt 9 and 10
fathoms at Low Water.

Directions for the Upgang Rock.
When you come from the northward you must keep Steas
Nab a little open with Kettleness point which will bring
you no nearer (nor must you come nearer) than five
fathoms and when you bring Coney-how west hill on with
the White House in Reeveland Dale (?) you are past the
Rock and may steer in directly for the Harbour.

Directions for anchoring in Sandsend Road.
Bring Mulgrave Castle over the great Red house in the
middle of Sandsend Town and Steas Nab about a Saile
breadth without Kettleness point and you may bring up
in 7 Fathom Water good clayey ground and may ride with
the Wind any way from the NW to the South.

Whitby harbour provided a good strategic haven for a large number of ships on an inhospitable coast, but it also held large numbers of laid-up vessels in winter; colliers, which did not sail between September and March, and whalers, which had to wait for the spring to thaw the polar ice. This time of laying up allowed repairs to be carried out, rigging to be replaced and caulking and careening to be done.

ENCROACHMENT ON THE HARBOUR

In a state of nature, such as prevailed in the early Middle Ages, Whitby harbour would have been a series of mudbanks and pools at low water, its fringes of sand and silts sloping gently upwards to ill-defined banks. Its use as a harbour and more particularly as a site for settlement were to have a dramatic effect on its shape and on its margins.

As we have seen, a number of streets were built out over reclaimed sands, stiffened by piling. This is particularly so on the east side where the shelf of usable land is narrow. On the west side there was more room and the cliff is lower but areas such as the east end of Baxtergate, New Quay Road and St Ann's Staith all show evidence of encroachment on the harbour.

45 *One of the capstans on the West Pier. When it was in use hauling ships in or out of harbour a set of long bars would be inserted in the square holes visible in the side and turned by casual labourers. The hawser was wound around the wide lower section. A ratchet at the base engaged with an toothed iron ring, to stop the rope being pulled back. Low wooden rubbing strips on the pier edge protected the hawser from chafing, but were replaced with railings when steam replaced sail, and there was no longer a need for manual hauling.*

The process is likely to have been this: first pilings driven into the harbour side to revet houses and properties, then the building of staiths in front of them. After a time the ground was more or less consolidated by the staith and a new stage of building out onto this would begin, initiating a gradual process of reclamation which might be hastened by the dumping of ships' ballast or of domestic rubbish to stiffen the piling.

The area known as Dock End has seen a gradual and continuing diminution of its water front. In early times the Bagdale Beck made its way into the harbour via a large and indeterminate creek known as the Slike (at Jarrow a similar feature is known as the Slake). This was colonised by shipbuilders from at least the late 17th century and some of their activities, such as the building of dry docks, will have helped to curtail it. Until 1886 it ran almost to the railway station at its most westerly point. The N.E. Railway Company filled in the western end at that date, and since then it has been reduced in size and its shape defined within vertical walls, its timbers replaced by concrete. There is every prospect of its gradual reduction continuing as a consequence of surrounding developments unless it is artificially protected.

A boat trip around the harbour will quickly convince the sceptical viewer that much of the apparently firm ground at the root of the West Pier is actually just a staging built out over the harbour. This is at least a second stage of encroachment since there was no staith at all in this area until the early 19th century, while the outer part forming the Fish Quay was for many years at a lower level than the roadway. Dredging was the solution to the maintenance of a deep channel for shipping but those harbourside structures which did not have their piles penetrating through to bedrock (and that included many of the older structures) were adversely affected by the erosion of the sediments which resulted from this action.

Nowadays two vessels, the dredging pontoon *Saltwick* (1993) and the hopper barge *Sandsend* (2003), work in partnership in the harbour, but for years one of the familiar sights of Whitby harbour was the dredger *Esk* as she went about her work, maintaining the deep channel. *Esk* was a grab dredger, with a swivelling crane mounted in the bows to lift out scoops full of fine silt which it emptied into a tank, for discharging into the deeper water of Whitby Roads outside the bar, at high tide.

She was acquired by Whitby Urban District Council in 1936 to work on harbour maintenance for about four months of the year and when not required at Whitby used to go on hire to other ports such as Middlesbrough and Bridlington. She was sold to Glasson Dock on the west coast for harbour duties there in 1993 but has since been scrapped.

Previous to this there had been a bucket dredger, using a continuous chain of buckets running through a well in the vessel. It was found that dredging too near many of the staiths led to undermining and risk of collapse, where these structures were only bedded in sands and silts.

46 *The large capstan at the end of the West Pier, provided with eight sockets for bars. It worked in conjunction with iron pulleys set in those embrasures in the round head most likely to be used, i.e. those on the harbour side. Like much of the surviving pier furniture, this probably dates from the early 19th century, although elements of it will have been replaced many times due to wear and tear.*

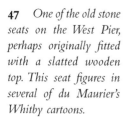

47 *One of the old stone seats on the West Pier, perhaps originally fitted with a slatted wooden top. This seat figures in several of du Maurier's Whitby cartoons.*

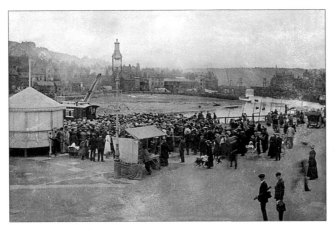

48 *A Suffragette meeting taking place on the Scotch Head in 1908. This postcard, which features a back view of two of my great-aunts, was sent by their mother to two of their sisters currently with their father on SS* Canterbury *at Rio de Janeiro! Whitby was a cosmopolitan place at that period.*

Apart from stronger and deeper piling the main contribution of modern times has been the stripping away of harbourside structures and the opening up of prospects, not always for the better, since many picturesque spots have been lost in the process. Viewed against the longer timescale of the weather and the tide with their continuing cycle of erosion and deposition most of the man-made structures are relatively new. It is not likely that we have seen the end of changes in the shape and size of the harbour.

WHITBY BRIDGE

Because of the way that Whitby lies on both sides of a tidal harbour its bridge, which links the two halves, assumes great significance. Indeed, without it the town cannot function and at times when repair or maintenance are taking place its want is very quickly felt. Until the opening of the new high-level bridge further upriver in 1980 the only alternative for traffic was to go round via Ruswarp bridge and Glen Esk. This makes it certain that a bridge was needed from early times. Arguments have been centred on these two questions; what was its exact location and how far back does it go?

So far the earliest written reference to the bridge appears to date from 1327. A will of that year refers to 'shops at the bridge foot in Whitby' and since it is not reasonable to refer to a bridge foot without there being a bridge we seem to have a clear, if indirect, piece of evidence that it already existed.

Further references occur in 1351 and subsequent years, when a grant of pontage was obtained for 'repairing and amending the bridge which is decayed and broken down'. Pontage was a royal grant enabling a landlord, or more usually a corporation, to take tolls on certain named commodities coming into or through the town for a set period (usually three or seven years) in order to apply the proceeds to work on a bridge. References to the decay of the bridge, though customary in such matters, and the successive grants of pontage which were obtained, suggest that the bridge really was in a bad state and that it was probably already quite old. How old, of course, we cannot guess.

If we examine other documentary evidence, such as the abbey cartulary, we find that at a date between 1190 and 1208 Reginald de Rosels allowed the abbot and monks to build a bridge between his and their land at Sleights. If Sleights bridge goes back to the late 12th century, is it not very likely that Whitby bridge, much more important to the monks, should be at least as old if not older? Absence of a specific mention in the records does not mean it did not exist.

49 *Whitby old drawbridge, engraved by E. Finden from a drawing by W. Westall. This is one of a large series published in 1829. The drawbridge, built in 1766 and replaced by a swing bridge in 1835, was a source of considerable difficulty to shipbuilders and masters who had to negotiate its narrow gap and counterweight beams set inconveniently at topsail height. Its condition was not improved by the habit of mooring ships to its piers and superstructure. As early as 1827 there was a scheme to build another, high-level, bridge further up river, a scheme which had to wait a century and a half to come to fruition.*

50 *'Whitby from the South' engraved by Fife after Westall, c.1833. The bridge, in the centre of the picture, appears to be the swing bridge of 1834-35 but a closer look shows that the engraver had first put in the uprights of the old drawbridge and then, in order to bring it up to date, presumably erased them. The 'ghosts' can still be made out!*

51 *The swing bridge of 1835, from a print published by Silvester Reed. The paper is watermarked '1850'. A carrier's cart and a coach are crossing over towards Church Street, while ships lie on the mud, drying their sails.*

Charlton thought that the earliest Whitby bridge lay at Boghall, where there was certainly a ford in the Middle Ages. It is thought that there was also a plank bridge for foot passengers beside this ford. However, the site cannot really be a contender for the location of the early bridge since the nature of fords and bridges is quite different. A ford requires a shallow and usually wide stretch of river with a firm bottom, while a bridge needs a narrow if deep channel with firm ground on either side. The bridge itself is usually carried on wooden piles driven into the bed of the river to provide stability. A permanent bridge at Boghall would make little sense. It is preferable to look at the present site, or somewhere very near it.

Wherever it was Whitby bridge became the subject of a number of bequests in the 15th century. Bridges were frequently supported by private charity and religious bodies in the Middle Ages. Bridge chapels were common, and many monasteries inherited responsibility for maintenance of bridges and causeways in fen country. Works of public charity carried out under the terms of a will were extremely common and indeed in the absence of any satisfactory local system of provision and maintenance they were practically the only means by which a community might be supplied with some of its most basic needs. In 1407, just to take one example, John Schilbotyll left instructions in his will for his executors to supply one oak for the maintenance of the bridge.

In 1541, just after the Reformation but in a will very much conditioned by the practice of the earlier part of his life, James Conyers bequeathed his shops on the bridge towards its maintenance for ever. It is clear that the medieval bridge was one of the type like old London bridge or the Tyne Bridge in Newcastle that carried shops.

Since many of the references are to the use of oaks in its repair we can assume that it was essentially a timber bridge, and probably a drawbridge like its successors, because of the need to bring ships through to the upper harbour. It is of course possible that the oaks were for piles to be driven into the mud for the support of a masonry bridge, but it is unlikely in that case that they would have been required so often for repairs. It makes more sense to envisage their use in the superstructure. Repairs went on throughout the 16th century. Late in that century it was estimated that forty oaks, worth £20, would be required.

Most authorities agree that up to this point the bridge lay on a somewhat different alignment than it does today, with its western termination further down Baxtergate close to the old chapel of St Ninian. This chapel would then make sense as a bridge chapel, where the faithful prayed before crossing, and paid donations towards its repair. This theory is tempting, and should be susceptible of proof or disproof by archaeology, but so far no clear evidence has been located. An unsuccessful search was made at the present bridge end when the block of shops known as 'Boots Corner' was demolished. However, excavations in 1999 on the line of the present western approach road to the swing bridge revealed part of a stone arch which had clearly led to one of its predecessors. It was thought to be later than medieval, but earlier than the drawbridge of 1766. It may well be the one referred to in 1609, when a surveyor was paid to 'try the ground for a new bridge', or possibly its successor. This does not necessarily mean that a radically new line was intended; even to rebuild the existing bridge would have needed some tests for pilings and abutments and in any case it is most likely that a replacement bridge would stand next to its predecessor so that there need be no break in use. Sixty oak trees were provided for the work in the following year, so the surveyor must have been satisfied.

52 *The old swing bridge, before 1909, looking towards 'Boots Corner', the Old Market Place at the foot of Golden Lion Bank and the Custom House. All the buildings on the left-hand side of the picture have gone. At one time there were matching buildings occupying the harbour side of St Ann's Staith, on the right of the picture.*

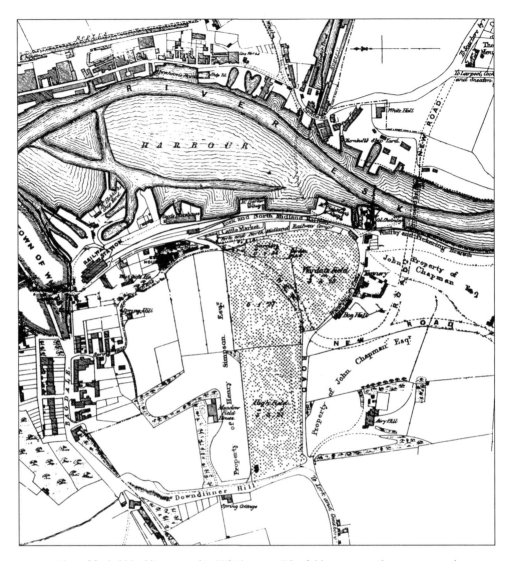

53 *Plan of freehold building ground in Whitby, 1853. The fields nearest to the river were to become the site of the Fishburn Park development, known universally in Whitby as 'The Railway'. The upper field had to wait longer, with late 19th-century houses on Prospect Hill (immediately to the right of Downdinner Hill on the plan) and mid-20th-century houses and an ambulance station further down Waterstead Lane. The new roads and high-level bridge were not built at the time, though the bridge opened in 1980 is on practically the same site. Meadowfield House, a Georgian building, was demolished in the 20th century and its grounds were given over to modern housing.*

Among papers presented two centuries later in another bridge controversy it is stated that in 1628 the bridge had been a drawbridge 'time out of mind'. It looks increasingly as though the same circumstances demanded a similar type of bridge in a similar place.

The replacement did not last very long in good condition. As early as 1640-42 it was reported to be once more in decay and in the latter year one Myles Cussan forcibly entered through the drawbridge while it was undergoing repair and 'threw the scaffolding into the sea'. This anti-social act makes more sense if we envisage Myles as the master of a ship, who was not prepared to wait for repairs to finish, and in his haste to take his ship through the bridge carried away the scaffolding.

Mariners were to be a constant source of damage to the bridge. Not only was it easy to collide with the raised leaves and counterweights in passing through, but many masters also apparently made a practice of tying up their vessels to the bridge supports, and thus weakened them. Not many, however, went to the lengths that Benjamin Coates, the shipbuilder, went to in 1746. Having built a new ship for Mr Coverdale in that year he was alarmed to find that it was several inches wider than the bridge gap through which it had to pass! He therefore petitioned that he should be allowed to chip away enough of the bridge supports to permit his ship to pass through! This seems to display a supreme disregard for the safety of the bridge.

Within twenty years the bridge was again rebuilt, again as a drawbridge. The new bridge of 1766 appears in many engravings. It had stone pillars instead of wooden ones, though undoubtedly these stood on oak piles. It cost £3,000 and had a gap 32 ft. wide.

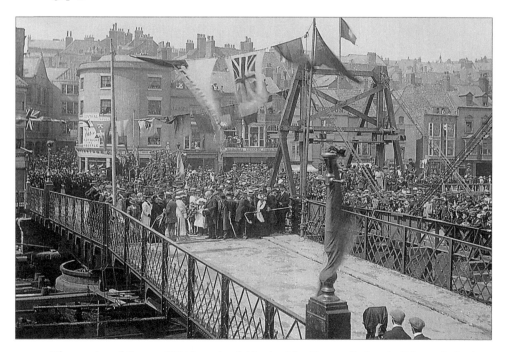

54 *The opening of the new Whitby swing bridge by Mrs Gervase Beckett in July 1908. In the background can be seen the temporary bridge used while building work was in progress.*

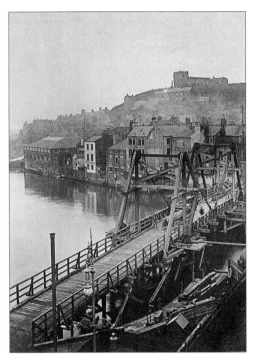

55 *The temporary bridge referred to above, from a postcard sent in March 1908.*

In December 1830 a hearse was passing over the bridge when a gust of wind threw the driver, John Brown, off the box and into the harbour, and he was never seen again.

As early as 1813 plans were put forward for a new swing bridge, designed by Mr James Peacock, which would have cost £8,000. This price was too high at the time, and the idea of replacing the drawbridge was postponed. Ironically, when it was put into practice 20 years later, to designs by Francis Pickernell, the cost had risen to £10,000. The new bridge, built 1833-35, broke for the first time with the tradition of a drawbridge. Instead its revolving leaves allowed a waterway of 45 feet, which gave the shipbuilding industry a renewed boost at a time when it was starting to run down. A grand opening ceremony was held on 25 March, with a procession, bands and banners. The vessel *William* was the first to pass through to seaward.

In 1906 the bridge passed out of county care and became a responsibility of the Urban District Council; this would seem to be an altogether retrograde step as far as the people of Whitby were concerned. Two years later a new electrically driven swivel bridge was begun, with a waterway of 70 ft. It came too late for Turnbull's shipyard at Whitehall which built its last vessel in 1902; the larger vessels required by shipowners would no longer fit through the old bridge gap. During its building a temporary bridge was added to the downriver side. The opening was carried out by Mrs Gervase Beckett on 24 July 1908. It is this bridge, essentially, with alterations and improvements, which still carries the traffic today.

It only remains to mention the high level bridge over the Esk near Boghall, which was opened in 1980. As long ago as 1827 the *Whitby Magazine* had prefigured this in a vision of the future, and a plan of building land on Fishburn Park in 1853 shows a similar bridge in a similar location. The advantage of the position, notwithstanding the great difficulties in finding good foundations, is that the roadway runs almost level across the steep sided valley and allows traffic to avoid the town to a great extent. Despite its building much traffic still continues to use the swing bridge and, short of a complete ban on traffic in the older core, will continue to do so.

Three

THE EARLY MONASTERY

Whitby as we know it – town, harbour and cliff-top abbey – is a product of many centuries of development. However, the reason for its first appearance was almost certainly the creation of a monastery here in the mid-seventh century. It was not just any monastery either, but a foundation of the royal house of Northumbria, the most powerful of the kingdoms of England at the time, and it was established in or before A.D. 657.

The royal connections ensured that even if accommodation were spartan the endowments of the monastery were substantial and secure. A large community was established here and prospered for the next two centuries. In the end it was an external cause – the invasion of Danish Vikings – which drove out the community and led to the abandonment of the monastery. It begins to seem more likely that it was a combination of economic and social factors that rendered the monastery increasingly untenable, rather than a single catastrophic event in A.D. 867.

Given the wealth and connections of the monastery it is probable that a small settlement grew up where the town now stands, especially upon the east bank of the Esk, in addition to the massive settlement formed by the wider monastery on the cliff-top. The harbour and the rich herring fishery must always have been a powerful attraction.

The abbey was at a place called 'Streanaeshalch', which may mean no more than 'Streana's Cliff'. There is a Strensall just north of York, and two occurrences of the name are recorded in Worcestershire in the Middle Ages, both close in form to the Whitby example. Bede, our earliest chronicler, however, adds another twist. He derives the name from 'Sinus fari', which he does not explain. Later historians have read this as Latin for 'Bay of the Lighthouse', presumably identifying 'fari' as the genitive of *pharos*, the regular Greek word for lighthouse. This interpretation need not seriously detain us since the words are sufficiently unlike for the connection to be philologically implausible. The idea of a lighthouse has, however, long been connected in the minds of local historians with a lost Roman signal station in the vicinity, which may account for its continued repetition.

ROMAN ANTECEDENTS?

In about A.D. 370 a series of strongly defended towers made their appearance along the coast of Yorkshire as part of the work of reconstruction by the Roman general Theodosius after a particularly bloody barbarian invasion of Britain in 367 known as 'The Barbarian Conspiracy'. Generally assumed to be signal stations, these towers all occupied high cliff-top positions with strategically important distant views out to sea, whence the threat of attack might be expected to come. Five of these towers are well recorded, at Filey, Scarborough, Ravenscar (known only from an inscription found at Raven Hall in 1774), Goldsborough and Huntcliff near Saltburn. Others have been suggested both north of the Tees and as far south as Flamborough Head, but evidence for their existence is so far wanting.

It has been suggested that Whitby takes its origin from another such signal station. This view is tempting because Whitby enjoys a strategically important position overlooking one of the few natural harbours on this harsh and inhospitable coast. Furthermore the 'fit' between late Roman structures and early Christian activities is often very good. In some cases standing Roman buildings may have become royal property, encouraging re-use for non military purposes. In other cases the attraction was undoubtedly the plentiful supply of well-cut stonework available from the ruins.

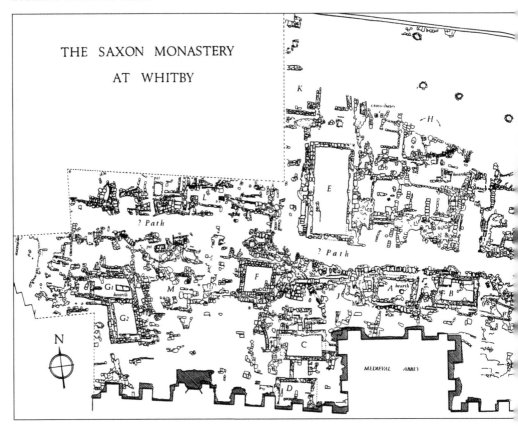

THE SAXON MONASTERY AT WHITBY

Tempting, however, as the view may be that the Northumbrian royal monastery stood on the site of a Roman signal station, we must regretfully abandon it for lack of evidence. Several archaeological excavations have attempted to discover the truth but so far no structural evidence has come to light, on or near the site of the later monastery. A number of Roman coins have been found, it is true, including 11 late examples from the abbey excavations, but these alone are inconclusive. The rate of erosion of the cliffs is very severe and could account for the loss of several acres of cliff top since Roman times, including the site of any signal station. If so then we shall never know for certain whether one ever existed. Three of the five known sites are suffering from erosion of the cliffs on which they stand, that at Huntcliff having almost disappeared.

EXCAVATIONS

However intangible the evidence may be for the existence of a Roman signal station, there can be no such doubt about the Anglian monastery founded in the seventh century. Not only do we have the testimony of the finest historian of the age – Bede, of whom more later – but also the evidence of archaeology.

Large-scale excavations on the site of the medieval abbey between 1920 and 1925, as part of the consolidation of the site, unexpectedly revealed traces of early

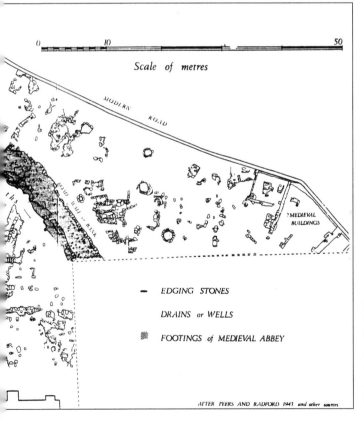

0   10   50

Scale of metres

MODERN ROAD

?MEDIEVAL BUILDINGS

—   EDGING STONES

DRAINS or WELLS

FOOTINGS of MEDIEVAL ABBEY

AFTER PEERS AND RADFORD 1943 and other sources

56 *Plan of the excavated remains of the Anglian monastery of Streanaeshalch by Peers & Radford, as reinterpreted by Prof. Philip Rahtz, omitting manifestly later structures and burials.*

buildings to the north of the abbey church. Other buildings also emerged to the south but no record of them survives. Those to the north consisted of shallow stone footings and wall bases which had in some cases carried timber or wattle and daub superstructures. Several rectangular and sub-rectangular structures were identified at the time or subsequently recognised from the mass of foundations on the plan. They seemed to be aligned to several paths trending north-west to south-east across the site.

On roughly the same alignment but further to the north was a stone revetted feature some five to six metres wide which the published account tentatively identifies as a roadway but which may in fact be a *vallum monasterii* or precinct bank. It must be admitted that this is not a wholly satisfactory explanation because early building traces seem to continue further to the north. Are they earlier, indicating a contraction in the size of the monastery, or later, indicating an expansion? The evidence is such that we can at present only speculate.

Unfortunately the excavation, like many of its date, was carried out by relatively unskilled labour under remote supervision, nor was there much of a concept of archaeological stratification, so all the structures appear on one plan, as though all of one date. It is most unlikely that over two centuries no change or development occurred. Excavations in 1984 and 1985 on the site of Whitby's sister monastery of Hartlepool serve to show just how complex and of how many superimposed phases such a site could be. At least two main phases may be discernible even so at Whitby; an earlier one of timber and turf buildings and a later one of partially stone construction.

Perhaps we should be glad of what little we know of the layout at Whitby but it is very clear that a major opportunity was lost and that a large amount of evidence has gone for ever as a result of unskilful excavation.

The Nature of the Monastery

Other excavations at the northern monasteries of Monkwearmouth and Jarrow have revealed layouts which, though incomplete, seem to indicate a degree of order and planning at variance with that of Whitby. This may be due to the later date of foundation of those monasteries or it may be because at Whitby the church itself was not found. The degree of order may have depended on proximity to the church, perhaps the central, and certainly the most important, feature of the whole site. At Whitby the early church probably underlies its medieval successor. Alternatively there may have been several churches within the monastery, given the size of the community. In this, early practice is quite different from that of the Middle Ages. I strongly believe that a central church of some size and architectural significance will one day be found in the vicinity of the medieval church.

Professor Cramp, in her reinterpretation of the site, has identified the purposes of a number of the buildings, particularly by a detailed study of the excavation finds register. They include what may be weaving sheds or a scriptorium as well as living accommodation. On present evidence there is no clear distinction between the male and female sectors as we might expect, knowing it to be a double monastery containing both sexes. When Bishop Trumwine was driven out of Abercorn by the Picts after the great Northumbrian defeat at Nechtansmere in A.D. 685, for instance, he and his entourage took refuge at Whitby, no doubt swelling the size of the community considerably and particularly its male constituent. One problem at Whitby is that in seventh-century Northumbria there were two models available for the structure and layout of a monastery, one based on Irish precedents and the other derived from Egypt via Italy. The Roman church was much influenced by the eremitic communities established in the Egyptian desert. After the Synod of Whitby (see pp. 66-7) the latter is likely to have been dominant, but at the date of foundation the position is less clear.

The story of Caedmon, which we will come to later, suggests a large and varied population of the monastery and its properties, including domestic servants, farm labourers and craftsmen, many of whom would be accommodated within the monastery, perhaps in separate zones. Recent excavations seem to suggest evidence for such zoning. At Coldingham, another contemporary monastery in Scotland, there are references in a story of Adamnan to *domunculae* or 'little houses' for prayer or reading. This description would suit the Whitby buildings quite well.

The importance of the monastery was no doubt very greatly enhanced by the burial within it of members of the Northumbrian royal house. There was St Hilda herself, the first abbess, and Elfleda and Eanfleda, her successors, King Oswy and even King Edwin. The latter had died much earlier at the battle of 'Hedfled', but his bones were recovered from their burial place and brought to Whitby for reburial 'to the south of the altar of St Peter and to the east of the altar of St Gregory in the same church'. This incidentally gives us the only topography of the monastic church at Whitby that survives and moreover it is given by a monk of Whitby, who might be expected to know the facts, in an early biography of St Gregory.

Whitby depended not only upon royal alms but also on the produce of the countryside. Some of this no doubt came from the toils of the abbey's own servants in the fields. It owned estates at some distance as well as relying on the produce of the fishermen and shellfish gatherers in the harbour below. The evidence for the latter comes from discoveries made in the 19th century in Church Street, immediately below the monastery.

ARCHAEOLOGICAL FINDS

If the excavation of the Anglian monastery left much to be desired there is no doubt that the quantity and quality of the finds was second to none. Indeed finds from the abbey fill textbooks for the period from the seventh to ninth centuries.

The abbey may have been one of the richest in Northumbria but with monasteries we have to distinguish between corporate wealth and individual wealth. A monastery such as Jarrow or Monkwearmouth could be corporately very wealthy but the inmates could still live a life of considerable austerity. Not so at Whitby. The scatter of small personal trinkets suggests that wealth lay at an individual level and that some at least within the abbey lived in comfort.

Of course, monasteries, particularly those containing nuns, had other functions in society than simply being powerhouses of prayer. They were retreats from the world – even kings retired to them from the bruising world of politics – and unmarried women of the royal house could live in them in safety. Royal princesses were frequently pawns in a cold-blooded game of dynastic marriage. Any who were, so to speak, surplus to requirements could be lodged in comfort and plenty, along with their attendants, in a monastery. This sort of arrangement may well have been in evidence at Whitby. Arguably it was one of the reasons for royal support – after all the ruling family would no doubt be counting on direct as well as indirect benefits.

As well as the more obviously personal finds there were building materials. Traces of baked clay daub from wattle-and-daub walling were common. Worked stones undoubtedly existed but were mostly robbed for re-use when the site lay in ruins.

Fragments of lathe-turned baluster shafts from window openings, like those from Jarrow and Monkwearmouth, hint at some late seventh- or early eighth-century building work of considerable pretension. From an analysis of the finds register Professor Rosemary Cramp has concluded that these, along with some important graves and inscribed memorial slabs, most likely originally inserted into walls, were all found in an area between the north transept and the north wall of the nave of the medieval abbey church. This suggested to her that the church of the Anglian monastery was in the same area and was disturbed by the building of its successor.

Peers and Radford suggest that important burials such as those of Elfleda and Cyneburga, whose memorial slabs were found in the excavations, were at one time in a *porticus* attached to the church, like that at St Augustine's in Canterbury.

Other burials lay grouped to the north and were marked by crosses, some of which carried inscriptions. One particularly elaborate sculptured fragment carved with a tree between two animals may well have formed part of a free standing shrine to some especially holy person, as was the custom of the period.

The most plentiful finds belong to two categories; those to do with books and writing, and those concerned with personal adornment. In the former category are decorative metal fittings from book covers and bronze styli for writing on wax tablets, as well as bone prickers used in marking out manuscript pages. Among the latter are pins, tweezers, elaborate strap-ends, brooches and combs. Other items are more specifically religious in character, such as fragments from portable shrines and hanging-bowls, jet crucifixes and rosary beads. Not all the objects published in the excavation report belong to the Anglian period. In the difficult conditions under which the report was written up mistakes were made. Among the pages are illustrated fragments of medieval musical instruments and at least one 16th-century cloak fastener!

Evidence for spinning and weaving comes not only from the discovery of spindle whorls and baked clay loom weights but also from a fragment of woollen textile. The monastery was probably self-sufficient in textiles as it was in many other products. Textile work – spinning, weaving and making up of garments – may have been one of the principal occupations of the nuns.

A very large quantity of pottery was also found including Frankish and Carolingian types imported from the Continent. These speak of links which were not merely the result of trade, for there was continued and widespread contact between Northumbria, Frisia and the Frankish territories through the activities of missionaries and through scholarly exchange. Alcuin, the great Northumbrian scholar and teacher, spent many years at the court of Charlemagne.

Finally the coins, which include both silver *sceattas* and bronze *stycas*, cover the period from *c*.700–850. Like the other datable finds they tend to preponderate in the latter years of the monastery's life and fill in a period for which written history is lacking. The finds from the 1920s excavations were for many years on loan to the British Museum, but in 2002 the collection was purchased by the Whitby Literary & Philosophical Society, some representative finds to be displayed by the British Museum and the Yorkshire Museum being left on loan.

The excavations of 1920–25 were very significant for our knowledge of the abbey of Streanaeshalch. There is some other information as well, however, from a variety of sources.

In 1958 excavations took place in fields to the north of the abbey. Only a series of test holes was dug, in order to determine whether levelling of the field surface could be carried out without damage to any significant remains. The excavators found traces of Anglian or medieval buildings over the southern part of the area and, though the evidence was inconclusive, it seems that the Anglian monastery may have stretched at least this far.

More recent excavations have taken the story on much further, although until full publication follows we have to rely on website and press release information, which may be reconsidered in the fullness of time. Most of the work has been carried out to minimise or mitigate damage to archaeological deposits caused by radical changes to the visitor management on the site. National recognition of the importance of the Abbey headland and a desire to interpret it better led to the building of a new car park to the east of the Abbey, thus removing casual parking from the Abbey Plain, the provision of a new visitor centre in the ruined Banqueting Hall of the Abbey House, and a network of footpaths around the wider site.

All of these required preliminary excavation to make sure nothing important was lost. The car park was resited by 1995, and the Banqueting Hall visitor centre open for 2002, with its 17th-century paved gardens revealed. To the south-east of the Abbey a large cemetery was located in 1997–8. The graves were laid out east-west and their general absence of grave-goods suggests that they are Christian. A ritual use of quartz pebbles in some of them may be a Celtic tradition. More importantly, a feature cutting into the top of one of the latest graves held a silver *sceatta* (a small Anglo-Saxon coin) of A.D. 700–40, which seems to indicate that the graves are earlier. Further finds were made to the west and north-west, around the Abbey House and on the cliff-edge, where a fragment of a cross was discovered.

At the centre of this cemetery was found in 2014 a small stone building interpreted as a 'chapel', though this name has too many modern connotations to be useful, as its purpose is unknown. It seems to have been respected by the burials and might possibly be a primary feature. The other big discovery was a deep and extensive ditch (some 3 metres wide by 1.8 metres deep) which was encountered at various points on the site and appears to be the boundary of the monastic area. Conceivably this can now be tracked throughout its surviving length by geophysical means.

All this new evidence suggests that the site occupied by the monastery was much greater than previously thought. Indeed, it begins to take on the proportions of a town, and certainly the little documentary evidence indicates that it was largely self-sufficient and contained herdsmen and shepherds, craftsmen and specialists, as well as novices, the sick and old, and, of course, the core of nuns and monks. There may well have been zoning to separate these various functions and to preserve the sanctity of the church and of the royal burial places.

BLACK HORSE YARD

A group of finds which is highly significant for our understanding of the monastery on the cliff above is that discovered between 1867 and 1876 at the rear end of Black Horse Yard on the east side of Church Street.

At its easterly end this yard runs up against the lower edge of the cliff face and abuts on a field known as Almshouse Close. All the evidence points to the objects having been tipped over the edge of the cliff among rubbish. According to the Rev. Haigh the deposits at the foot of the cliff were no less than seven feet deep in places and seemed to consist principally of organic material, including animal bones and shellfish remains. This appears to represent a long accumulation of kitchen rubbish but the finds which survive in Whitby Museum are altogether more important individually and come from other areas of the monastery than just the kitchens. Perhaps material from various parts of the abbey had been allowed to accumulate first in a midden before being tipped over the cliff.

The finds include spindle whorls and small whetstones, bone spoons and a jet bead. Three items in particular draw our attention. These are an inscribed bone

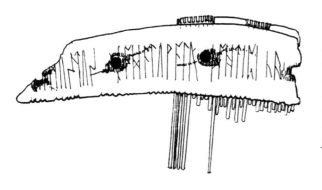

57 *Anglian bone comb from the so called 'kitchen midden' deposit in Black Horse Yard, Church Street. Perhaps liturgical in use, it derives from the monastery on the cliff above and bears a fragmentary runic inscription.*

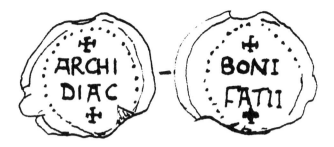

58 *Lead 'bulla', found in Black Horse Yard, Church Street. It bears the name of the seventh-century Archdeacon Boniface and would have come to the monastery of Streanaeshalch attached to letters or documents from the papal curia.*

comb, a lead bulla and a bronze comb. The bone comb has a runic inscription which has been translated by Page, the greatest living expert on the subject, as: 'My God, may God Almighty help Cy—'. The last word is incomplete and may be a personal name. The lead bulla bears the inscription; 'BONI/FATII ARCHI/ DIAC', which refers to the Archdeacon Boniface. There were several Archdeacons of this name at Rome in the papal curia and the object dates from either *c.660* or *c.685*. It would have come from Rome attached to a document, as a mark of authenticity, and it is very tempting to think that it was in some way connected with the Synod of Whitby. Many official documents, however, must have come this way over the years and we can have little idea of their contents. There is still a strong personal connection in that such an important document would certainly have been read and handled first by the abbess, perhaps in this case by Hilda herself.

The bronze comb is of an exceptionally rare type, thought to be unique until other examples came to light first at Aalsum in Frisia (Holland) and then at Cologne in Germany. It is not yet clear which is the traveller, though the balance of probability points now more to the Whitby comb being a continental import than the other two being of English origin. There is plentiful evidence for contacts between Northumbria and Frisia, especially via missionary monks.

The discovery of two elaborate combs at Whitby raises images of personal vanity among the inmates of the monastery. It is very much more likely that special combs of these types were used ritually by the priest, ceremonially combing his

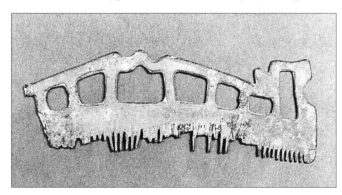

59 *Bronze openwork comb found in Black Horse Yard. Such combs are exceptionally rare and may date from the ninth or tenth century AD. Others have been found at Aalsum in Friesland and at Cologne in Germany.*

hair before celebrating mass. An elaborate ivory example is among the relics of St Cuthbert preserved at Durham.

BEDE AND HIS HISTORY

The great eighth-century historian Bede gives the monastery considerable coverage in his *Historia Ecclesiastica*. There are four main stories he has to tell: the founding of the abbey, the Synod of Whitby, which took place in A.D. 664, the life of St Hilda and the story of Caedmon.

We will examine the story of the founding first; it was directly or indirectly a fulfilment of a vow by King Oswy, a grateful return for his victory at the battle of the Winwaed, a river identified as 'near Leeds'. The battle took place in 655 between Oswy and his great rival, the pagan king of Mercia, Penda, and his Welsh allies. It could so easily have gone the other way, but Penda was killed and Mercia's power temporarily broken. Moreover, it was seen as a Christian victory, and led to the conversion of Mercia. In celebration 12 monasteries were founded, six each in Bernicia and Deira, the two components of Northumbria. Hilda was made abbess of one of these, Hartlepool, and was given the king's daughter, then a child, to bring up as a nun. Two years later she acquired, according to Bede, an estate at Streanaeshalch, and built a monastery there. This makes the foundation of the Abbey at Whitby about 657. The princess moved with her and was eventually buried here, along with her father, mother and grandfather. These royal connections can have done the Abbey, and Hilda's standing, no harm at all.

The Synod of Whitby was one of a number of synods or meetings of Church and State held in the seventh and eighth century to establish church policy; this one was to prove important in church history and it is significant that Whitby was chosen as the place for it to be held. In modern terms we would say that Whitby had a convenient geographical position for the various protagonists and also had appropriate facilities for a conference. In the event it had to be able to accommodate not only Oswy and his son Ahlfrith, no doubt with sizeable retinues, but also a roll call of the most notable clergy of the day: Colman, Agilberht, Agatho, Wilfrid, James, Romanus and Cedd. Abbess Hilda and her followers also no doubt played their part in the discussions and in the enactment of the verdict, but Bede does not look beyond the words of the main protagonists.

The actual subject matter of the synod seems extremely arcane to us today. It hinged on the calculation of the date of Easter and on the correct form of the tonsure to be worn by monks. However, as is often the case in religious disputes, the real argument was about something not even on the agenda. It centred on the issue of which tradition, that of the church of Rome or that of the Celtic church of Ireland, should now be respected in Northumbria and, by extension, in most of England. If this seems an odd or one-sided debate it should be pointed out that the Irish church through its early missionary activities had become enormously influential in England. Oswy and Hilda belonged to the Irish tradition along with Cedd and Colman; the cards appeared to be heavily stacked against the Roman side.

A lengthy and academic debate took place but in the end Wilfrid played the trump card for the Roman side, essentially by an appeal to emotion, rather than logic. He argued that the words of Christ to Peter: 'Thou art Peter, and upon this rock I will build my church … and I will give unto thee the keys of the kingdom of heaven' clearly gave the highest approval to the church of St Peter – that is, the church of Rome. The supporters of the Irish church could field no such high authority and so Oswy was convinced. As he declared:

> … since he [St Peter] is the doorkeeper I will not contradict him: but I intend to obey
> his commands in everything to the best of my knowledge and ability, otherwise when
> I come to the gates of the kingdom of heaven, there may be no one to open them.

The king allowed himself to be converted to the Roman tradition and naturally others followed suit. Colman, discredited, returned to Scotland with a few followers. The Roman party thus in a short space of time extended their influence over the strongest and most flourishing kingdom in England.

To understand the significance of the synod we have to look at the years immediately following. The church gained rich gifts of land and property in consequence and was governed by a strong central administration, unlike the loose and localised control of the Irish church. The Roman tradition ruled supreme in England thereafter until the Reformation.

Behind all the speeches and cool reasoning we can envisage the excitement and turmoil at the abbey. The arrival of the king, the search for accommodation for the important clerics and other guests, the preparation of extra food and the buzz of conversation in Irish, Old English and Latin, must have long been remembered at the abbey. So also would be the conference hall, perhaps the abbey church itself, packed with anxious faces, wondering what the royal verdict would be.

Hilda was herself a royal princess. She died at her abbey of Streanaeshalch in A.D. 680 at the age of 66, having, according to Bede, spent half of her life nobly in the secular state and half in monasteries. Her monastic career had begun with her conversion to Christianity by St Paulinus at the Northumbrian court of King Edwin. Serving first in an East Anglian monastery, she had intended to devote her life to service at Chelles in France but she was recalled by Aidan and established a small monastery on the north side of the river Wear – we do not know its name. Later, after two years spent at the abbey of Hartlepool, she was given the task of founding or reorganising the abbey of Streanaeshalch – Bede is ambiguous as to whether it was an entirely new foundation.

There is also some internal contradiction as to the length of her service before she came to Whitby, but there is no doubt that she devoted the rest of her life and all her energies to ruling the abbey. Hilda represents a fusion of the native and Anglian traditions of the period since her father was a minor Anglian noble and her mother was British. She was probably bilingual and her British blood no doubts explains her attachment to the traditions of the Celtic church.

She was a great teacher as well as ruler of her monastery. No less than six future bishops were among her protégées. Many of the members of the monastic community

60 *Caedmon of Whitby, as depicted on the Caedmon Cross, dedicated on 21 September 1898, by the Poet Laureate, Alfred Austin. The cross was sculpted by Messrs Beale of Newcastle in memory of Whitby's first and greatest poet. Understandably striking an Anglo-Saxon attitude, Caedmon is being instructed in the art of extempore verse by the angelic presence above his left shoulder.*

were probably first generation Christians, like herself, and there can be no doubt about the enthusiasm of their belief. Later members of the community may not have held such high ideals.

Bede's account of Hilda's death provides some background information for the organisation and development of the monastery. Two miraculous visions were used by Bede to illustrate her sanctity but the stories appended to them are perhaps of more interest to us for the incidental light they shed on more everyday affairs.

The first tells of a nun called Begu, who had served the monastic life for some thirty years and who had recently moved to the new monastery of Hackness, which Hilda had established shortly before. She was resting in the dormitory when she heard in the air the well known sound of a bell and saw, as she thought, the roof of the house open and the soul of Hilda being borne away into heaven.

Not only do we gain from this the knowledge that Streanaeshalch spawned at least one daughter house, a fine but weathered stone cross from which survives in Hackness church, but also we have here the first literary reference to the use of church bells.

Another witness to a vision of St Hilda's death was a woman who at the time was staying in the remotest part of the monastery where women taking up the monastic life were on trial, clearly a sort of novice house. This adds something more to our knowledge of the topography of the abbey, although it would clearly be difficult to identify such a building from its archaeological remains. It does suggest some zoning of the site by function, as we have seen.

As if Whitby had not had enough of visions, some years later another was vouchsafed to the great St Cuthbert on his last visit to the area. He had come to see Elfleda, Hilda's successor, about the consecration of a church on the abbey estates, perhaps at a place called 'Osingadun', which some have identified as Easington. At dinner he went pale and dropped his knife. Upon being asked what he had seen he replied that he had seen the soul of a holy man from the abbey being carried off to heaven. There was no immediate explanation but the next day a messenger came while Cuthbert was celebrating mass and announced that the day before one of the shepherds, Hadwald by name, had fallen from a tree and been killed.

This story is unconvincing from the miraculous point of view since the vision and the event do not seem to tally very closely and the cynic might observe that in a large community with the usual mortality rate of pre-Conquest England to forsee the death of an un-named member of it would not be particularly difficult! However it is of interest to note the wide estates which the monastery possessed and also the incipient parochial structure evidenced by the new church.

Farm servants lived upon and worked these estates, probably under a simplified version of the abbey's religious rule. One of these was a man named Caedmon, whose story is another miracle which provides background colour to the organisation of the abbey.

Caedmon was an elderly man who worked on the abbey estates looking after the cattle under the supervision of the steward. His name is British, so he may have been of British descent, like many of his contemporaries in Northumbria. It was the custom to hold a feast once a year to which all the servants of the abbey were invited and for all in turn to take up the harp and give a song. Since Caedmon knew no songs he would retreat at such occasions to his house. On one occasion he had gone out to see to his cattle when the time came for singing and then gone home. He dreamt that night that a man told him to sing. He replied in his dream: 'I do not know how to sing; that is why I left the feast and came here; because I could not sing'.

The stranger replied: 'Nevertheless you are to sing to me', and told him to sing about 'the beginning of created things'. Caedmon spontaneously composed and sang verses in Old English:

> Now must we praise Heavens's ward,
> The Lord's might his intentions
> Work of the Glory Father He each wonder ordered
> Eternal Lord First Creator
> He first made for children of old
>
> Heaven as a roof Holy One created
> This Middle Earth Mankind's Guardian
> Eternal Lord after created
> For man a country
> Praise the Almighty.

It is almost impossible to render the flavour of the Old English into modern English since the original depends to such an extent on alliteration and rhythm.

Next morning he told the steward of his new gift and was quickly taken into the presence of the abbess and a number of her learned men. He told his story and sang his song. The assembly gave him sacred history or doctrine to put into verse, which he quickly did. In due course he joined the monastic community himself and put his gift to good use, taking texts and ruminating upon them 'like a clean animal chewing the cud', an apt metaphor for a former cowherd.

Even the story of Caedmon's death provides us with a little information. He spent his last days in a building where they used to take those who were infirm or seemed near the point of death. It is clear that the abbey was a large and elaborate complex of small buildings, each with its own separate purpose, unlike the buildings of the medieval abbey which each contained many rooms.

The written history of Streanaeshalch largely comes to an end with Bede, who wrote his *Historia Ecclesiastica* in A.D. 731. That is not to say that nothing happened afterwards – merely that our sources for specific events at the abbey dry up.

THE END OF THE ANGLIAN MONASTERY

It is usually claimed that Streanaeshalch fell to Viking raids in the year A.D. 867, along with much of the rest of Northumbria, and thereafter lay in ruins. Whether it happened as suddenly as this is open to question. It may have suffered a slow strangulation such as that of Roman Britain, when the influences which had supported it, and the relatively peaceful environment which had nurtured it, collapsed. Some of the archaeological finds, including coins, date specifically from the eighth and ninth centuries, showing that religious life went on at least that long, though with what vigour we cannot tell. The monasteries of Northumbria, which had in their time been beacons of light in a dark world, went out some time in the ninth century, not to be relit until after the Norman Conquest.

William of Malmesbury states that King Edmund took away the bones of St Hilda from Whitby to Glastonbury in *c.*944. It is impossible to check this, although some have cast doubt on whether he had the ability at this time to carry out such an action, given the dangerous political situation. The story suggests that the holy places of the north were still known and their memory kept green in southern monasteries where the effects of Viking raids had been less or non-existent.

Between 1072 and 1078 the site of Streanaeshalch was reoccupied by monks from Evesham under Reinfrid, a former soldier in the Conqueror's army. The description of those times by William of Malmesbury is of great interest: 'There were at that time, in the same place, as aged countrymen have informed us, "monasteria" or oratories to nearly the number of forty, whereby the walls and altars, empty and roofless, had survived the destruction of the pirate host.'

Presumably the remains of the forty oratories were the most resilient parts of the last phase of buildings on the site. We cannot project this number backwards in time with any certainty since the size of the abbey is unlikely to have been static and may well have declined with the decline of Northumbria. The description, vague as it is, is different in kind from those of Simeon of Durham regarding Wearmouth and Jarrow, and may indicate that Whitby's buildings were neither large nor rectilinear as they were.

As we have seen, after the destruction of the monastery the site of Streanaeshalch stood empty and derelict for some two centuries. Newcomers from Denmark settled in the area, naming the ruins on the cliff top 'Prestebi' and the settlement below 'Witebi'. 'Witebi' survived and when the abbey was restored after the Norman Conquest both Streanaeshalch and Prestebi were forgotten; it was as Whitby that both town and abbey were to be known.

Four

THE ABBEY

REFOUNDATION BY THE NORMANS

It was to the ruins of Prestebi on the cliff top above Witebi that a Norman monk named Reinfrid came with a few companions in about 1075. Reinfrid was an old soldier and may even have been part of William's army that did such terrible destruction to the north of England in 1070. Some people have seen in his actions the motive of expiating crimes of which he was now ashamed. Whatever his background he was at the time of his arrival in Whitby a monk of Evesham who had set out with two companions in 1073-74 to revisit the lost shrines of the north. Between them they refounded the famous monasteries of Jarrow and Wearmouth and then Reinfrid set off for Whitby, which he probably already knew.

The ruins of the 'monasteria or oratories' which he found there may have offered a temporary home to the first monks but they soon started to build in a new style. It is arguable whether in those first few years the community had the wherewithal or the stability to begin the stone church which excavations revealed in the 1920s. It was usual practice to build in timber to start with and to replace buildings as finance and numbers allowed, working in a prearranged way from choir to nave and nave to cloister.

Reinfrid may have been a holy man but he was less notable as a judge of character, or perhaps his humility worked against him. At all events he allowed himself to be supplanted as head of the new monastery in a very short time by one Stephen, a plausible but unstable monk who quickly fell out with William de Percy, the owner of the land on which the monastery stood. Trouble in the new community led to secession from Whitby to Lastingham by the unruly Stephen and other monks may have taken temporary refuge at Hackness until the position was steadied by the appointment of Serlo de Percy, brother of the founder, as Prior. It is unlikely, therefore, that serious building began much before the end of the 11th century.

If you wish to gain an impression of the appearance of the first Norman church at Whitby then go to Lastingham where the parish church represents the east end of the monastery left unfinished by Stephen in 1086, when its monks left for York. They may well have built to the same specification as had been intended for Whitby before they had left.

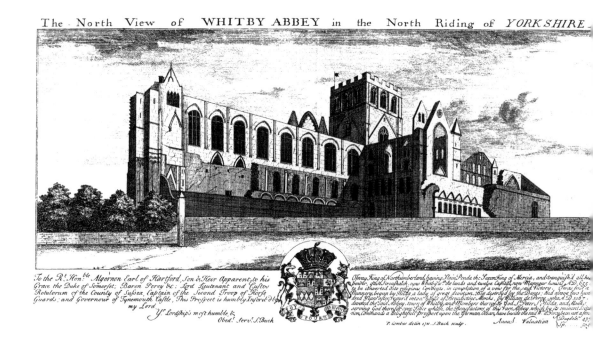

61 *The earliest view of Whitby Abbey, engraved by Samuel Buck after a 1711 drawing by P. Combes. Although curiously lacking in depth and wrongly titled (it is in fact a view from the south-west) it is very useful in that it shows areas like the nave arcade, the west end and the south transept before they collapsed. Oddly enough the impressive east gable, one of the most notable features of the ruin today, is depicted quite wrongly. This may be a result of the engraver using someone else's drawing, and not understanding it correctly.*

Reinfrid had been fortunate in gaining the sympathy of William de Percy; they may have been soldiers together. However, Stephen's high-handed actions had alienated his goodwill. With the accession of William's brother Serlo as Prior after the death of Reinfrid in 1087 the stage was set for the monastery to grow and thrive. In 1095 William set off for the Crusades, from which he never returned, leaving as a parting gift the raising of his monastery's status to that of abbey. Three years later this had been achieved and Serlo himself departed in retirement for the small Priory in Fishergate, York, which had recently come into the hands of the Whitby monks. Serlo was succeeded by his kinsman, another William de Percy, as Abbot of Whitby.

HISTORY OF THE ABBEY

The abbey's history after the Norman Conquest was by no means as illustrious as it had been before. Hilda's monastery had been at the front edge of intellectual life in the brightest kingdom in the western world; its successor was content to occupy a much more humdrum position.

There were notable abbots and worthy monks, but none who was outstanding intellectually or morally. Abbot Richard de Burgh, 1148-75, was loved by his community and Abbot Thomas de Haukesgarth, 1322-54, was a strong disciplinarian and kept a firm hand on the reins, much needed after the laxity of his predecessor, but there was no St Bernard or Ailred, a charismatic leader with a reputation in the wider world.

In the 12th century, however, the affairs of the abbey prospered. There were in 1175 no fewer than 38 monks, whose names are listed on the death of Abbot Richard: Thomas the Prior, Ralph I, Martin, Aschetin, Richard I, Bartholomew, and so on down to Michael. Ralph was the favourite name, with no fewer than four monks bearing it, no doubt to the great inconvenience of the others.

By 1320, when Archbishop Multon carried out a visitation of the abbey, it was deeply in debt. He forbade monks from going out of the abbey with bows and arrows or keeping hunting dogs in the monastery, a sad comment on their worldliness! The abbot, of course, had his own hunting parks, so he was presumably immune from the criticism.

The rise and fall of the abbey's fortunes can be seen reflected in the buildings. These were the outward and visible sign of the abbey's ability to attract and use

62 *This is the point in the north wall of the abbey nave where work stopped in the 13th century and was not resumed until the fourteenth. A buttress covers the junction of the work but the windows to the left are lancets while those to the right are in the Decorated style of the following century. Presumably there was a temporary wall closing off the end of the nave at this point until the work could be completed.*

capital, and depended to a certain extent on how persuasive the abbot could be with his great lay contemporaries. It was the buildings, too, that symbolised the great wealth in land which fell into the hands of the monasteries in the first century or so of their existence.

As land supplies began to dry up so the ambitions of the abbots encountered problems. The effects of the Statute of Mortmain in 1279, which stemmed the flow of land into monastic hands, were compounded in the 14th century by a serious shortfall in the labour market resulting from the Black Death and associated with changing social attitudes.

Whitby, like many other monasteries and the world in general, suffered the ravages of the Black Death in 1349. No statistics survive for its effect on the town but it is known that approximately 45 per cent of beneficed clergy died as a result of it in the diocese of York. If Whitby got away with less than one third casualties then it was extremely lucky. Numbers in the cloister were never to be so high again and the worst effects, for the abbey, were felt among the abbey servants, who could now exploit their rarity value to command higher wages or alternative employment. Consequently large parts of their lands began to be put out to lease, though, as we shall see, the monks kept the local granges in their own hands at least as late as the 1390s.

63 *'Whitby church the ancient Streanshal' from a drawing by the famous antiquary William Stukeley. Unfortunately its exact date is not known, but it belongs to the period of c.1725-1750. What are we to make of this, one of the earliest views of the abbey? At first glance it seems wholly wrong, but a second glance suggests that we are looking from the north side at an abbey virtually complete except for its roof. The north door in the transept, and the lack of one to the nave, are patently wrong. Numbers of windows, with indications of tracery, are approximately right, on the other hand. It looks like a hurried sketch, done partly from memory. Reproduced by courtesy of the Bodleian Library (MS. Top.Eccles.d.6 fol.8.v).*

64 *Whitby Abbey from the south by S. Hooper, 1785. The great west window still stands, and, more importantly, a large part of the west wall of the south transept.*

In the 1530s the value of the abbey's possessions was reckoned at £437 2s. 9d. per year, a figure large enough to exempt it from immediate closure (reserved for houses worth less than £200 per year), but on 14 December 1539 it was surrendered to the King's Commissioners by Henry Davell, the last abbot.

Shortly before this Sir Christopher Jenny was writing to Cromwell, who oversaw the Dissolution, to tell him some hearsay about the abbot selling livestock of the abbey and making many secret leases and grants of annuities. This was a common complaint, for as abbots saw the end in sight many started to dispose of property, partly with a view to feathering their own nest and partly in order to cheat the king of the spoils.

The surrender of the abbey was, at least in part, a result of badgering of Davell's aged and feeble predecessor by Gregory Conyers. A local man, who had held lay office in the abbey and who 'hath the most living of our house of any man', Conyers hoped to steer the abbey's great possessions into his own hands, but in this he was deceived for the site was leased after the monks had been ejected to Richard Cholmley, Knight, who bought it outright some fifteen years later in 1555 and whose successors were to hold it for several centuries to come.

At the surrender the abbot, Henry Davell, received 100 marks as a pension and the prior, Robert Woddus, had £8. Twenty monks, all of whom were priests (i.e. in Holy Orders) received pensions of between £6 13s. 4d. and £5. Their names were as follows: William Nicollson, Thomas Thorpe, Thomas Hewett, Thomas Stavyler, Robert Warde, Henry Barker, Robert Peirson, William Styll, John Watson, Matthew Patche, William Newton, William Froste, Robert Baxster, William Kyldaile, William Colson, Robert Lydley.

ABBEY LANDS

All medieval monasteries except friaries depended on the ownership of land for their continued survival. In the 12th and 13th centuries many of them worked their own land using their own paid labourers, supervised by the cellarer, the monk whose duty it was to make the lands pay, but in the 14th century and later it became usual to lease the land out to tenants on a long-term basis. The bulk of monastic land was acquired before 1279 when the Statute of Mortmain recognised the widespread fear that too much land was falling into the hands of the monasteries and effectively put a stop to further gains. Thereafter many monasteries spent much time and effort in rationalising their holdings by exchanging distant properties for others nearer at hand and consolidating what they had for the convenience of diminishing resources of labour.

Whitby had acquired a very substantial amount of land as its foundation grant and subsequent acquisitions tended to lie in the same area so that in due course it owned a mainly coastal strip of land focussed on four centres: the vicinity of the abbey, around Hackness and Scarborough, along the northern edge of the Vale of Pickering, and a scatter of small possessions in Cleveland up to the Tees. This group included a small cell with its own prior at Middlesbrough, then a hamlet of two farms with no indication of the meteoric growth it would enjoy later. Whitby also had more distant properties, including land in York. The area around the abbey was a geographical entity known as 'Whitby Strand', running from the Thordisa Beck at Sandsend in the north to Blea Wyke near Ravenscar in the south.

Some of these lands reflect the property which the pre-Conquest monastery had owned, particularly in and around Hackness. This may indicate the founder's conscious attempt to recreate St Hilda's monastery as an act of piety or it may show that the boundaries of landholdings in this area had an extraordinary tenacity despite all the warfare and conquest which had intervened.

Most of the land was held as strips in common fields, with the usual share of other rights, such as meadow and woodland for pasture; the monks also drew their income from mills such as Cock Mill, Ruswarp Mill and Rigg Mill, fisheries such as the one in the Esk at Sleights called 'Fish Hekkes', 'vaccaries' or cattle ranches such as Stoupe and Keasbeck at Harwood Dale, grazing on the high moors and of course the town and port of Whitby with its rich herring-fishery.

65 *Whitby Abbey from the west by S. Hooper, 1785, a companion piece to the other Hooper engraving. The interest of both is their relatively early date and hence their depiction of more surviving detail than those of a few years later.*

Churches also provided a useful source of income; the monks had rights in a number, including of course Whitby parish church, but also as far afield as Crosby Ravensworth in Westmorland, where they had a grange as well. In the customary medieval way the monks would take the tithes and other income intended for the support of their churches and install a vicar to oversee the religious duties.

At Fyling the abbot had a hunting park, still traceable on the ground at Demesne Farm (NZ940033). Land on both sides of the Ramsdale Beck was enclosed with a massive stone wall which still survives in part, older than all the other field walls which run up to join it. The farm at Park Gate marks the original entrance to this deer park.

Some of the land which the monks owned they consolidated into single large farms called 'granges', copying the very successful system employed by Cistercian monks. These lay largely outside the normal open-field cultivation, though some of the land undoubtedly derived from this source, and allowed the monks to develop their land in their own way, without the need to fall in with the wishes of other strip owners. As a result of this several of the granges became specialised, concentrating on particular stock or crops.

In 1301 the abbey had at least seven granges in a relatively small area of its heartland, as well as a number in more distant possessions. These seven were at Eskdale, Stakesby, Whitby Lathes, Larpool, Fyling, Hawsker and Normanby. Lathgarth is also named later and may be an alternative name for one of the others. Most of these were concerned with arable farming and also stored the corn tithes collected from lay properties in the area.

The grange of Whitby Laithes or Lathes can still be recognised, about a mile to the south-east of the abbey at NZ921096. East of the modern farmhouse are earthworks of a moated site with other earthworks of enclosure banks, perhaps for cattle. In 1394 £23 was spent in repairs to this grange, which at that date was still operated by the monks, producing wheat, oats and hay. In that same year several pounds were also paid out for washing, shearing and salving sheep and for women making cheese at the grange. By 1540 it was on lease for 40s., and ultimately came into the hands of Sir Richard Cholmley in 1555.

RELATIONSHIP WITH THE TOWN

The relationship between the abbey and the town at its feet seems to have been one of almost total domination. We have seen in an earlier chapter how one abbot granted a borough charter to the town and his successor managed to have it set aside. This seems to be symptomatic of the relationship: the abbey wished to have no independent township on its doorstep and the isolation of Whitby served only to emphasise the abbey's pre-eminence.

We gain much of our information from evidence of legal actions, so it is not surprising that our views are coloured by suspicion that the monks were grasping and litigious. They had to be so, for they had around them landowners of an unscrupulous nature who would snatch whatever they could reasonably expect to get away with. However, in the defence of their rights the monks often seem to have gone too far.

John de Richmond, the abbot, and Peter de Hartlepool, bursar, were brought before Star Chamber in 1378, charged with beating and wounding a Whitby shipmaster, Nicholas Penok, and taking from him salt and nets. This perhaps amounted to an over-zealous seizure of tithes, which happened quite often.

The fishermen must have been sorely tried by the rapacious servants of the abbot, who attempted also to take tithes of catches landed at Whitby by Filey boats, thus bringing Whitby Abbey into dispute with the equally rapacious Bridlington Priory, which attempted the same with Whitby boats landing their catches at Filey.

Whitby fishermen also had to pay a rent for 'spredeles', the important and indeed vital right to dry their nets on the beach; at times the rent became unreasonable and they had to go further afield to carry out this activity.

Another Star Chamber case, of the 16th century, makes bizarre reading. The inhabitants of Whitby stated that it was their immemorial custom to make a bonfire on the eves of Midsummer, St Peter and St Thomas [22 June, 31 July and 20 December], and for the mariners and fishermen to process through the streets carrying a blazing tar barrel, singing and making merry. On the occasion in question the abbey servants had set on them and beaten them, at the orders, it was claimed, of the abbot. Apparently to make amends the abbot had invited them to have ale on St Thomas' Eve but when they climbed the narrow approach to the abbey (the Church Stairs?) the abbey servants had once more set on them and driven them back into the town. Such an entirely believable story of trickery suggests that relations must have been strained to the point of non-existence.

Irksome though the duties imposed on the townsfolk were and unreasonable as some of the demands might be, there was a great measure of continuity in the abbey's rule, far greater than there was ever likely to be with a secular landlord. By and large the influence of the abbey was peaceful and benevolent, and there must have been an enormous gap left in the administration of the town when the monks departed, never to return.

THE ABBOT'S BOOK

The abbey charters and other related documents were published in 1878–79 in two large volumes by Canon J.C. Atkinson of Danby. These monumental works contain a great deal of value, but are not easily accessible to modern research because they are mostly in the original Latin, with minimal translation and commentary.

The first volume is based on the ancient book now in the Museum of the Whitby Literary & Philosophical Society and commonly called 'the Abbot's Book'. It came to the Museum from the Strickland family, latterly owners of the abbey site, and they had it from the Cholmleys, who presumably had it from the abbey itself. (Another similar book, which Atkinson also used, is now in the British Museum.)

This ancient book, consisting of 144 leaves of vellum, is approximately 222mm x 152mm in size, by 64 mm in thickness and is bound in oak boards; it represents the title deeds to most of the abbey's possessions together with other documents and records of the early history of the abbey, such as the 'Memorial of Benefactions' which is certainly earlier than 1180. The texts are mostly in Latin, but there is some old French. Here the abbey's scribes wrote their records and memoranda, in expectation of legal challenge.

From this cartulary comes much of our knowledge of the ancient landscape and the history of settlement around Whitby. Great lay landlords such as the de Percys rarely kept such a record of their possessions, and rarely enjoyed them in such unbroken succession as did monastic corporations. If the abbey had never existed we should know next to nothing of the town in the Middle Ages.

THE ABBEY BUILDINGS

At first sight from the north the abbey seems to be substantially complete; after all the church has walls on three sides standing up to roof level and apparently needing only the restoration of the roof itself to be once more in working order.

66 *'Whitby-Abbey, Yorkshire', an engraving published in July 1798 by S. Walker. The view shows the great west window still standing, though it had fallen five years before. Also of interest are the marks of various rooflines on the central tower. Below the main roofline is the evidence of a lower roof which presumably covered the nave while building work was in progress.*

From the south the view is quite different; on this side the church itself is deficient and the domestic buildings almost totally missing.

Reinfrid and his community were in no position to build grandly; probably timber buildings had to satisfy the early monks until their differences were settled and a period of stability began. It is unlikely that the monks built in stone before the end of the 11th or the beginning of the 12th century. What we see of the church today is the shape it took during its time of finest flowering

The Norman church with its apsidal presbytery and transepts with eastern apses was found only by excavation. They in turn had been replaced in the 1220s by an eastern limb of a plain rectangular form, but on a much larger scale, in an Early English style of great severity but much beauty. This rebuilding may be associated with a growing cult of St Hilda – many monasteries at this time rediscovered the veneration of their saints, or as cynics might put it, woke up to their commercial possibilities.

Not only the east end but the two transepts and the first three bays of the nave, the area containing the choir, belong to this rebuilding phase, which went on for a long time. That the community ran out of money for the work or turned its attention to other things is clear from the fact that between the third and fourth bays of the nave there is a complete change of style; the Early English with its tall pointed lancets gives way to a more florid type of window with a larger opening and ornate tracery, appropriately known as Decorated. There is over a century between the work of the east end and the new western part of the nave.

If we examine old illustrations made before the fall of the central tower in 1830 we can see that it too was of 14th-century date, though it stood over a 13th-century crossing. On its western face appear two rooflines; at a higher level the steep line of the 14th-century roof and, much lower down, that of a temporary roof covering the unfinished work of the previous century.

At the west end of the church, the principal approach for visitors, a great Perpendicular window was inserted in the 15th century, occupying the whole of the west wall of the nave above the west doorway. There may have been other work of this date, but the loss of most of the south side including the domestic buildings has removed all the evidence. Buck's engraving of the abbey from a drawing of 1711 seems to show windows of similar date in the clerestory of the south side of the nave.

If we wish, we can put a historical context to the progress of the building; the choir was begun in the time of Abbot John de Evesham (1211–22) and carried on by his successor Roger de Scarborough (1222–45). This early work involved the demolition to ground level of the Norman east end as far as the transepts; the nave was permitted to remain for the time being, although the builders of the early 13th century managed to align their work askew to the Norman nave. Why this was done has remained a vexed question. It can hardly have been due to ineptitude and may well be something to do with the difficulties of replacing a building on the same site without losing the continuity of use.

Abbot John de Steyngrave (1245–58) continued with the transepts and the lower stage of the tower (the crossing) after a gap of a few years. Then there is a hiatus; work does not recommence on the western part of the nave until the 1330s, under Thomas de Haukesgarth (1322–54). A brief was obtained to raise money throughout the Diocese of York in October 1333. Gifts must have come in fast for building work began within a few months. In November a great gale brought down the new nave to its very foundations. Despite this setback the west end was eventually completed, along with the noble tower which probably acted as a lantern to light the choir.

Some writers refuse to believe that the west end had remained unfinished for almost a century; however the western part did not serve much useful function at this time. The monks had their choir which ran through the crossing into the first bays of the nave, and they had chapels in the eastern limb and in the transepts. In many Benedictine houses the nave was parochial – in other words it served as a parish church – but at Whitby the parish church was only a stone's throw away.

In the 12th and 13th centuries the abbey servants might have worshipped in the nave, especially since the Yorkshire monasteries of many orders were heavily influenced by the ways of Cistercian houses. There, lay brothers – manual servants with some of the attributes and responsibilities of monks – had the use of the nave as their church. By the 14th century, however, servants of this kind were few in number. The nave may have been reserved for lay visitors to the abbey, and so was not critical to its functioning, but the unfinished work may have been an embarrassment to the monks.

Very little is left of the domestic buildings. The Norman church had a passage immediately to the south of its south transept, probably giving access to the monks' graveyard to the east. As rebuilt the church with its larger transepts oversailed this and the passage was buried, only to be relocated in the excavations of the 1920s. At the west end are traces of the Norman outer parlour, giving communication between the cloister and the outside world. Its position indicates that the Norman nave was every bit as long as its successor.

There are fragmentary remains of the cloister itself, 88 ft. from east to west, the other dimension unknown. Everything else lies outside the boundary of the site, but it surely deserves to be examined by some non-destructive means such as resistivity survey to locate the whereabouts of buried foundations. Around the cloister we would expect to find on the east side the chapter house, where the whole community met for the allotment of praise and blame and to transact its business, the warming house, where the only open fire in the monastery was available on cold days, and the dormitory at first floor level, where the monks slept. On the south side would be the kitchens and refectory while the west side housed the prior and the cellarer's office, and perhaps favoured guests.

Beyond the cloister would be the infirmary for sick and aged monks, the guest house, and the abbot's house, where the abbot lived in state like a great secular landlord. There was certainly a gatehouse, enabling the precinct to be closed off at night; it may have stood near the top of the Church Stairs. In the same area lay the Almery, where scraps of food and other gifts were given to the poor, its site probably marked today by the youth hostel.

THE DECAY OF THE ABBEY

After the monks had left the roof was stripped of its lead, the windows of their glass, and the bells, vestments and treasures were carted off for sale or destruction. It was in this state that the abbey stood for many years. Perhaps it was fortunate in this, because in some counties the king's receiver took his instructions more seriously and rendered the buildings completely uninhabitable by demolishing them to the ground, or else the buildings were sold off to form the core of a grand new house. In Whitby's case there is no evidence that the townspeople began to rob the walls for their stonework until decay was quite far advanced.

67 *Whitby Abbey from the north-west, from a print by J. Greig published in 1812. This shows well details of the north transept and the north side of the central tower; oddly the decorated windows of the nave immediately to the right of the three lancets are shown as a mere hole in the wall, though window tracery survives there today.*

The process of destruction, begun in 1540, was rapidly accelerated by Sir Francis Cholmley when he started to build his new house near the abbey in about 1580 and his successors, who built more substantially, continued it. As the house lay to the south of the abbey they took the stone from those parts of the ruins that were most immediately accessible, in this case from the domestic buildings which lay to the south of the cloister. To this day this area is still the most incomplete section of the abbey.

It can be seen from the surviving ruins of many monastic sites that stone robbers were quite daunted by the dangers and difficulties of pulling down high walls. Where someone was prepared to make a start, others would follow, so that there is often a contrast between almost wholly preserved areas and areas where destruction is total. Once a wall was robbed to ground level those in search of good stone might transfer their attentions to other parts, or carry on digging until they had removed the foundations as well.

Unlike many monastic ruins Whitby Abbey has had not only stone robbers to contend with but also fierce winds off the sea. The sandstone on exposed faces is often picked into holes by the force of the winds and great storms over the centuries have caused no little damage to the fabric. Even before it was a ruin there are records of storm damage, such as in 1333 when a gale brought down the whole of the newly built nave.

68 & 69 *A pair of lithographs showing the Abbey before and after the collapse of the central tower on 25 June 1830. The quality of the drawing is not very good; the interest lies in the story recorded by the Whitby Repository. According to this the artist, J. Brown, was sketching the ruins, left for a while to have some lunch, and when he returned found that the central tower had fallen just where he had been sitting!*

We can catalogue the process of decay not only by contemporary reports but also by an analysis of the large number of topographical engravings which the abbey's romantic position has encouraged. The most comprehensive, if not the most accessible, source is Dr T. English's magisterial two-volume work on Whitby prints. (As a child I was fascinated by the abbey ruins and in particular by their appearance in the 18th century, as seen in this book. This fascination survives with me yet.)

In terms of date, though not of quality, the most important surviving print of the abbey is that produced by Samuel Buck in 1711. Samuel and his brother Nathaniel were a well-known team, visiting and sketching ruins of monasteries and castles each summer and engraving from their drawings each winter, producing over 400 such engravings in total. Since their engravings usually antedate any others of a particular site by over half a century we can allow them a little licence, like the inclusion in the background of gentlemen's houses, where they saw the possibility of a sponsor.

In the case of the Whitby engraving Samuel Buck was following a sketch by P. Combes (of whom little is known) and his own drawing in his sketchbook contains little detail. This could explain the curiously 'flat' technique which makes the abbey look as though it had been cut out of cardboard. In particular the gables of the transepts and choir, with their turrets, do not seem to be in three dimensions at all. Furthermore the view, described as being from the north, is actually from the south-west. These are the negative points; on the positive side the view shows the whole of the nave surviving, together with part of the cloister. The central tower stands in all its glory and so does the south transept. Not much sense can be made of the east gable, which Combes had perhaps only lightly sketched, nor of the curious wall which seems to run east of the south transept, unless it is intended to be the sacristy. At the west end an odd four-light window in the side of the turret may represent a louvred bell chamber, since the central tower was purely a lantern and never intended for bells.

Among the Lansdowne MSS. in the British Museum is Samuel Buck's Yorkshire sketchbook in which are a number of preliminary drawings, details and completed sketches of Yorkshire scenes and houses, dating from the early years of the 18th century. On f326 is 'Whitby Abby', a sketch prospect of very poor quality with curious perspective, showing the abbey perhaps still roofed, the church and Whitby Hall (Abbey House) and the roofs of the town below. There is no detailed sketch of the abbey itself, which is presumably why Buck used another artist's drawing of the ruins as a basis for his engraving.

Of similar date, but undated, is a sketch of the abbey by William Stukeley, now in the Bodleian Library, Oxford. (MS top.eccles.d.6,f8v.) It adds little to our knowledge, but is of interest for its early date. What a pity that neither of these artists, who at best could give very detailed information, has much to offer.

Within a few years the ruins began to change dramatically. In 1762 the south wall of the nave fell and in 1793 the rest of the arcade. Three arches of this arcade were reconstructed from the fallen masonry during the restoration of the site in the 1920s and now stand rather oddly against the northern boundary wall. The following year saw the collapse of the great west window during a storm.

The most disastrous fall, however, was that of the central tower on a calm hot day in June 1830. Luckily, due to weaknesses in the south-west corner, it fell in that direction; had it not done so much more of the fabric would have fallen with it. The collapse of such a landmark inevitably attracted its own folklore. It was said that a chimney sweep had climbed the tower shortly before and stolen the copper weathervane from the top and that this had precipitated the fall.

Dr English gives an amusing story of how a boy playing in the garden at Meadowfield witnessed the fall, running indoors to tell his father, who promptly cuffed his head for telling untruths! According to the *Whitby Repository* for 1832 a young artist named Brown was sketching the ruins at the time and had gone off for his lunch. The tower fell as he was walking back across the field. In confirmation of this story a pair of lithographs, taken just before and just after the event, was published by Greenwood & Co., from drawings by Brown.

In 1839 part of the presbytery collapsed. The fall involved an arch and pillars of the south wall of the choir. Casual robbing of the stonework continued all this time. An 18th-century vicar, James Borwick, on his own initiative had all the elaborate abbey tombstones destroyed because, he claimed, his parishioners were re-using them and not paying a fee!

Excavation and Restoration

Some limited restoration took place before 1841, perhaps in response to the 1830 and 1839 collapses. It was remarked that the fall of the tower had nicely opened up the view of the ruins from the south! Towards the end of the 19th century the owner of the site, Sir George Strickland, made some half-hearted attempts to clear the ruins of fallen masonry and to carry out some very limited repairs. This work included the blocking of the north door, a buttress to support the south-west corner of the presbytery and timbers across the presbytery at triforium level to support both walls. The abbey at that time presented a picturesque but incoherent appearance, with great heaps of stones, especially where the tower had fallen, covered with turf and with flowers and saplings growing out of the walls.

An unexpected threat to the ruins loomed suddenly out of the mists of the North Sea in 1914 when, within a few months of hostilities being declared, two German battle cruisers, forming a detachment of a small fleet sent to lure the British Grand Fleet out on to newly laid minefields, opened fire on Whitby with their 11- and 12-inch guns. As we have seen, the damage to houses and property in the town was quite extensive, but the west end of the abbey also took a direct hit, bringing down the top of the west doorway.

The results of this raid, oddly enough, were not wholly bad, because soon after the war was over H.M. Office of Works took over the site and started to excavate and repair the ruins. We have already seen the results in the unearthing of the seventh-century monastery; this was only part of an ambitious programme of work which involved the laying of light railway tracks through the ruins to move the heavier overburden (and with it, unfortunately, much of the archaeology!) and the stabilising of what remained. A number of local men provided their labour on this lengthy project.

Clearance and excavation were carried out as two stages of the same operation. The vast masses of super-incumbent stonework, fallen from above, were removed using a light railway and dumped elsewhere on the site. Tumbled stonework lay up to 2.7 metres deep over the floor of the abbey, especially where the tower had fallen. Large parts of the western tower arch lay intact where they had collapsed, while three bays of the nave which fell in 1762 were still firmly cemented together.

When the surface had been cleared excavations began. It was not the usual method of Sir Charles Peers, who directed operations, to look below

70 *The east end of the Abbey church as drawn by Edmund Sharpe in 1868 for 'Architectural Parallels'. This is a very detailed series of drawings, catching the Abbey at a time between the major stonefalls of the early 19th century and its restoration.*

the latest floors, but he did so here. Inside the crossing and choir of the abbey church he found the apses of the Norman predecessor of the standing church, a few courses high, where they had been demolished in about 1220. Further to the north were even more exciting and unusual discoveries. As we saw in the last chapter the Anglian monastery of Streanaeshalch lay here, in the form of stone buildings and parts of the precinct bank. Unfortunately the quality of excavation and techniques available were insufficient for the full comprehension of what was being found and a tremendous opportunity was lost. Supervision of the digging was remote and the recording of it primitive.

Peers and Radford finally produced a publication of the work on the Anglian remains nearly twenty years later under the very adverse circumstances of wartime. The medieval site has never seen proper publication. All that we have are the successive official guidebooks, together with a number of site photographs.

Much of the excavated site was refilled and levelled, the Anglian remains being considered too insubstantial for consolidation. Standing masonry was a different story, however; H.M. Office of Works was good at this sort of thing. Walls were strengthened by pressure grouting of their rubble fill and phosphor-bronze cramps, which would not expand or distort, were put into the stonework to stiffen it. Stonemasons selectively refixed fallen masonry and painstakingly rebuilt the west doorway, damaged in the bombardment.

When this work was complete it was a very different abbey that was opened to the public, its remains displayed and, to a very limited extent, interpreted. Despite the continued effects of weathering the ruins now have an assured future and are protected from the worst aspects of deliberate damage.

In the last few years the Whitby Headland Project has seen considerable changes made to the site. Excavations have taken place away from the medieval abbey ruins to tie down parts of the earlier history of the site, while car parking has been largely banished from the Abbey Plain. Instead a new car park has been built further to the east, beyond the ruins, and a new entrance provided to the site from this side, in the 'Atlantic Wall' school of concrete architecture. Most dramatically, the ruined Banqueting House of the Cholmley mansion, abandoned and roofless since a storm in the 18th century, has been elegantly refitted to carry interpretive displays on the abbey, its stone forecourt excavated and laid out as originally designed. The opportunity was not taken, however, to extend the displayed and conserved area of the medieval abbey ruins, nor to investigate the underlying Anglian remains within the central core.

Five

SHIPPING

SHIPBUILDING

Whitby has a long tradition of shipbuilding. On the foreshore on both sides of the river and on staiths and mudflats from Dock End to Larpool a steady stream of ships was built and launched from the 17th century onwards. Sizes varied from fishing vessels and trading sloops of 20-30 tons up to ship-rigged vessels of 500-600 tons, limited only by the width of the bridge which divided the harbour into two parts.

In a peak year more than a dozen ships might be on the stocks at the same time. Many were sturdy vessels designed for the coal trade, in which Whitby specialised. They were 'coal cats' or 'collier brigs', bluff in the bow and flat in the floors for maximum capacity and designed to take the ground safely while unloading their cargoes on exposed beaches. Others were timber ships, bringing back a precious cargo of shipbuilding timber and tar from the Baltic. This was one of Whitby's few regular imports, required because of the lack of suitable timber in the vicinity. These vessels unloaded their cargo through timber ports cut in the bow and usually had to lie off in Whitby Roads until they had been sufficiently lightened to come in over the bar.

As demands changed so did the ships. Whalers, specially strengthened for battles with Arctic ice; privateers, armed against French and American ships; transports, built for maximum load capacity in the wars with France; convict ships, off to New South Wales, Van Diemen's Land and Norfolk Island; emigrant ships, with quarters for the hungry and penniless families leaving to start a new life in the colonies of Australia, New Zealand, or Canada; all these had their turn and Whitby could build them all.

When steam propulsion became established paddle steamers were added to the repertoire; H. & G. Barrick built *Streonshalh* in 1836, and she rapidly came into her own as a harbour tug. The shipbuilding industry made a successful transition to iron when that replaced wood – Turnbulls launched their last wooden sailing ship at the Whitehall Shipyard in 1871 – and again when steel replaced iron, but its days were numbered because of size limitations placed on it by the bridge. A dramatic reduction in the number of shipyards took place in the 1830s with a downturn in trade and again in the 1860s when the market for wooden vessels dried up. As Dora Walker so picturesquely put it: 'The shadow of smoke on the seas was hardly noticed, but the sudden offering for sale of all O'wd Gideon Smales's brigs struck the warning note…'.

Screw steamers made their appearance in Whitby in 1864 and became the stock in trade of Turnbull's Yard until the last, *Broomfield*, was launched in 1902. During the last few years of shipbuilding several vessels in excess of 5,600 tons were launched here. This was the very uppermost limit of size possible in Whitby, and even so guiding the 'light' hulls through the opening of the old swing bridge must have been a very tense affair. Indeed it seems almost miraculous today. Eventually shipbuilding ceased because the County authorities would not widen the bridge. Ironically it was only six or seven years later that the new swivel bridge was built, with an opening of 70 ft. By then there was no shipyard to need it.

SHIPBUILDERS

Whitby has a long tradition of ship-building probably going back into the Middle Ages, but next to nothing is known about the earliest days. The recorded history of shipbuilding begins, for all practical purposes, with the arrival on the scene of Jarvis Coates in about 1697. A change of scale and importance probably coincided with improvements to the harbour at this time. Shaw Jeffrey records another late 17th-century ship-builder, William Chapman of Ruswarp, but there is tantalisingly little known about him.

It is not easy to pick out for certain ships built by the earliest Whitby shipbuilders since in general the early registers do not record builders, but we do know that in 1717 Coates built *William and Jane* of 237 tons.

He was succeeded by his sons, Jarvis Coates jnr. and Benjamin. Benjamin followed his father in the yard at a place called the Walker Sands, near the Bagdale Beck. The topography of this part of the harbour is so totally changed that it hardly makes sense to use modern names at all. The site is now all dry land near the railway station. Jarvis jnr.

71 *One of the finest Georgian houses in Whitby is 23 Baxtergate, now solicitors' offices. Luckily it managed to keep its original railings despite wartime scrap demands. Originally the home of the Coates family, it may have been built by Benjamin Coates, the shipbuilder, who amassed quite a fortune.*

opened a new yard further upriver, near Boghall, but quite soon became bankrupt. Benjamin almost certainly built the vessel *Benjamin's Conclusion,* owned by him in 1756-57. His will shows him to have been an extremely wealthy man, supporting his bankrupt brother and leaving large sums to a wide range of relatives. His executors were to sell his ship, named above, to George Ware, his niece's husband, for the sum of £1,500, if he would have it.

On the other side of the river, above Spital Beck, was the shipyard of William Coulson, who came here from Scarborough in about 1735. His yard later became the Whitehall Shipyard, the longest lived of all the Whitby yards, which built its last large ship in 1902.

Coulson died in 1750, quite young since the baptism of his daughter is recorded only in 1746, and a detailed and interesting probate inventory lists the goods in his yard at that time:

(Household goods, omitted)	
In the Brew House	
A parcel of old bad rope, a small	
parcel of occam, some props and wedges	
	2s. 6d.
(Items omitted)	
In the Ship Yard	
20 ring bolts, 8 sett bolts,	
2 iron horses, 2 quart(er) saws, 4 whip saws	
2 triangles with falls and blocks,	
a crane	£3 3s. 4d.
In the Ship Yards	
Timber plank, Dantswick plank, a keel	
piece, 2 sterns, oddments and materials	
in the whole	£413 0s. 0d.
A new pram	£20 0s. 0d.
2 boilers	£30 0s. 0d.
Total (of all)	£518 15s. 4d.

The inventory contains the raw materials of wooden shipbuilding; rope, oakum and pitch for caulking seams, iron fittings, saws for cutting whole trees into planks, and 'triangles' or sheerlegs for lifting heavy items. Parts of ships were clearly ready, such as the keel piece and sterns. The presence of 'Dantswick' plank, presumably a Baltic pine or fir exported through the port of Gdansk, is clear evidence for Whitby's need even at this date for Baltic timber. At the time of his death it seems that Coulson had no complete or nearly complete vessels on the stocks.

Some of the shipbuilding companies had long lives. Various members of the Barrick family worked from 1781 to 1865, while Thomas Fishburn, and later his son Thomas, in partnership with Thomas Brodrick, were building ships from 1748 until 1822. The Langbornes, from whom the Langborne Sands took their name, were in business from c.1760 until 1837.

On the other hand many ships were built as a matter of opportunism by men or companies which went on to do other things when the economic climate changed. Some of these associations were very short-lived, perhaps representing a temporary pooling of resources by individuals who afterwards went their own separate ways. Peter Cato, for instance, who launched his first ship in 1802, was in business with Smales in 1808 and 1816-17, with Ingram Eskdale in 1803, with Lacy and Eskdale in the same year, and with J. Jackson in 1823. His untimely death came in 1829 through falling off the quayside into a lighter moored below.

Smales & Co., and Gideon Smales, built ships between 1807 and 1815 but were also substantial shipowners and manufacturers of ships' fittings. John Spencelayh, who launched ships between 1819 and 1827, was in business as a sailmaker by 1840.

Some of these 'builders' were undoubtedly skilled craftsmen who oversaw all stages of the work and gave Whitby its excellent reputation in the shipping world. Other names are clearly those of sleeping partners, who saw the business as an excellent investment for their surplus capital, or who financed a small speculative venture on their own account when the times seemed right.

In Whitby the all-pervading influence of the port meant that capital, which might elsewhere have gone, for instance, into textile manufactory, here naturally found its way into financing shipbuilding. Though it cannot at present be proved, it seems likely that it was not just the large capitalists who saw the benefits of a thriving shipbuilding trade but also widows with small nest eggs, solicitors investing on behalf of clients for annuities etc., and even small farmers who brought surplus cash with them on market days to buy shares. For example, Caleb Dale, yeoman, left three 32nd shares in ships in 1703, while Thomas Perry, 'merchant or factor', left two 32nds and a 16th share, and Elizabeth Morrison, widow, left a 16th and two other shares, proportion unspecified, in 1715. None of these had any known connection with the sea, and no doubt saw a portfolio of different shares in shipping as a safe way to dispose of surplus cash. Nor were all those with shares in Whitby ships local. The wealthy Lancaster West Indies merchant James Moore left two 8th shares in 'the new ship now building at Whitby' to two of his sons in his will of 1810. Unfortunately this ship cannot be identified by name in Weatherill's lists, unless it is the ship *James* of 419 tons. It was customary to divide ships and their gear into 64ths, to spread the risk if any one vessel sank, individual shareholders taking a number of shares in different vessels. However, as can be seen above, multiples of 64ths might be taken too.

Probably the best known of Whitby's shipbuilders was Thomas Fishburn, who built *Earl of Pembroke* of 368 tons in 1764, *Marquis of Granby* of 462 tons in 1769 and *Marquis of Rockingham* of 336 tons in 1770. These are better known as *Endeavour, Resolution* and *Adventure,* renamed when they were acquired by the Admiralty and used by Captain Cook on his voyages of discovery. The aptly named *Discovery,* the fourth of the quartet, was built as *Diligence* of 295 tons by George and Nathaniel Langborne in 1774. *Endeavour,* bought by the French after Cook's voyage, later ended up a wreck at Newport, Rhode Island, where her remains could still be seen at the end of the 19th century.

These were by no means exceptional vessels, but were chosen because they were reasonably new and also of rugged construction, capable of being beached. Cook himself was of course familiar with their qualities, having served his apprenticeship in Whitby vessels, but more importantly, at the time of his first voyage to the South Seas, their qualities were known to the Admiralty, which chose them. Whitby colliers were a common sight on the Thames at the end of their run down the North Sea.

In 1790-91 Whitby built 11,754 tons of shipping and was therefore the third most important builder in England, after London and Newcastle. Thirty-one ships of over 200 tons formed part of this total. In 1792-93 Whitby had risen to be the second largest builder in England. These figures are quite extraordinary, considering that Whitby had so few natural advantages and had a much smaller population than its main rivals (12,215 inhabitants in 1821). By 1804-5 the total was down to 9,950 tons and Whitby was fifth in the league. During this period 22 ships over 200 tons were built.

In general the number of ships built in a single year fluctuated from 10 in 1809 to 39 in 1802. Between 1800 and 1816, 331 ships with a total tonnage of 77,891 were launched, an average of 19 ships totalling 4,582 tons per year.

As late as 1838 there was a revival of trade after a depression in which several builders had gone out of business, and no fewer than 25 ships were launched, including 10 of over 100 tons. This was no doubt aided by the opening of a new swivel bridge in 1835. Not only was the 45 ft. gap it provided appreciably wider than the 32 ft. gap recorded by the historian Young for its predecessor, but it was also less dangerous to sailing vessels than the old drawbridge of 1766-67, with its counterweight beams projecting just at topsail height.

The scale of operations as late as the mid-19th century is indicated by the 1851 Census Enumerators' Returns. In Baxtergate, for instance, was Thomas Hobkirk, aged 36, employing 10 men and 16 apprentices in his shipyard. Henry Barrick, aged 65, had 40 men and two apprentices, while Thomas Turnbull, living in Skinner Street and aged 31, employed no less than 54 men in his yard. It was in about this year that Turnbulls took over the old Whitehall shipyard, where they were to remain for the next half-century.

Earlier shipbuilders lived near the harbour, where they could oversee their men in all senses of the word. Thomas Fishburn built Esk House above his shipyard, while Thomas Hutchinson and after him the Barrys had a large house nearby, where the bus station now stands. A painting in Whitby Museum appears to show Esk House and the shipyards in the late 18th century. The house known as Whitehall, on the other side of the river, played the same role to the shipyard of the same name.

The size of the various workforces before Census figures become available is far from clear. However, MacGregor records 265 shipwrights and caulkers in

1804. Some of these would of course have been involved in repair work, as well
as new building. A table of shipbuilders (Table 1) and their dates indicates which
proprietors were coeval, but we cannot produce a similar table for their workers.

TABLE 1
Whitby Shipyards, *c*.1697-1902

1. Bagdale Beck
Jarvis Coates (-1697-1739)
Benjamin Coates (-1739-1757)

2. Angel Inn Yard
Thomas Hutchinson (-1763-)

3. North Part of Bagdale Beck
T. Hutchinson (-1763-1787)
Robert Barry (-1775-1793)
John & Francis Barry (-1787-90)
John Barry (-1792-1826)
Robert Barry (-1815 1830
[Bought Y. & N.M. Rly 1845]

4. South Part of Bagdale Beck
Henry Barrick (-1781-1814)
Thomas Barrick (-1786-1827)
Henry Barrick (-1827-1866)
[Bought by N.E. Rly. 1866]

5. Further Upriver (Boghall)
Jarvis Coates jnr. (-1717 bankrupt)
Thomas Fishburn (-1748-1777)
Fishburn & Brodrick (1781-1823-)
[Bought W. & P. Rly. 1836, trans. to
Y. & N. M. Rly. 1845]
Dry dock used until 1902

6. Dock Company's Land, Church Street
Used by:
Reynolds & Co. (1790)
Reynolds & Holt (1792-1796)
Holt & Richardson (1804-1819)
H. & G.Barrick (1828-1865 bankrupt)

7. North Part of Dock Co. Land
Peter Cato (-1802-1829)
Smales Bros. (-1866-1871)

8. Whitehall Shipyard
William Coulson (1735-1750)
Ingram Eskdale (-1787-1807)
Eskdale, Smales & Cato (-1803-)
Eskdale, Cato & Co. (1803-1808)
W. S. Chapman & Co. (-1799-1817-)
Chapman & Campion (-1800-1803-)
R. Campion (-1822-1841)
J. & W. Campion (-1838-1842 bankrupt)
T. Turnbull & Sons (1844-1902)

9. West of River, gained from Harbour
William Simpson (-1760-)
William Hustler (-1760-1777-)
Nathaniel & George Langborne
(1774-1813)
J. Langborne & Co. (-1811-1837)
William Hobkirk (-1824-1850)
Thomas Hobkirk (-1850-1862
bankrupt)
[Bought N.E. Rly Co.]

10. Larpool, above the oil house
Jonathan Lacey (-1800-1803)
Gideon Smales (-1807-1816-)
John Spencelayh (-1819-1827)
Thomas Turnbull (-1840-1844)

Sources: Weatherill, Ancient Port
of Whitby; Parish Registers; Trade
Directories

MacGregor also records the rise in building prices. *Henrietta* of 251 tons, built
in 1777, cost a little over £13 per ton. By 1818 *Fame* of 300 tons cost almost £20
per ton, an indication of the inflation due to the Napoleonic Wars.

PORT TRADES

Supplying the shipbuilding and repair industry was a large body of specialist
producers – block, mast and pump makers, ships' chandlers, ships' carpenters, riggers,
rope and twine manufacturers, sailcloth manufacturers, sailmakers, and timber and
raff merchants (the latter were wholesale seasoners and suppliers of shipbuilding
timber). Many of these were themselves sizeable employers of labour. In addition
to these was a whole series of trades which may well have worked on ships but
could also have had a domestic function. Among these are painters, unspecified
carpenters and provisioners. Table 2 shows those directly or indirectly employed
in the shipbuilding trade in 1823, from Baines' *Directory* for that year.

TABLE 2
Employment in Shipping and Allied Trades, 1823

Block, Mast & Pump Maker	(3)	Sail Cloth Manufacturers	(3)
Boat Builders	(3)	Sail Makers	(4)
Ships' Chandlers	(6)	Ship Builders	(7)
Carpenters – House & Ship	(15)	Ship Chandlers	(2)
Master Mariners	(37)	Ship Insurance Brokers	(5)
Painters – House, Sign & Ship	(12)	Ship Owners	(71)
Pilots	(12)	Timber & Raff Merchants	(5)
Riggers	(2)	Wharfingers	(4)
Rope & Twine Manufacturers	(6)	Miscellaneous (Customs, Harbour Master etc.)	(5)

Total 202

Source: Baines *Directory*, 1823

A glance at Pickernell's map of 1841 or the 1852 60-inch Ordnance Survey map is particularly instructive. If we examine the area around Spital Beck we see, in addition to the Whitehall Shipyard, a ropery, a sailcloth manufactory, three sail lofts, three timber yards and a timber pond. Clearly the specialised trades clustered round the users.

There were five roperies working in Whitby in the early 19th century, all on the fringes of the town because of the need for long uncluttered alleys for the rope-walks. The two largest were on the east side, one on the cliff-top above Boulby Bank, 440 yards long (i.e. able to make ropes a quarter of a mile long), and the one running parallel to Spital Beck. A plan of the former in 1737 indicates that it was then open to the air with a gravelled walk apart from a work-house covering the simple machinery at the northern end of the site. Later rope-walks tended to be enclosed under a long roof.

Sailcloth was mainly manufactured in small units set up in yards within the old town, but one was rather more ambitious. This was a set of buildings tucked into Stakesby Vale by Robert Campion and called Campionville. It started as a sailcloth factory in 1757, but by 1814 Campion had added a spinning mill (Hope Mill), a range of seven cottages and a villa called Campion Villa. This is no Saltaire, but nonetheless an interesting small-scale example of a mill colony. The villa, now the *Arundel House Hotel*, five of the cottages, now Arundel Terrace, and the sailcloth factory survive, the latter now a furniture warehouse. The rest was demolished when the railway embankment was built across the site.

Provisioning of ships was another important trade. Local farmers supplied beef, particularly from old bulls which were killed and salted to feed the ships' crews. Local bakers produced ship's biscuits, the carbohydrate element in many meals at sea, which kept reasonably well in difficult conditions. The greatest bustle of this kind occurred in spring each year when ships which had lain up all winter made ready for sea on 1 March.

One of the earliest improvements to the port of Whitby in the 18th century was the building of dry docks. The Dock Co., established in 1730, built a single dry dock at the foot of Green Lane on the east side of the harbour soon after its foundation and added a double dock in 1734. The Dock Co. did not itself build ships, but let out its docks to those that did.

Thomas Fishburn attempted to build another dock at his shipyard on the other side of the river but found the ground was too soft and unstable. In 1757 he successfully built one upriver at Boghall. The Langbornes constructed another dry dock in their shipyard near the Bagdale Beck in 1760. Thomas Barrick built another in 1812 and Robert Campion added the last in 1818. A further dry dock, which does not seem to appear on any map, was excavated in the Church Street car park in 1998, at a point almost opposite the old end of the Bagdale Beck. The stone-built dock had a semi-circular end and contained the dismantled timbers of a brig and a coble. It has been dated to 1755 and is thought to be the work of William Simpson, although one wonders whether it can be equated with the abortive attempt by Fishburn, mentioned above.

The purpose of these docks was ship repair, which was probably always more lucrative than building. Wooden ships required frequent attention to the caulking between the planks, and, in the days before wire rigging, the heavy hemp rope needed regular adjustment and replacement. When ships were in harbour for any length of time it was usual to 'rig down' – to send down the topmasts and spars and to renew standing rigging. Timber also required regular painting or tarring.

Minor repairs to the hull could be carried out by crew members if the ship were beached on soft sand and pulled manually over on to one side. There was always a risk of the ship being caught by the tide and filled, especially if caulking or repairs were incomplete, or being struck by a storm. This is where dry docks came in. Ships could be floated in on a high tide and propped. When the tide fell the dock gates were closed and the ship left dry for work to be carried out on the hull. Winter was the usual time, when much shipping was laid up and necessary repairs could be carried out. Constant wear and tear on wooden hulls meant that there was a steady demand for the dry dock facilities, marked by a 'queue' of vessels awaiting their turn. In enumerating the dry docks functioning in his day, Charlton states, '… all of which docks meet with so much encouragement and employ, that seldom any one of them is long empty, or without a ship in it'. A fine photograph by Frank Sutcliffe shows the brig *Margaret Nixon* dry-docked at Whitby in the late 19th century.

NOTABLE WHITBY SHIPS

Whitby produced many fine ships with interesting stories. Space does not permit us to describe more than a few here.

Sea Adventure, built in 1724 of 248 tons, probably by Jarvis Coates, came ashore in the middle of a Lincolnshire field on a flood tide, 86 years after her launch. *Volunteer* of 1756 was another veteran, with no less than 45 Greenland whaling voyages to her credit, on one of which in 1804 she brought back 18 whales. *Columbus* of 1832, built by H. & G. Barrick of 467 tons, was an emigrant ship sailing to Quebec; she survived at least until 1883.

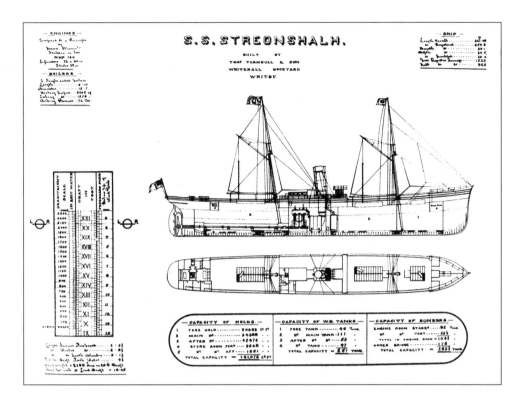

72   Lines of S.S. Streonshalh, *launched on 22 December 1877 by Thomas Turnbull & Son at the Whitehall Shipyard. She invites comparison with the small coaster carved on a pew in the parish church.*

73   *Detail from a rather mysterious engraving by Haynes of York, showing the harbour from above Whitehall. It dates probably from the 1740s. In the middle distance stand the buildings of the Whitehall shipyard, perhaps incorporating parts of the medieval hospital. Beyond are ships in the dry docks near the foot of Green Lane, rigged down while under repair (their topmasts and yards sent down). On the lower edge of the cliff is the Ropery, at this stage a long open alley with gantries across it.*

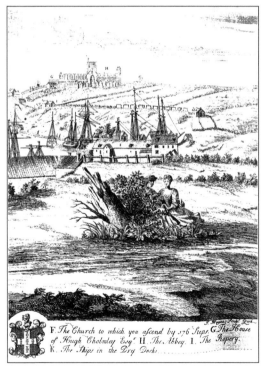

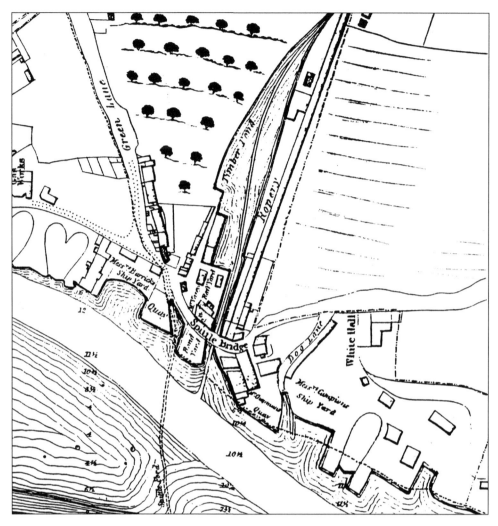

74 *Detail from Pickernell's map of 1841, showing the dense concentration around the Spital Beck of ship-wrighting activities, such as the dry docks, ropery, timber and raff yards, and two shipbuilding yards, those of Barricks and Campion.*

Liberty and Property, built in 1752 of 380 tons, survived all the rigours of the sea until 1856 when she was stranded on the island of Gothland. Even at the time she was recognised as being notably old-fashioned. There is a contemporary half-model of her, and a modern rigged full model, in the Merseyside Maritime Museum at Liverpool.

Two very large ships built by Fishburn & Brodrick in 1795 and 1801 respectively were *Coverdale* of 579 tons and *Culland's Grove* of 599 tons. Among the large armed vessels designed as privateers, carrying letters of marque which allowed them to attack enemy shipping, or at least to be able to sail on their own, outside the convoy system, were *Esk* (1781) of 629 tons and 44 guns and *Yorkshire* (1776) of 650 tons burthen and 16 guns. The latter seems drastically under-armed for her size.

Other large vessels of over 500 tons were *Indefatigable* (1799) of 549 tons and the unfortunate *Centurion* (1811) of 536 tons, lost within a year of her launch. *Esk* and *Centurion* were both products of the yard of Fishburn & Brodrick, who clearly specialised in the building of larger vessels.

Phoenix (1816) of 324 tons, built by W. S. Chapman at the Whitehall shipyard, was the last whaler to sail out of Whitby. Although some whalers were converted from other vessels they were very specialised in that their hulls were heavily strengthened against the Polar ice. They were also often away for very lengthy periods and carried a larger crew and larger quantities of supplies than ordinary merchantmen. In 1837 *Phoenix*, while under tow out of the harbour by the paddle steamer *Streonshalh*, had the misfortune to run aground behind the East Pier. She survived this to be refloated and sold to Scarborough, but never sailed to Greenland waters again.

Palatine of 507 tons (1841) was sold to Liverpool and in 1851 lengthened to give a tonnage of 615. It seems quite extraordinary how often shipwrights would lengthen or radically alter a ship, even to the extent of rebuilding ships that had burnt to the waterline, such as *Nautilus* of 1778, burnt out in 1795 but re-used to build *Wakefield* in 1797-98. With warships the process of complete rebuilding might occur several times, resulting for all practical purposes in an entirely new ship.

One middle-sized vessel comes to our attention for different reasons. *Whitby*, built in 1770 of 302 tons, is recorded by a delft-ware ship-bowl in Liverpool Museum with a portrait and the legend 'Success to the Whitby 1772'. Owners

75 *A Liverpool delft-ware ship-bowl with the legend 'Success to the Whitby 1772'. The vessel portrayed is a typical plain-stemmed collier bark; it can probably be identified with the vessel of that name built at Whitby in 1770 of 302 tons and lost in May 1827. Reproduced by permission of Liverpool Maritime Museum.*

or masters frequently commissioned such bowls before an important voyage. A whaler in 1786, *Whitby* was lost in 1827.

Very large vessels were fairly unusual. Although Whitby built a substantial number of large wooden ships over 400 tons, the largest as we have seen was 650 tons and the majority were much smaller. Indeed, small sloops and schooners of under 100 tons probably formed the greater part of the output. One Whitby vessel built in 1777 and now famous for other reasons is *General Carleton*, whose wreck was found and excavated on the Baltic coast near Gdansk in the 1990s. This excavation produced a quite outstanding set of finds, especially the hats and clothing of some of its Whitby crew. The wreck took place in 1785.

With the advent of iron shipbuilding and of screw steamers in 1871 sizes immediately began to increase. *Whitehall*, Turnbull's first screw steamer, was of 1,100 tons. By the turn of the century several vessels in excess of 5,600 tons had been launched. This was the absolute limit set by Whitby bridge, through which the hulls had to pass. With *Warrior* and *Theodor Wille* of 1901, both of 5,700 tons, Whitby reached its peak and also its swan song. At this point it ceased to be an active competitor in the field of shipbuilding. *Broomfield* of 1902 was Turnbull's last ship, and at a mere 3,860 tons the end of a centuries-long tradition of high quality.

One of the strangest vessels associated with Whitby was not built there, but can still be seen on the Scaur between Whitby and Saltwick. She is the *Creteblock*, one of a class of Admiralty tugs built just after the First World War from concrete. *Creteblock* was built at Shoreham in 1920 and was brought to Whitby in 1934 for dismantling. After languishing in the Upper Harbour for some years the hull was patched up in 1947 for towing out to sea, to be sunk in deep water. However, the weather proving adverse, she was beached on the Scaur and blown up. The remains are remarkably resilient and have lain there ever since!

THE SHIPPING TRADE

Several things combined to encourage the shipping trade of Whitby. In the medieval period most of the shipping serviced the domestic needs of the town and of the abbey: coal, fish and probably heavier goods which were difficult to bring by road.

However, it was the development of the alum trade which was to act as the first spur to growth in the shipping industry. Production of this valuable commodity, the raw materials for which were shale, coal, brushwood, seaweed and urine, was ideally suited to the North Yorkshire coast. Thomas Chaloner established his first alum works at Slapewath near Guisborough in 1604. Coal was brought into Whitby or direct to the alum works themselves which had spread to Saltwick, Kettleness and Sandsend, and alum was shipped out.

Unloading facilities were primitive on this rocky coast and many of the coal and alum vessels were quite small. When a great landslip occurred at Kettleness

76 *The launch of S.S.* Whitehall *at the Whitehall Shipyard on 20 June 1871. She was the first of many screw steamers built at this yard and represented a revolution in shipbuilding at Whitby.*

in 1829 the *Little Henry,* a sloop of 64 tons, was loading at the alum works and it was on board her that the families rendered homeless took refuge. She must have been fairly typical of the size of vessel employed in this trade.

Access to the loading facilities at most of the alum works called for high qualities of seamanship. In the event of a storm blowing up vessels were on a lee shore with no means of escape. Rudimentary harbour works existed at several of the alum works, such as Saltwick and Boulby, it is true, but they offered little protection from an onshore gale.

Every year vast fleets of colliers sailed from the Tyne and Wear to the Thames bearing the produce of the coalfields of Northumberland and County Durham. Some ships called at intermediate points and unloaded coal on beaches and foreshores wherever the demand occurred. Returning ships occasionally carried a paying cargo; most however took on ballast in the Thames in order to retain seaworthiness. Huge quantities of Thames gravel and chalk were taken off into lighters at the coal ports and at Sunderland the ballast accumulated to form huge mounds. All the profits of the voyage were therefore concentrated on the outward trip; the return brought only expense in loading ballast and then unloading it at the other end. The story of the colliers is well told by Roger Finch in *Coals from Newcastle.*

77 Diamond *of Scarborough, a small ketch, photographed by Frank Sutcliffe while unloading coal in the time-honoured way on Sandsend beach in 1887. The vessel was beached stern-first and propped when the tide fell, her coal being simply shovelled out into waiting carts. Poor people would eke out their supplies of coal by picking up forgotten lumps when the process was finished.* The Sutcliffe Gallery.

Much of this collier fleet was owned at Whitby and Scarborough. Whitby's share grew steadily throughout the 18th century from 8,300 tons in 1702 to 47,900 tons by 1788. In 1702-4 Whitby had the third largest ownership of colliers numerically, with ninety-eight. A letter from the shipowners of Whitby to those of Newcastle in 1717 suggests by its tone that the former had a very strong influence in the trade.

The collier fleet tended to sail only in the summer months, between 10 March and 29 September. Demand for coal was obviously strongest in winter, but the risk of storms was correspondingly greater in that season. Insurance for shipping in the winter months was so high as to be prohibitive and most colliers were laid up in consequence.

Whitby's involvement in the coal trade probably stemmed from two factors. It possessed at high tide one of the best harbours of refuge on the East Coast, an area noted for its sudden storms and generally inhospitable shore. This harbour was greatly improved by taking a toll on all goods shipped or landed here but more particularly by the passing toll on all colliers except Yarmouth vessels. Even in 1696 Whitby was said to be able to hold '500 sail of ships' and up to one hundred vessels were known to have entered on one tide alone. As many as 600 are said to have passed Whitby in one day in 1846. The other factor was shipbuilding, as we have seen. Defoe noted in 1724: '… they build very good ships for the coal trade, and many of them too, which makes the town very rich …'.

Many of the builders were also owners, and the careers of many Whitby seamen led them into eventual ownership. With such a large and regular trade it is not hard to see why collier ownership became important, although the evidence does not suggest that either masters or owners found it especially lucrative. Indeed a set of accounts for an unnamed Whitby collier in about 1756-9, published by Humble in 1972, makes very depressing reading. Perhaps like many accounts they were designed to play down the profitability for some purpose?

The traditional vessel for the trade was a brig or snow, or often a cat-built bark, sturdily built for maximum capacity and the ability to stand square when beached. Brigs and snows had two masts – the latter with a small trysail-mast immediately behind the main mast – while the bark carried three, including a small mizen. At this date differences of nomenclature were often based on hull-form rather than on rigging, which became usual in the 19th century. A good example of a bark was *Earl of Pembroke* before she was converted to serve in the Royal Navy as H.M.S. *Endeavour.*

Whitby shipowners found another valuable source of income from hiring their vessels to the state to serve as transports for troops and equipment in times of war. This occurred particularly in the 1750s, the last quarter of the 18th century and the first quarter of the 19th. Most in demand were the larger ships, of 300 tons and upwards. There were, of course, great risks to the ships, but these were insurable, or at least the owners would receive compensation in the event of their loss.

The owners found the hire of their ships as transports very lucrative, since payment was fixed and reliable – 10s. per ton in 1775, 13s. per ton in 1783, and as much as £3 3s. per ton by 1795. Between seventy and eighty Whitby ships out of 251 in 1779 were transports, while out of 221 transports surveyed between 1799 and 1807 no less than 23.7 per cent of tonnage had been built in Whitby. The quality, sturdiness and load-carrying characteristics of Whitby-built ships were no doubt the reason.

It is difficult to assess just how many transports Whitby provided since they were registered in London during their period of service. There can be little doubt that Whitby was building many larger ships specifically for hire by the government as transports. A number of them were captured by the French. Only sound ships were hired, and for these demand was high.

Not all ships which were hired as transports spent their whole working lives in this role. In the 1750s and '60s some of the transports were former whalers

78 *Wrecks of the brigs* Mary *and* Hope *lying on the foreshore in front of the Battery after a storm in 1851, from the* Illustrated London News, *11 October 1851. This sort of fate was all too common for the small vessels serving the coal trade; every storm caught a few on a lee shore and the next day the shore was covered in wreckage. Not all ended up in such public view as these.*

which had been taken out of service. Presumably some of them survived to return to whaling afterwards.

From the 1780s a new possibility for ship-hire opened with the creation of the penal colonies in Australia, Tasmania and Norfolk Island. Many Whitby ships of the largest size were chartered for the long voyage, such as *Indian* of 522 tons in 1810, *Indefatigable* of 549 tons in 1815, or *John Barry* of 520 tons in 1819. Journeys could take between three-and-a-half and eight months. *Indefatigable* could carry two hundred convicts. Ships usually left from London or one of the south coast ports, the convicts having been brought from prisons all over the country to the hulks in the Thames and thence aboard. Only those thought fit enough to stand the rigours of the voyage were transported.

SEAMEN AND SEAMANSHIP

We have already seen the evidence for the Navy's interest in Whitby shipping shown by the selection of ships for Cook's three voyages. Many of Whitby's seamen also served in the Navy, by no means all by choice. There is no doubt that the activities of the press gang, which was never made legal, carried away many merchant seamen, sometimes only after a fierce struggle. Gaskin gives a number of examples in *The Old Seaport of Whitby,* while there are also stories of Whitby men lying low in Cock Mill Woods, fed secretly by wives and sweethearts, until the press gang had moved on. The press gang bore particularly heavily upon whalers, as they carried large crews, and were vulnerable as they returned to port at the end of a voyage, often heavily laden.

Many sailors, however, probably found service in the Navy a natural progression in their career. Probate inventories indicate a large number of Whitby sailors serving in men-of-war. Many of them were owed wages at their death, or else we should know nothing about their naval connection. Most seamen were paid in arrears, so there is nothing sinister in the fact that the Navy owed them money.

Three men, John Gray, Matthew Porrit and Gregory Scrafton, all died in October 1740 aboard H.M.S. *Superb.* We cannot now tell whether they were all pressed men or volunteers but since they all died together they were probably messmates. The ship was at that time with a fleet on a mission to watch the Spanish coast, but no actual engagements are recorded. *Superb* was herself a captured French warship of 60 guns. In October 1740 she was caught in a heavy gale 70 leagues westwards of Start Point and badly damaged. Perhaps this was the occasion when the three Whitby sailors met their deaths.

Of all the jobs available to the menfolk of Whitby that of seaman – or 'mariner' – was the most obvious. While there were many fishermen, they did not register as highly in the social scale or make such an impact as seamen who disappeared for months on end and returned to swagger along the staithside with money jingling in their pockets.

Since Whitby had no obvious hinterland it looked seawards of necessity. Whitby supplied seamen for its own ships, those of other ports, and the Royal Navy, as we have seen. Many of them must have spent their entire lives before the mast, but a proportion worked their way through to a master's berth and finally to ownership, ending up as respected and wealthy members of the community. Two examples help to illustrate this.

Henry Taylor was born in Whitby in 1737 and at the age of 13 was bound apprentice for six years. A number of voyages followed, mostly in the North Sea coal trade but including two to Stockholm and one to Norway. By 1756 he was free, and after two more voyages he sailed as mate to Riga in 1758. He did not become master until 1760, refusing an earlier offer on the grounds that he was too young! After becoming master and part owner he gave up the sea to become a ship-and-insurance-broker at North Shields at the age of thirty-five.

My own great-great-grandfather, George Willis, also began in a fairly unpromising way. Born in 1821 of a poor family, son of an able seaman, he sailed first at 13, making two Atlantic crossings, the second to New Brunswick. After seven years apprenticeship to Captain Clark in the brig *Henry* from 1835 until 1842 he sailed successively as AB and mate, in 1848 becoming mate of *Abbotsford*. In that same year Gideon Smales took him on as master of *Ethel*, which he had bought lying in London Docks. He served eight years as master and became part owner of the brig *Active* in 1856. *Active* was lost in 1872 on the island of Aland and he bought the brig *Lancet* for £1,215. He retired in 1881, selling *Lancet* and other part shares in shipping which he had accumulated. He never made a fortune, but all his five sons followed him as master mariners, and some of them did rather well for themselves.

Here again we can see the progression from apprentice to AB, AB to mate, master and owner. The speed and eventual success of these careers can be put down in part to the large number of vessels each with a small crew and to the frightful rate of attrition of this fleet through storms and other natural disasters. Those who showed promise might very quickly achieve promotion in these circumstances. A master mariner carried heavy responsibilities – for large amounts of money, for gaining appropriate cargoes, for navigation, and ultimately for the lives of all the crew. Men who went to sea at 13 grew up rapidly in that harsh environment.

In the days of sail getting a ship into or out of harbour could be one of the most difficult and dangerous parts of a voyage. Until the sails filled and the ship had enough way to steer it could be unmanageable and capable of

79 *Whitby from the north-west, an engraving published in 1837. Many artists have attempted this view along the beach towards the West Pier. At the date of this engraving the beach was a place for hauling up boats, drying nets or unloading coal. It was not yet the domain of bathers and visitors. Many a wreck has lain on the shore at this point. From time to time the wreck of the* Skane, *a Swedish vessel which ran aground here in 1916, has made its reappearance due to alterations in the gradient of the beach.*

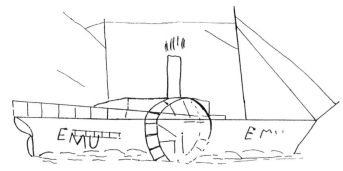

80 *The paddle-steamer* Emu *carved into a rear pew in the north transept of the parish church. Built on the Tyne in 1871, she came to Whitby in 1873 and was a familiar sight as a tug and in the 1880s as a passenger carrier, running a regular service to Scarborough.*

running into and damaging other ships as well as itself. Smaller ships would put on topsails to catch what wind there was in the harbour and would use 'sweeps' (very large oars) to row themselves out over the bar. This was a favourite tactic with fishing luggers but even larger vessels sometimes did this. Most larger vessels put out boats to tow them down harbour by oar, while capstans and rubbing strips on the West Pier were used for warping vessels out. Available men on the pier could also be used as bow hauliers to pull out the ships by main force. There was still a difficult moment when the vessel began to feel the seas but had not yet caught the wind. A contemporary description of getting the whaler *Esk* to sea in 1813 noted that 'by the assistance of a rope to the pier, two foy boats and a light breeze of wind we were drawn safely without the piers at 5pm'.

Coming in was equally bad, for ships would try to enter the narrow gap between the piers at as great a speed and with as much sail as they dared, in order to maintain way up the harbour. Frequently, if the tide was running across the gap, they would misjudge it and hit the end of the pier or run aground on Collier Hope. Unluckier still were the ships that went behind the East Pier and took the ground on the rocky Scaur, for they stood little chance of survival. It was a feat of great skill to judge exactly how to enter the harbour in bad weather and the masters who misjudged it did not often get a second chance.

In the harbour itself there was another obstacle in the form of the bridge. Not only was it very narrow but until 1835 it was common for ships to foul their rigging or topsails in the raised drawbridge leaves and counterweights.

The launch of the paddle steamer *Streonshalh* in 1836, though an omen of what was to come, must have seemed like a godsend to sailing masters, since she and her successors were independent of the wind and could tow sailing vessels in and out of harbour in relative safety. Thereafter paddle steamers carried out dual work, acting as tugs in the harbour and carrying parties of holiday-makers out to sea or along the coast when this was more profitable.

Even motor ships have difficulties in docking at Whitby and over the years I have seen many an embarrassed vessel forced to sit it out on the mud, waiting for a high tide to lift it clear, after misjudging the dredged channel!

EVIDENCE

In view of its heavy involvement with shipping it is not surprising that Whitby produced a number of important marine artists, although several of them subsequently moved away to work in more lucrative places.

George Chambers (1803-40) was articled to a house painter but as a boy he sold ship portraits to whaler crews. He later moved to London. Other members of the Chambers family also achieved some notability in marine painting. They included George, junior (b. 1830), William Henry (b. 1833) and William, the brother of George, senior, born in 1815. George is said to have been responsible for the wall-paintings showing Whitby and its shipping in the *Prospect of Whitby* inn, at Wapping Wall on the Thames, where he lodged on first going to London, although nothing now survives. There is considerable confusion over the issue, and Chambers' biographer, Russett, suggests that Crawford's inn, where he did the paintings, was *not* the *Prospect of Whitby*, but another Wapping inn.

Michael Scurr (1800-64) was another Whitby artist who settled in Wapping, London. Thomas Dore, who

81 *Graffito of a brigantine cut into the Newholm Pew in the north transept of the parish church. The vessel is very lightly incised and seems to be marked 'Lucy'; the carvings lie thickly intercut and so it is not absolutely certain which inscriptions go with which drawings.*

82 *A brigantine carved into a pew in the nave. Though apparently unfinished, the carving is very spirited and shows interesting details of sails and rigging.*

is known as a marine painter in Liverpool, died in 1887 in Whitby Infirmary. Perhaps in his latter days he had also painted there.

The most notable Whitby family of painters is undoubtedly the Weatherill family. George, Mary, Sarah Ellen, Elizabeth and Richard were responsible for many Whitby views, including a large number to do with ships. Richard also wrote the definitive history of Whitby shipping. The best collection of Weatherill paintings can be seen in the Pannett Art Gallery. George's work has become very popular and collectable over the last few years. What may be his signature is cut into the parapet at the end of the East Pier in handsome capitals.

Henry Redmore of Hull (1820-87) painted marine scenes along the East Coast including some very fine paintings of ships off Whitby. These can be seen both in the Pannett Art Gallery and in the Ferens Art Gallery at Hull.

There are a number of naive ship portraits in the shipping gallery at Whitby Museum. They are very much in the style of those painted at Naples and in the Sound, the passage which forms the entrance to the Baltic, which were frequently offered to masters of vessels passing through. Typically they show what at first seem to be three ships but which on closer examination turns out to be the same ship from various viewpoints.

In later days the photographs of Frank Sutcliffe show the period of changeover from sail to steam, including many veterans of the age of sail. They also incidentally show how densely the harbour could be packed, especially during the visits of the Scottish and Cornish fishing fleets.

Another source of information comes from the remarkable series of carvings in Whitby parish church. Over forty representations of ships, from small sloops to brigantines and steamships, are cut into the backs, seats and bookrests of the box pews, especially of the east gallery. One carving, of a paddle steamer, is identified as *Emu,* a regular visitor to Whitby in the 1870s and 1880s. We must presume that these carvings were cut by apprentices and the like, during the long services and perhaps particularly in the winter when most shipping was laid up. They are of varying quality from crude to extremely accomplished, and serve to illustrate the range of shipping to be seen in Whitby in the 18th and 19th centuries. They also show the large part shipping played in Whitby's communal consciousness, since graffiti of other subjects in the parish church are few in comparison. Other ship graffiti appear on the galleries of St Ninian's church in Baxtergate.

Ship models are also a useful source of information. The bracket half-model of *Liberty and Property,* discussed above, is in Merseyside Maritime Museum and is probably one of the earliest such models in existence. Whitby Museum has a very fine collection of ship models. Of these the best are probably those in the Walker Collection. Examples of Whitby-built ships are *Wilberforce,* W. Hobkirk's first ship of 1838, *Skipio,* a brig built by Fishburn & Brodrick in 1809, and *Columbus* of 1832, by H. & G. Barrick. There are also a number of half-models, especially of ships built by Smales Bros. and by Turnbull's, together with plans of many of the latter's steamships, such as S.S. *Streonshalh, Whitehall,*

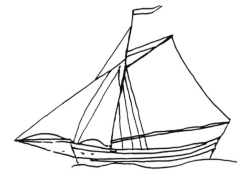

83 *A sloop carved into a pew in the north gallery. In the late 18th century Whitby was building many small trading vessels of this kind, of about 60-80 tons. The artist has managed to convey the essence of one in a few powerful lines.*

Thordisa and *Cosmopolitan*. Hull Town Docks Museum has a model of the Whitby whaler *Harpooner*, built in 1769 of 341 tons. To my eye this is a very bizarre and ugly model, giving a quite wrong impression of a whaler's proportions.

Whitby Museum has, in the H. W. Smales Collection, a number of line plans of ships built by John and Robert Barry. Among these are *Orient* (1810), a brig of 110 tons, *Brilliant* (1813), a ship of 237 tons, and *Clio* (1813 or 1816), a sloop of 82 or 86 tons. The latter is an unusual survival of what must have been one of the commonest types of vessel built in Whitby, requiring no special building facilities. Many of these smaller ships were built as a speculation on the staith or on the foreshore and launched unceremoniously at a convenient high tide. Many found a role in supplying coal and kelp to the alum works.

Some of these smaller vessels such as the sloops *Lively* of 1786 and *Alert* of 1802, of 49 and 43 tons respectively, were re-rigged during their long lives. The former was photographed before 1886 by Frank Sutcliffe, rigged as a billy-boy, while the latter became a schooner. Rigs were certainly not immutable and, indeed, considerable changes often took place, including the stepping of additional masts. This is not surprising given the need for continual overhaul of hemp rigging. During the 19th century in particular there was a trend towards simpler fore and aft rigs, requiring less hands to manage them. Many older square-rigged vessels were re-rigged as schooners or barques at this period.

LIFEBOATS

Whitby's first lifeboat was acquired as early as 1802 when Francis Gibson, Collector of Customs for the port, approached Lloyds of London for assistance in forming a lifeboat station there. Lloyds gave £50, the remainder of the £160 was raised locally, and the new boat, built by Greathead, the lifeboat pioneer, arrived in Whitby on 15 September. It was to be kept in a boathouse near the West Pier, opposite the Scotch Head.

In 1822 this boat was replaced by two new ones, one of which was to be kept hanging from davits on the Tate Hill Pier, on the east side of the harbour. The stone bases of the davits survived until recently. The cutting of the Khyber Pass in 1847 entailed the moving of the west side lifeboat house a little further to the south, to where the Lifeboat Museum stands today.

These early lifeboats carried out many rescues over the years; they were all of the pulling variety, relying on oars for motive power. In the wild conditions which tended to prevail when their services were called on it required very powerful oarsmen to thrust them through the mountainous seas. When the wind was onshore, driving vessels onto the rocky coast, it was very difficult to get the lifeboat out between the piers or off the slipway into the teeth of the wind. Oars also got in the way of coming alongside the stricken vessel. Seamanship of a very high order was demanded. There were casualties, too. In 1841 four lifeboatmen were drowned when the lifeboat was overturned while going to the rescue of two fishing boats.

Of all the incidents dealt with by Whitby lifeboats none is better known than
the tragedy which struck on 9 February 1861. In the words of the Rev. William
Keane, writing to *The Times* newspaper that day:

> We have had a fearful storm today. Half a mile of our strand is already strewn with
> several wrecks; a new lifeboat launched a few months ago was manned by the finest
> picked seamen of Whitby. Five times during the day they have braved the furious sea
> and five times returned from vessels in distress. A sixth ship was driven behind the pier.
> The men, exhausted though they were, again pulled out, but, before they had gone
> fifty yards, a wave capsized the boat. Then was beheld by several thousand persons,
> within almost a stone's throw but unable to assist, the fearful agonies of those powerful
> men, buffeting with the fury of the breakers till, one by one, twelve out of thirteen
> sank, and only one was saved. There were ten widows, forty-four fatherless children
> and two dependants left.

Only Henry Freeman survived. He was on his first day in the lifeboat crew
and was saved by his cork life jacket, which was of a new type. A monument to
the disaster, in the rather curious form of a model Greek temple, can be seen at
the west end of the parish church.

One result of the disaster was the joining of the Whitby Lifeboat Association
with the R.N.L.I. and the dispatch to Whitby shortly afterwards of one of the
institution's self-righting lifeboats.

A great number of rescues has been achieved over the years. There is only
space here to look briefly at two of the most remarkable of them. In January 1881
the Whitby brig *Visitor* sank in heavy seas off Robin Hood's Bay and her crew
took to an open boat. The Whitby lifeboat could not be got out by sea into the
face of the fierce wind and waves. Despite the deep snowdrifts 200 men from
Whitby and Robin Hood's Bay set to work to clear the road between the two
places while others hitched horses to the launching carriage and by main force
dragged the lifeboat the six miles over steep gradients and bad roads to launch it
at Robin Hood's Bay. Even after this it took two attempts and double the usual
crew to rescue the stricken sailors. A reconstruction of this epic rescue attempt
took place in 1999.

Another great rescue took place in the early days of the First World War when
the hospital ship *Rohilla* of 7,409 tons struck the Scaur near Saltwick Nab. She had
been following a course close inshore to avoid minefields and the usual navigation
lights on the piers had been dowsed because of the state of war.

The story of the subsequent events has been told many times; readers who
would like to know more are directed to the several excellent accounts of the
wreck. Briefly, it was thought impossible to launch either of the Whitby lifeboats
in the prevailing conditions but by morning coxswain Langlands had the idea of
carrying and dragging the lifeboat under the Spa Ladder at the shoreward end
of the East Pier. Despite the difficulties this was done and 145 men and women
hauled the boat along the Scaur to Saltwick. Thirty-five people were rescued
from the *Rohilla* in two attempts before the lifeboat was damaged too seriously to

84 *The scene of the great lifeboat disaster in 1861 as depicted by the artist of the* Illustrated London News *for 23 February 1861. A viewpoint somewhere off the end of the West Pier has been chosen, looking back towards the Battery and the West Cliff.*

make any further attempt. Other lifeboats were called in, including the Teesmouth motor lifeboat. Eventually the last 50 survivors were taken off by pouring oil on the water to enable the lifeboat to come alongside.

Many perished in the wreck and the lack of a motor lifeboat stationed nearby was probably a contributory factor, despite the heroism shown by the crews on this occasion.

Subsequently Whitby has had a succession of motor lifeboats, the most recent of which is the Trent-class boat *George & Mary Webb*, which in 1996 replaced the powerful Tyne-class *City of Sheffield* supplied in 1988. The former lifeboat *Mary Ann Hepworth*, used from 1938 to 1974, can still be seen in summer, taking visitors on trips out to sea. Increasingly important in recent years has been the inshore lifeboat, an inflatable which can travel fast in shallow water to rescue people trapped by the tide or victims of pleasure-boating accidents.

A visit to the Lifeboat Museum is worthwhile, to see the relics of nearly two centuries of rescues and a preserved rowing lifeboat on its carriage.

Six

FISHING

Fishing has long been important to Whitby. Fish was probably the staple diet of the Anglian monastery and was to remain an important commodity, of international concern, throughout the Middle Ages. The harbour provided a safe haven in bad weather but specially adapted boats worked off beaches, wherever there was a living to be made and wherever they could be pulled up out of the reach of winter storms.

The types of boats used varied considerably. The main influences on their design were the sea conditions, the landing conditions, the type of fish being sought, and finally the amount of money their owners could afford to spend. Life was adapted to the migratory habits of fish such as the herring, vast shoals of which began to appear off the port in August-September. Salmon, cod, ling, crabs and lobsters were all taken in their due season, each requiring a different bait or technique.

In early days shellfish were gathered for food off the scaurs. Mussels were plentiful on this rocky coast. By the 19th century most shellfish were gathered by the women to bait long lines for their menfolk and such was the demand that mussels had to be brought in large quantities by train from Lancashire and from Boston in Lincolnshire. It is probable that local stocks of shellfish were simply outstripped by the demand for bait at this period. Limpets ('flithers') were also used but were definitely second best. In Whitby shellfish are seen as bait, not as something to eat.

The most characteristic fishing vessel of this coast is the coble. It is certainly an ancient design and its name occurs as early as the Middle Ages. The coble is a boat of variable size from about 17 ft. up to 40 ft. in length but can be recognised by its high sharp bow, its low, steeply angled transom and its flat bottom with bilge keels. Larger cobles are known as 'ploshers'. Traditionally they are measured not by overall length but by the length of the 'ram plank', the oak centre plank which runs from the curve of the bow to the transom. The overall length can be up to thirty per cent more.

A coble's shape is entirely a product of its original purpose – beaching stern-first on a sandy shore. The deep forefoot grips the water and holds the head to the waves while the stern can run gently on to the sands, its two 'draft keels' taking the strain. Cobles could be rowed or sailed. In sailing a relatively small dipping

85 *The sailing coble WY 97, Gratitude, lying on the harbour mud at low tide. She sits squarely because of her flat bottom and twin keels under the stern. The high peaked bow and raked transom stern can clearly be seen. Such cobles were once a common sight, with their tan dipping lug sail, steeply raked mast and long flat oars on throle pins for pulling. Following a move to motorised vessels with wheelhouses there has been a return of interest in traditional sailing vessels of this sort, but mainly for pleasure.*

lug was set, occasionally with a foresail rigged to a temporary bowsprit. Rowing involved three flat-sectioned oars on single throle pins. In some areas two men rowed to starboard while a third rowed over the port quarter. In Whitby two or three pairs of oars were often used.

Excavations in the remains of a dry dock in Church Street in 1998 revealed the lower planks of a coble which had lain there since perhaps the 1780s, along with parts of a dismantled brig. It is unusual for small fishing vessels to survive, and particularly interesting that this coble seemed very similar to more modern examples, as though little development had taken place in recent centuries. This example seemed to have no mast step, so that, although she was missing the upper strakes which might have held evidence for oars, she was most likely powered by oars only.

Sail has long ago given way to motors and now most larger cobles are decked and have a wheelhouse to give some protection from the elements. On the

Northumberland coast many cobles are built with a lower bow than those of Yorkshire. Some protection from the weather is offered by a canvas awning or 'cuddy' stretched over the forepeak. Cobles of this type can be seen today at Staithes, only 10 miles north of Whitby. In the 19th century, however, conventional cobles of the Yorkshire type fished from here in large numbers.

Inshore fishing involved not only cobles. Double-enders of a similar size, known as mules, were once very common. Their lines were better adapted to taking heavy seas from astern. Their modern descendants are now to be seen, like the coble, mostly in a motorized version and with simplified lines.

The inshore fisherman's year revolved, and still does to a certain extent, around the various catches in season – salmon and trout between March and August, lobster and crabs outside those times, and the perennial cod. Salmon and trout were caught in nets, lobster and crab in pots, and cod and ling on baited long lines – 200 hooks to a line, each 10 ft. (three metres) apart. A coble would carry six long lines or 240 pots in four strings of 60 each. Baiting and preparing the long lines was women's work. They had to open and 'skane' (soak) the mussels, fix them to the hooks, and then coil the line so that the hooks did not foul as the line was paid out. Each coil of line was fastened down to a wicker 'skep' for carrying. In more recent times fishermen have fitted their boats with mechanical haulers for pots but long lines do not lend themselves to mechanised hauling and have largely passed out of use on the east coast.

Nowadays many coblemen hire out their vessels to anglers who arrive in droves on summer weekends. Fishing on wreck sites, where fish tend to shoal, is especially popular. Angling from the piers and their extensions is also popular. At certain times of year vast masses of sprats shoal around them, forming extraordinary silver patterns in the water. Mackerel feed on the sprats and further out larger fish wait to feed on the mackerel.

Salmon and sea trout are taken with nets, buoyed up with cork floats. Both the season and net size have changed since the late 19th century, when nets were six to eight feet (two to three metres) deep. Not only did the depth increase to 30 ft. (about 9.5 metres) but the mesh size went up to five and six inches (14-15 cm.).

The migration of herring led to a corresponding migration of fishermen. Whitby fishermen at one time followed the herring down the coast, which probably accounts for the note in the accounts of the Overseers of the Poor at Leverton, near Boston, in Lincolnshire in 1570: 'Given to ... Cook and petro Robertes of Whytebay marioners. xii d'.

During the 19th century Cornish and Scottish boats began to arrive in Whitby in pursuit of the herring shoals, and continued their annual visits well into the 20th century, though the First World War greatly changed the economic climate for fishermen. Their distinctive rig and dark sails made them a notable feature of the harbour for a few weeks each year. The Cornish boats were luggers, their Scottish counterparts zulus and fifies. These large vessels fished the grounds some 60 miles offshore.

The Cornish luggers were excellent and fast sailers. Finch records how in 1910 three such luggers made a passage of some 600 miles in 70 hours. When under full sail they carried two masts and a long raked outrigger over the stem. On the fishing grounds they lowered the mainmast onto crutches and set a small mizzen to keep the vessel head to wind. Scottish zulus came from the Moray Firth area while the fifies came from a little further south. Very large vessels – zulus up to 75 ft. overall and fifies some 10 ft. shorter – both had a similar sail plan but zulus had a sternpost raking at 45 degrees or so in contrast to the vertical stempost of the fifie. They carried massive masts and spars with minimal standing rigging, a bonus in crowded harbours where damage could easily occur. Large crews meant that there was little pressure for mechanical handling devices.

In 1991 and various successive years the fifie *Reaper*, preserved by the Scottish Fisheries Museum at Anstruther, was a visitor to the Whitby Regatta, its huge masts and tan sails a vivid reminder of scenes in the harbour over seventy years ago.

Most of the herring were preserved in salt or ice. Scottish women followed the fishing; in teams of three accompanied by two male coopers they moved from harbour to harbour gutting the herrings as they came in. The men made the barrels and packed the fish into them. Bought up by wholesalers and middlemen, the herring were dispatched by rail. This pattern began to change with the First World War, though vast shoals reappeared in the 1950s.

Not all herring were preserved this way, however. A substantial number were kippered using woodsmoke. Kipper houses were established by the Whitby Herring Company at Tate Hill Pier in 1833. The artist Mary Ellen Best stayed in Whitby on several occasions and one of her paintings, dated 1838, shows the interior of the kipper house. Even today Fortune's kipper house in Henrietta Street still uses the traditional method. There is no more delightful sensation on a warm summer evening than to stand on the cliff above and smell the distinctive smoke, unless perhaps it is to eat the end-products!

In kippering the fish are split, gutted, washed, dipped in brine and fixed to sharp hooks on battens running up to the roof of the kipper house. When the space is full oak chips and sawdust are set to smoulder on the floor below. All holes and doorways are blocked and the fish are steeped for 12 hours in the thick smoke. The interior of the kipper house is thick with a black tarry deposit from the fish oil and wood tar. Kippering preserves the fish for long periods as well as giving it a delightful flavour. At one time holiday-makers sent kippers packed in wooden boxes to less fortunate friends and relations still at home, but the rising cost of postage has largely put paid to this custom.

As well as cobles Whitby has long been home to larger fishing boats which worked out as far offshore as the Dogger Bank and had more accommodation and a larger crew. In 1817 Young noted that Whitby only had nine full-time fishermen. The explanation seems to be that during the 18th and 19th centuries – the period of Whitby's greatest prosperity as a shipbuilding and shipowning port – the fishermen were gradually pushed out. If negative evidence can be

86 *Hauling salmon nets between the West Pier and the beach. As well as carrying the usual 'WY' registration mark this coble also bears an 'SF' mark to show that it is licensed for salmon fishing.*

accepted, then the complete absence of any fishing boats from among the fifty or more vessels recorded as graffiti in the parish church seems to indicate how thoroughly Whitby had become a shipping rather than fishing port in the late 18th and 19th centuries.

Fishermen and their boats migrated to Staithes and Robin Hood's Bay, and many of the larger boats which fished the Whitby area were owned at Staithes. This state of affairs had not been prevailing for long. From the earliest records of the abbey, ships from Whitby had been involved in fishing. In 1248, for instance, a dispute with St Leonard's Hospital in York was resolved by the abbey sending 3,000 herrings there each year. In 1394 a vast shoal of herrings made its appearance, bringing with it a number of foreign fishing boats, foreshadowing the shape of things to come. In the 15th century Scarborough and Whitby boats worked the cod grounds as far away as the Faroes and Iceland. This practice continued into the 17th century.

Of considerable importance to the economy of the town is the fish market, the means by which the fishermen sell their catch to the dealers and middlemen. There have always been fishermen who have sold some or all of their catch direct to the public, as they still do on Redcar sands.

Young tells us that the fish market was originally in Sandgate but moved in about 1790 to the foot of Brewster Lane, at the upper end of the Fish Pier. Later it moved across the river to Coffee House End and was held in the open air. Since the late 1950s the auctioning of the catch has taken place in the same area in covered sheds, conveniently close to the derrick used for hauling fish boxes out of the boats and on to the quay.

Pier Road itself dates from *c*.1786 and was built out over sands, with a stone revetting wall. A timber fish quay built in 1914 fronted this but dredging near it gradually caused road, wall and timber deck to subside. In the late 1950s its replacement had become urgent. The new Fish Quay is both higher and wider than the old one and level throughout with Pier Road. As well as the Fish Market it contains an icemaking machine and lockable stores for fishing gear.

In the period 1928-47 the wooden decking at Dock End was also replaced and New Quay Road developed. The dock itself, a sheltered mooring for smaller fishing boats, was much reduced in size to create car parking, another stage in the gradual diminution of the mouth of the Bagdale Beck, which has been going on for the last three hundred years.

In the 20th and early 21st century the port and shipbuilding trade of Whitby has once more given place to fishing boats as well as pleasure craft of all sorts.

87 Reaper, *a fifie built in 1902 and now owned and restored by the Scottish Fisheries Museum at Anstruther, on a visit to Whitby during the 1991 Regatta. Fishing vessels of this sort were once common annual visitors to Whitby, following the herring. With their massive pole masts, huge tan sails and strong hulls they made an impressive sight in the harbour.*

The earliest larger vessels recorded are the so-called 'five man boats'. Documentary evidence for them first appears in 1541, though they were probably
old-established even then. They were of about 30-40 tons and larger than the
largest cobles. Young describes a typical example in his day (1817) as 46 ft. long,
16 ft. 8 in. beam, and 6 ft. 3 in. deep, clinker built and decked. Of 58 tons, it had
three masts and spread four sails, carrying two cobles on its deck.

Many of these vessels followed the herring down as far as Yarmouth and then
were laid up over winter in Whitby harbour, along with those belonging to other
places along the coast which lacked a safe anchorage. The men would go on
fishing through the winter in cobles. These larger vessels carried either nets or
long lines, depending on what fish they sought. Despite their name they usually
carried a crew of seven. Five, including the owner, took a full share of the profits.
The owner took another share for the boat and all these men provided their own
gear. Another man, without gear, took a half share, while a boy, who provided no
gear and took no share, learned the trade.

Distinctive types of vessel seen later in the century were the Staithes 'Yacker'
and the Marshall lugger, introduced, according to Dora Walker, by the Whitby
boatbuilder Robert Marshall in about 1850. These had two masts and carried a
crew of five. A gate in the starboard bulwark allowed the launching of a single
coble carried on deck. Minimal accommodation was provided for the crew who
lived and slept aboard for long periods.

Late in the 19th century increasing competition led to the introduction of
'Dandies' which were ketch-rigged and needed only three men to manage them.
The competition came from steam trawlers from other ports, which were not
only more efficient but cheaper to run.

After the First World War keel boats made their appearance. With motors and
auxiliary sail, and also a wheelhouse to give some protection from the elements, they
were safer and could venture further out. Ring-netting, using two boats, replaced
drift-netting. In the summer Scottish boats arrived in Whitby to fish local waters.
During the 1960s the Scottish fleet began to include larger steel stern-trawlers
and in time some of these were sold on to Whitby owners. Nowadays the larger
vessels are mostly stern-trawlers and the keel boats are no longer in evidence. As
with cobles, however, the use of motors and enclosed wheelhouses has tended
to blur the distinctions; locally developed hull-forms, designed for sailing and
beaching in very specific circumstances, have given way to a wide variety of types
with better weather protection and requiring less maintenance, which now make
up the fishing fleet.

Quotas on catches have also led to diversification. Over-fishing of the North
Sea has led to quotas in all sorts of fish. The herring, whose huge numbers formed
the staple commodity of the fishing industry, is suffering long-term decline, both
through over-fishing and through a cyclical process which has historically left a
record of alternating glut and scarcity. Herring for kippers are now bought from
Scotland or even Iceland. Larger foreign vessels from all over the world exploit the

88 *Fortune's kipper house in Henrietta Street. Although Whitby kippers have been made since the 1830s, the early kipper houses were situated at the head of Tate Hill Pier. Fortune's was established in 1872; the room at the street front is the shop, while the rear forms the kippering shed. Rows of split herrings hang here on battens over smouldering oak chippings and sawdust and thus acquire their delicious taste.*

formerly rich fishing around the British Isles using the latest technology. Widespread trawling is indiscriminate in what it catches. Now even cod is under threat from over-fishing. The effect of quotas has been to reduce the size of the fishing fleet and to take many boats out of commission. Whitby's fishing fleet is now but a shadow of its former state. Fish processing has in recent years become a successful growth industry in Whitby, and Whitby scampi is on the menu everywhere.

Pictures of growth or decline in the fishing industry are difficult to establish. It is not even very easy to determine how many fishermen there are. It is traditionally a seasonal and variable occupation, with many part-timers and amateurs as well as the old-established fishing families. The last large-scale survey of Whitby in 1958 found it impossible to establish the true number of fishermen, or even of boats. What is manifestly clear is that no longer do Whitby fishermen have to face only the uncertainties of sea and weather, of fish prices and fluctuating stocks, but also the actions of distant bureaucrats and the insatiability of world markets.

Seven

LOST INDUSTRIES

Visitors to Whitby see a town with little obvious industry apart from fishing and the relatively small port trade. Things were once very different and Whitby was at the centre of a number of substantial industries determined by its position and geology. Among these were extractive and processing industries such as jet, alum, Roman cement, ironstone, and building stone; whaling and whale-processing followed from Whitby's shipping interests. Salt may also have been extracted here, though the evidence is tantalisingly slight. In the absence of a rich hinterland it was mainly these raw materials which Whitby exported, along with fish and dairy products, and it was these commodities, especially alum, which helped to develop the port's shipbuilding and shipowning capacity.

Many of these industrial activities were on a gargantuan scale and involved the moving of huge quantities of material. Alum, for example, was a valuable commodity but very wasteful of raw materials. It is reckoned that 100 tons of alum shale would only produce some three tons of refined alum, until the basic chemistry was better understood. The remaining calcined shale waste, to say nothing of the soil and rock overburden, was left close to the quarrying site on beaches and clifftops where it survives to this day, a sterile layer which blocks plant growth.

Although jet extraction went on for a shorter time and was on a smaller scale, cliffs and valley sides for miles around are scarred by the rows of small adits made by the jet miners in following the elusive deposits.

Building stone came principally from Aislaby quarry but the opening of the railway line to Pickering revealed useful deposits of other rock which could be brought out through the port of Whitby. Rich deposits of ironstone were located at Grosmont in the Esk valley, leading to a brief but large-scale industrialisation of that area. Further and richer deposits in Cleveland, particularly north of Skinningrove, were worked until recently.

Deep-lying deposits of potash were discovered near Stainsacre and at Boulby in the late 1960s and the latter are now exploited by Boulby Mine.

The whaling trade, though lucrative, has left little mark on the landscape. All the processing yards have gone and the products were mostly perishable. A number of whale jaw arches used to adorn the area but most have succumbed to the weather. That which stands on the West Cliff is symbolic of the former trade but is in fact the jawbone of a Norwegian-caught whale, brought here only in the 1960s.

Whitby's contact with the interior was negligible until the 20th century. Bad roads and steep gradients, difficult to traverse in winter, did not encourage much contact. Pannierways carried most of the traffic until the mid-18th century and they were not well adapted to the carriage of heavy or bulky goods. The coming of the railways was more influential in bringing into Whitby the products of its hinterland than distributing Whitby-made goods to a wider world. It was sea traffic that scored heavily, being well adapted to carrying large heavy cargoes. This in turn encouraged shipbuilding and allied trades.

The effect of this heavy industrialisation is often so great that we do not even recognise the magnitude of the scale. Whole cliffs have been changed beyond all recognition. Access ways to the shore and landing places have altered the shape of the coastline. At Ravenscar the former alum works are intercut by a railway line, a brickworks, and an inclined plane from a ganister quarry on the moor above, all confused by landslips and coastal erosion.

These are the surviving effects but we should remember also the shorter term effects. Large scale industries such as these required workers, whose housing has also largely disappeared. Ships and harbours served the works. Breakwaters and piers have mostly fallen victims to the sea since abandonment. Alum required huge amounts of coal and large quantities of seaweed to burn for potash, so beaches were rented and harvested systematically.

What are now desolate cliffs and foreshores, once the brief holiday period is over, were once thronged by seaweed gatherers, bait gatherers (known as 'flither pickers'), jet miners and fossil collectors. We should add to this picture the numerous fishermen drying their nets, the poorer people gathering driftwood for fires and sandstone for scrubbing floors, and the children picking up coal spilt on the beaches where colliers berthed.

It has often been claimed that the Cholmley family, and especially Sir Hugh, were key figures in Whitby's rise, through their introduction of the alum trade and through harbour improvements. A recent assessment, however, suggests that they followed the trend, rather than leading it, and that as lords of the manor they were net beneficiaries rather than benefactors.

JET

Jet is one of Whitby's most famous products. Indeed many people who have never been to Whitby know of Whitby jet. It is a type of fossilised wood, related to both coal and lignite, from an ancient tree similar to the modern araucaria or monkey-puzzle tree. Such trees flourished in the forests of the Jurassic period, some 180 million years ago. Unlike coal, jet does not occur in predictable seams. Its preservation as a fossil was relatively chancy and although the strata in which it is found can be readily identified it occurs as discontinuous lumps.

89 *A Whitby jet worker at his bench. He appears to be carving by hand though many photographs of jet workers show only the polishers at work with their wheels.*

Early jet workers discovered enough raw materials to satisfy them on beaches and under cliffs, wherever the jet had been eroded out. They discovered that it cut relatively easily and moreover would take a high polish, producing that distinctive deep black known as a result as 'jet black'.

Jet was first worked in quantity by the prehistoric people known as the Beaker People, who used it for buttons and toggles, and slightly later, during the Bronze Age (*c.*1800-700 B.C.), it was in demand for ornaments such as necklaces. Good examples of the latter can be seen in Scarborough Museum and at the Yorkshire Museum in York. At Scarborough is a necklace from a barrow at Man Toft, Egton, consisting of 35 shaped beads and spacers.

From some necklaces we can tell that the craftsman was attempting to copy some other material such as amber, for the spacers are frequently marked with lines exactly where the strings would be seen passing through a semi-transparent substance. Jet, then, was worked as an alternative to other soft and workable substances such as amber and shale, but it was widely traded and no doubt highly prized for its colour and perhaps for the magical qualities it was assumed to possess.

Jet workshops were established in York in Roman times and many ornaments have been found there. As it was a cosmopolitan city we must be careful not to assume that all jet in York came from Whitby. Spain also had supplies of jet and the Romans were adept at bringing the luxuries of their empire to markets.

In Anglo-Saxon times jet continued in popularity, and there are many objects of jet from the site of Streanaeshalch. These include small crucifixes and beads, just the sort of religious item that continued to be made in jet throughout the Middle Ages. Interestingly, a number of jet discs and a part-finished jet bangle show that jet was being worked actually on the site of the monastery. They bear the marks of turning on a pole lathe. It is hard to see these bangles as anything but fashionable female jewellery, suiting the high-born ladies who lived here as nuns.

All this work was done on a very small scale, however, and casually found jet was probably sufficient for the purposes. It was around 1800 that a Captain Tremlett, a naval pensioner, saw the opportunities of turning jet items commercially, rather than carving everything. With two experienced jet workers, Robert Jefferson and John Carter, and a turner called Matthew Hill, he slowly managed to develop the business. By about 1850 it was firmly established and the Great Exhibition of 1851 helped to publicise the products.

The next thirty or forty years were the heyday of the jet industry, coinciding so exactly with the Victorian taste for mourning and for sombre jewellery and accessories. As well as the turners of jet there were carvers, polishers, rough jet merchants and jet miners. Workshops were established, particularly in the yards of upper Church Street, Baxtergate and Flowergate, and conditions in them must have been bad even by the standards of Victorian sweated labour. Hundreds of men and boys were employed for long days in cramped conditions among the dust and dirt of the workshop. Apart from the photographs which show some of the workshops, and of course the jet objects themselves, little survives, but a recently located workshop complete with all the grinding and polishing wheels is currently on show in Church Street near the top of Tate Hill Pier.

The products which were turned out were often of astonishing quality, even if the florid artistry does not accord with modern taste. Skilled carvers and turners had the pick of the best pieces of jet; beads were made from the offcuts and smaller pieces. Demand for rough jet exceeded capacity and miners went in search of the elusive material, following the geology to find the top Jet Dogger, a thin limestone which overlay the best deposits. Adits were cut into cliffs and hillsides below this level and the Dogger formed a fairly secure roof to the tunnels. No explosives could be used, for fear of damaging the fragile substance. Large pieces were sometimes found, but all too often there were impurities in them, such as iron pyrites.

Sir George Head describes the work of the jet miners in 1835:

> A man very often not only works alone all day in such a gloomy state of confinement, but reaches his solitary dungeon without assistance, merely by the perilous expedient of a rope rove round a stake fixed on the summit of the cliff: by the rope he lets himself down, and at the end of his day's work pulls himself up again.

The industry collapsed as quickly as it had risen. Changing taste and supplies of cheaper substitutes such as vulcanite or glass attacked the economic base and by the early 20th century the industry was a shadow of its former self. It is as a small craft industry, capable of meeting demand from the available supply of rough jet, that it survives today. Antique jet commands high prices.

ALUM

Alum was once one of the principal products of the North Yorkshire coast. Charlton declared in 1779: 'Our staple commodity is allum, an article wherewith we furnish the greatest part of Europe ...'.

It is a double sulphate of aluminium and potash or aluminium and ammonia. Originally produced in the East and then near Rome, it was highly prized as a mordant for cloth, giving the dye a better colour and greater fastness, and in the tanning industry for rendering leather more supple and waterproof. It was also used in paper-making, and was at one time believed to have numerous medical properties. Its origins in this country are confused. Several attempts were made to produce it in England in the 16th century but it was first successfully made at Slapewath near Guisborough, under the control of the Chaloner family, in 1604.

It was soon recognised that the shales of Cleveland, and particularly the coastal exposures, provided the best source of raw materials. By the 17th century production was in progress at a number of points along the coast, on both sides of Whitby, as well as inland. Coastal sites benefited from the ease of transporting the finished product outward and the huge quantity of coal that was essential for its production inward.

The process was both lengthy and complex. It was not aided by the absence of scientific and chemical knowledge at the time – the chemical explanations for the process were not fully understood until the mid-19th century – but a body of empirical knowledge was established by close observation and by trial and error. The main constituents were derived from the alum shale of the Lias. Aluminium silicates and iron pyrites were both present in the alum shale and it was the job of the alum makers to combine the sulphur from the iron pyrites with the alumina, separating the required chemicals from the impurities and other by-products. To do this alum shale was dug, stacked on brushwood and burnt. The breakdown of the shale and iron pyrites was partially exothermic, giving off its own heat, so more shale could be piled on top until the mound was huge and burnt for months. Brushwood was used in this part of the process but coal was needed for later stages.

When the burning was complete, the calcined shale was steeped in pits of water to extract the required constituents. After steeping the liquor was run off into a series of settling tanks while the used shale or 'mine' was dumped, often over the cliff. A good illustration of this stage of the work can be seen in *The Costumes of Yorkshire,* published in 1814. The liquor gained strength at each stage, and progress was measured by checking its specific gravity.

Next the liquor was run off via troughs or pipes to the Boiling House, often some distance away, where it was boiled in large lead pans, set over iron plates. Boiling was carried out using small coal which produced a vigorous heat. This stage consumed large quantities of coal which was usually brought to the works by sea. The liquor still needed the addition of potash or ammonia. This was done by the separate process of collecting and burning seaweed or by collecting stale human urine, which contained about two per cent ammonia. Such were the demands for kelp that seashores around the country were leased and gathering was on a commercial scale. When the kelp lees or urine were added there was a slight effervescence, because carbon dioxide was a by-product of the mixture.

90 *Mulgrave Castle, set in a high wooded position beyond Lythe village. It was and is the seat of successive Lords Mulgrave who, like the Cholmleys on the other side of Whitby, exercised patronage and control over the town for many centuries. The house, seen here in an engraving of 1829, was built in the Georgian style but romanticised in c.1790. The original Mulgrave castles, a motte and a ruined stone keep, still survive in the grounds.*

The final stages involved letting the liquor settle and cool, during which crystals of alum began to form. The 'mother liquor' was put through the boiling process again and again, producing alum and 'slam' (iron, silicates, etc. which were unwanted), while the water evaporated. By-products of the alum, such as the 'slam', used in the manufacture of bottle glass, and Epsom Salts were also sold. The end product was put into barrels, though there is some evidence that barrels were opened up after settling had taken place and the crystals were ground to powder (known as 'alum flour') with edge-runners first, and taken off by sea.

By the late 18th century alum makers were experimenting with soapers' ashes as a source of soda or potash instead of kelp lees. It seemed to be effective and also cheaper, since the waste from one process was being used in another. The alum works at Sandsend also experimented for a time with sending barreled liquor off to Shields for boiling and the addition of ammonia. It probably saved on the transport of coal but did not answer because the carriage of so much water in the liquor could never be cost-effective.

Walter White describes a visit to Sandsend alum works in 1858, and

> a low, darksome shed, where from one end to the other you see nothing but leaden evaporating pans and cisterns, some steaming, and all containing liquor in different states of preparation … In going about the works it was impossible not to be struck by the contrast between the sooty aspect of the roofs, beams and gangways, and the whiteness of the crystal fringes in the pans and the snowy patches here and there where the vapour had condensed.

During the 19th century other methods of producing alum became available, while the invention of aniline dyes rendered it less useful. The last of the alum works to close were those at Kettleness and Boulby, in 1871.

At the peak of production many alum works had been functioning under a variety of ownership. Most were run by skilled agents for local landowners such as Sir George Cooke, Hugh Cholmley and Lord Mulgrave. A cartel worked for many years to tie production to demand and pay owners for setting aside their works at lean times, in order to keep the price up. It was said to be difficult to maintain because at times when the price of alum was high outsiders were encouraged to cash in quickly, without any thought for the longer term.

Carriage was almost exclusively in Whitby vessels, usually sloops of 50 tons or so, capable of carrying about the same burden and able to lie safely on the rocky shore. They brought coal, kelp and urine to the works and took off the refined alum. *Violet*, *Fox* and *Active* are mentioned in documents of 1784-85 and we have already seen how *Little Henry* took off the frightened inhabitants of Kettleness during a landslip there in 1829.

Port Books also record the incoming raw materials and outgoing alum. In 1690-91 Berwick shipped in some 60 tons of kelp to Whitby while in 1731 coal was brought in from Sunderland and Newcastle and firkin staves from Hull, for barreling the alum. In 1682 alum was sent out to Exeter and in 1731 to London, Newcastle and Alloa. These are merely sample years in the history of an important and widely connected trade.

Berthing facilities were primitive for the vessels serving the alum trade, which took great risks in coming aground on this dangerous coast. At Saltwick slight remains of a stone breakwater, perhaps that licensed in 1673, can still be seen, while at Boulby a vertical shaft gave access through the cliff to the shore. At Peak there are remains of a haven and buildings on the lower cliff, possibly even originally defended by guns. Vessels carrying valuable cargoes such as alum were always at risk from prowling privateers in the 18th century. 'Rutways' also survive in a number of places, with boulders cleared away and tracks matching the distance between cart-wheels hacked into the shale of the foreshore. This aided heavily laden carts, especially when the tide may have been lapping round the wheels.

Few traces survive on the sites of accommodation for the workers. Married men probably walked to work from nearby villages and unmarried men, on the evidence of other industries like ironstone mining, probably lived in communal hostels on the site. At Peak as well as the substantial house near the works (the agent's house?) there was in 1860 a row of cottages and a row of allotment gardens. Workers were paid either by the day or by piece-work. Skilled workers might be contracted by the year and were paid every six months, in June and December.

Those works nearest to Whitby and most important to it were Boulby (NZ 752197), Kettleness (NZ 832159), Sandsend (NZ 860130), Saltwick (NZ 916108), Stoupe Brow (NZ 960032) and Peak (NZ 973023). Remains can be seen at all of these, mainly heaps of characteristically reddened waste shale and in some cases traces of wharves or harbours. Most of the sites invoked gravity to their aid by staging the processes in a downhill sequence from the quarries to the boiling houses and from there to the shore.

Sites at Boulby and Peak have undergone long-term excavation and, in the latter case, through the ownership by the National Trust, consolidation, helping in the elucidation of this complex process which went on over two and a half centuries and laid the foundations of our chemical industry.

91   *Saltwick Bay at low tide. The shape of the cliffs has been dramatically sculpted by centuries of alum working and vast heaps of discarded shale reddened by calcining form parts of the Nab. In the foreground is part of the breakwater built to protect ships loading alum at the works. Other fragments survive below the cliff at the extreme right of the picture.*

ROMAN CEMENT

Another minor industry associated with the alum works was the manufacture of Roman cement at Sandsend. In the late 18th century one James Parker had obtained a patent for making a powerful cement by grinding stones gathered from some southern beaches. His patent ran out in 1810 but by chance an architect called William Atkinson, who was aware of this product, came on a visit to the Marquis of Normanby at Mulgrave Castle. He was actually working on designs for the castle at the time. He recognised that the stone nodules rejected by the alum workers at Sandsend would probably make a similar cement. A former corn mill at Eastrow was pressed into service for grinding the stones which were first calcined in a kiln very much like a limekiln, fired with coal.

The nodules occur naturally in the upper levels of the Alum Shales and were regarded by the alum makers as an undesirable contaminant. Today many such nodules can be seen in the Alum Shale at Saltwick Nab. As well as being put on one side by the alum workers, these stones could be found under the cliffs where they had eroded out, or on the foreshore. As the demand increased these nodules had to be sought from further afield. Fishermen and others gathered them from as far away as Staithes, Loftus and Grosmont. Sir George Head, who visited the works in 1835, wrote:

The stones, all round and smooth, taken from below the high water mark, are shot from the vessels which bring them over board into the sea at high water, as near the land as possible whence they are carted, at low water, to the kilns …

The main source of stone dried up with the closure of the alum works in the 1870s and mining into the top of the Alum Shales took place at Deepgrove near Lythe, all done by hand without the aid of explosives. As early as 1821 the Earle brothers of Hull obtained the agreement of the Marquis to their collecting cement stones from the shore in his domains, and these stones were taken on to Hull for calcining and grinding.

The cement made at Sandsend, known as 'Mulgrave Cement', was manufactured until 1933 when the mill and kiln closed down. In 1847 William Wood of Wandsworth had obtained an exclusive supply of it within London, so many London houses must be built − or rendered − with it. In that year the profit of the works came to over £1,200, not bad for such a small concern. What made the cement desirable was that it set quickly and could be used under water, most useful in harbour works and the like.

IRONSTONE

Another important extractive industry which has left huge scars on the landscape of the Whitby area is ironstone mining. It has a long history, going back into the Middle Ages. Early antiquaries misunderstood the physical traces which it left and interpreted them as evidence of prehistoric settlements. The 'Ref-holes' of Westerdale and the 'Killing-Pits' of Danby were in fact earthworks left by lines of medieval bell-pits following the seams of ore across country.

92 *Alum-making on the coast near Whitby, from the 1885 edition of Walker's 1814* Costumes of Yorkshire. *The men appear to be steeping burnt shale ('mine') in long tanks as part of an early stage in the process. The cliff behind is terraced for extracting the raw shale.*

93 & 94 *Obverse and reverse of a Director's pass in ivory for the Whitby & Pickering Railway, dated 1833.*

Bell-pits were a primitive form of mining in which a narrow vertical shaft was dug leading into a wider vertical hole. The miners were lowered in by ropes and the ore was lifted out in the same way; they extended the sides of their pit as far as they dared short of causing a collapse. This method was suitable for shallow deposits and had the advantage that the pits could be reasonably ventilated. When one bellpit was exhausted another was opened nearby, the spoil from the new one filling the old.

95 *A horse-drawn railway coach, probably* Premier, *approaches the mouth of the tunnel at Grosmont in about 1835. The building to the left is the* Tunnel Inn, *more recently known as the* Station Hotel. *The white bridge is typical of the early bridges on the line, built of Baltic fir, later replaced in steel or masonry. This oil painting is in Whitby Museum.*

96 The last remains of the Weighing Machine House of the Whitby & Pickering Railway near Boghall. It is something of a scandal that this early building of 1835 should have been allowed to decay. Indeed it is not too late to consolidate its remains and protect them from further decay. Another small stone building of similar date once stood on the opposite side of the track.

Exploitation of the ore on a larger scale did not develop much until the 19th century. In Cleveland the main seam of the Middle Lias provided the basis, and is now effectively exhausted. The seam was two to three metres thick and was mined by horizontal shafts into hillsides and by vertical shafts from the surface. Around Skinningrove the ground is honeycombed by miles of parallel shafts. A visit to the Cleveland Ironstone Mining Museum here is very instructive in understanding the details of mining methods and the hard lives of the miners.

The beck which empties into the sea at this once idyllic spot is still coloured ochre by its passage through the mines, while further up the valley a railway viaduct, undercut by these mines, was converted to an embankment by the dumping of thousands of tons of mine spoil.

At Port Mulgrave a small harbour was constructed in the early 1850s by Palmers of Jarrow, who operated a drift mine there. All harbour installations except the jetties were removed in 1934. Above, on the cliff, is a row of cottages which began life as a communal lodging house for the miners.

When the Whitby & Pickering Railway was constructed ironstone was located at various places in Eskdale, particularly at Grosmont in 1836-37. A new village for the miners grew up near the railway and brickworks and limekilns operated here too. It was not the main seam but rather the pecten and avicula seams which were exploited here, producing some 25-29 per cent metallic ore. Ore was initially sent to the Tyne Iron Company and the Wylam Iron Company, but by the 1860s it was being smelted in the village. Prosperity was short-lived, however, the ironworks being offered for sale in 1891. Attempts to revive it were equally short-lived and the village, which had a population of 1,600 at its peak, began to empty. Visitors to the North York Moors Railway there now see little obvious evidence of the former industrialisation, although the scars are all around.

As for other extracted materials, the route linking the mines to inland users was highly unsatisfactory. The Whitby & Pickering Railway brought goods down to Whitby where further carriage was by sea. Later on the coastal railway line and special mineral lines carried the ore from coastal mines to the blast furnaces of Middlesbrough.

BUILDING STONE

One of Whitby's more significant exports was stone for building. It came from the lower deltaic series and was in the form of a freely workable sandstone from the 'washout channels' in the delta of an ancient river. These channels had filled with sand which became a rock virtually devoid of bedding planes. As well as being workable this stone had the virtue of hardening as it weathered and of resisting the effects of immersion, so it was very useful in harbour works.

This stone was used almost universally in Whitby, one of the rare exceptions being the late Georgian house at Airy Hill where a carboniferous limestone was brought from West Yorkshire, no doubt at great expense. It was ashlared in several of the houses in Bagdale and St Hilda's Terrace but can also commonly be seen in walls and humbler buildings with the herringbone tooling so characteristic of the area. It weathers to a variety of colours, from buff to dark brown, and can be seen in all its shades at the abbey, though here can also be seen a grey sandstone from Sneaton, along with a dark brown ironstone probably quarried close to the site. Indeed, one wonders whether the fishpond due east of the abbey church began life as a quarry. Other possible sources are quarries on the cliff edge above the Scaur and in the Abbey House area.

The main source for this lower deltaic sandstone was Aislaby, three miles to the south-west. The quarry here no longer functions but in its day its products were sent by sea from Whitby to build Margate and Ramsgate piers, the foundations of London and Waterloo bridges, Covent Garden Market and London Docks, to quote but a few examples. Houghton Hall, too, was built of Aislaby stone in 1720, carried from Whitby to King's Lynn by sea. Whitby piers were built from the same stone, which was available in very large blocks. Some were absolutely huge. William Scoresby wrote of single stones of 100 cubic feet or six tons, but in the building of the West Pier in 1814 a stone of 12 tons was used.

These blocks, like all those which came from the quarry to the stone wharf in the upper harbour, were carried on wagons pulled by oxen. Holt, in *Whitby Past and Present*, describes the awful sensation of meeting a stone wagon in the narrow Waterstead Lane. The oxen leaned outwards as they pulled and occupied the whole road, obliging pedestrians to scramble out of the way. Atkinson describes the sight of oxen and horses yoked together, pulling a stone cart up the steep Stonegate Hill at Lealholm, where there was another quarry.

In 1834 a Whitby Stone Company was formed, with its wharf at Boghall. It was a by-product of the new railway to Pickering, the works for which had uncovered many different building stones; these were brought down by inclined plane from the quarries at Lease Rigg, above Grosmont, and thence by rail to Whitby for shipment.

Many minor quarries existed. Of these the most interesting is probably that which worked out the whinstone of the volcanic dyke known as the Cleveland Dyke which crosses the Moors. This provided an extremely hard stone useful for road making. The great linear quarry can be seen on the moor between Whitby and Goathland, but the Dyke was also crossed by the Whitby & Pickering Railway, which first rendered it accessible.

THE GREENLAND WHALE FISHERY

According to a guide book of 1787: 'Whitby affords another excursion, that persons of curiosity will think amusing; especially soon after the Greenland ships return from the Whale Fishery …'.

The Greenland whale fishery came late to Whitby, beginning only in 1753 and continuing, with several breaks, till 1837. Whitby was never the most important port to send ships to Greenland; Hull, London, and Scottish ports could outnumber the Whitby vessels. Nevertheless, Whitby won a good reputation in the field, some of the ships bringing back many whales as a result of better technique. Among the masters who made Whitby's reputation were the Scoresbys, father and son, and Captains Kearsley and Johnson, of *Henrietta* and *Aimwell*.

Whalers always referred to their prey as 'fish', though whales are not fish at all, but mammals. The Greenland Right Whale was the type they sought, but they would take others if they could. They also killed seals, for their fur and to a lesser extent for their oil, and

97 *Salt Pan Well Steps, leading up onto the lower slopes of the cliff from Church Street. At the foot of these steps once stood a pump set up by William Scoresby in 1819 (now in Whitby Museum). The name of the steps may record Sir Hugh Cholmley's attempt to establish a salt industry here.*

narwhals as well. The ships sought the edge of the ice in Greenland or the Davis Straits. Whales were harpooned from open boats, each crewed by seven or eight men, and chased through the icefields until they were exhausted or dead.

The boats towed the dead whales back to the ship where they were quickly 'flensed' – cut up with sharp long-handled knives – before they started to decompose. The fat or blubber was quickly put into barrels to keep it during the voyage, while the jaws and 'baleen' were removed for later use. There was no further use for the rest of the carcase, so the men would push it off or sink it. Whales decomposed very rapidly and the stench was frightful.

Ships left their home port in the spring, so as to reach northern waters as the ice melted. They would follow the whales through the summer months, barrelling the blubber as they went, and return in the autumn. Vessels returning after a successful voyage would carry a garland at their masthead, a hoop of ribbons and streamers. It was the custom for boys to race to be the first to climb the rigging and remove the garland when the ship docked.

If there were times when ships came home loaded with whales there were other times when the ships did not return at all. The treacherous ice could close around a vessel, crushing it or locking it in through the winter. Some owners only supplied enough provisions for eight months at sea, and if the ship took longer the crew could die of starvation, cold or scurvy. In the extreme cold men often cut themselves with the sharp flensing knives and developed gangrene; frostbite was also common and had the same effects. The ships were overcrowded and lacked light or ventilation, especially in the fo'c'sle, so conditions were never conducive to good health at the best of times.

98 *A section from Emmanuel Bowen's strip-map of 1720 showing the road up onto the Moors via 'Rushworth' (Ruswarp) and Sneaton, and thence, via Saltersgate, to Pickering. This is well to the east of the present main road via Eller Beck and Blue Bank.*

A crew of fifty or so was usual, twice or three times as many as for the equivalent collier. There would be a proportion of boys and the crew would be very young on average, since the work required stamina and fitness. The majority of the crew were from Whitby but most ships called at Orkney or Shetland on their way to Greenland to pick up provisions and a few crew members. There is a good description of the 1772 voyage of *Volunteer*, written by William Kidd, surgeon.

The greatest number of ships to go whaling from Whitby in one season was 21, in 1787-9. As time went on the catches gradually increased but could never be relied upon. In 1814 *Resolution*, Capt. Kearsley, took 28 whales yielding 230 tuns of oil, a record for the port. It has been reckoned that in a successful four-month voyage a whaler could earn as much as in two years' service as a collier. *Camden* and *Phoenix* were the last ships to go whaling from Whitby. In 1837 the latter was setting off on her voyage when she was driven behind the East Pier and went aground. Although refloated, she never went whaling again.

Esk, built in 1812 of 354 tons, was another famous ship. She had served Captain Scoresby well, and under his guidance survived a desperate battle with the ice in 1816. Under another master she was not so lucky, being lost with all hands but three in 1826 on the shore at Marske, near Redcar, not far from home.

Whaling ships were not specially built: most were just solid vessels which were suitable and these were usually strengthened by extra layers of planking and with great baulks of timber within to give them the stiffness to withstand the pressure of ice. This was referred to as 'doubling' and 'fortifying'. Some vessels acted as whalers while it was profitable and went on to act as transports if that paid better, especially in the 1750s and 1760s, so clearly there was no great degree of specialisation. They had to carry an enlarged crew for a long voyage, as well as extra stores, and had to leave room for the many barrels of whale blubber.

Once the blubber was brought back to Whitby it was rendered down into oil. This process made a fearful stench and the four oil houses were relatively well out of the town, around Boghall and Larpool. One stood at the bottom of Waterstead Lane. The oil was in considerable demand and a successful trip could make an owner's fortune. It was even used to make gas for street lighting in Whitby for a while, between 1825 and 1830, though ultimately it could not compete with coal gas for price or convenience, the smell being appalling in a confined space.

The tough whalebone also had many uses, in the days before plastics. One particular use was in providing the stiffening in ladies' stays. Sometimes the individual stay busks would be carved with designs and initials by seamen for their lovers. It was said that the advent of coal gas and soft stays was the death of the whaling industry.

Whalebone, or more properly whale jawbone, arches were once common in the district. Arches stood at Sleights and in Spring Hill; a whole shed was found to have been set on seven pairs of jawbones, used rather like crucks, when it was demolished in the 1930s. It stood next to Mortimer's Lodging on the north bank of the Esk, near the Scarborough viaduct.

An unlikely by-product of the whaling was the bringing back of polar bear cubs. Scoresby trained one such, like a dog, despite its fierce nature. Another lived in the Ropery, beside the Spital Beck, in the 1790s. Large crowds gathered to watch whenever it was allowed out for an exercising swim in the harbour!

TRANSPORT

As we have already seen, transport out of Whitby for many centuries was principally by sea. Then as now the high moors imposed a substantial barrier to the movement of goods, especially in winter. Roads over the moors are still frequently impassable after a few days of snowfall, and few years pass without a number of motorists, cut off by the snow, taking refuge at the Fylingdales defence establishment.

In the Middle Ages and as late as the 18th century the main traffic with the interior was by means of packhorse. For miles around Whitby modern footpaths follow the lines of the packhorse tracks. You will frequently see the characteristic sandstone flags, either forming the path or else tucked under the hedgerow where they have been overgrown by bushes and walkers have followed a new line. In many places the flags marked the pannierman's route, his horses following a softer path to one side.

The stones have usually worn hollow and have been turned over or replaced; the paths follow ancient lines but are often composed of replacement stones. Good examples can be seen at Featherbed Lane, between Briggswath and Aislaby, or through Arncliffe Woods, between Glaisdale and Egton Bridge. In Whitby itself there are numerous survivals, such as that crossing Ruswarp Fields from Mayfield Road, or the one through Meadowfields to Spring Hill, or even one followed by the modern road in Downdinner Hill and the north side of Bagdale.

Goods were carried inland on a string of pack-ponies each with a pair of panniers, led by the pannierman. The lead horse, the 'bell horse', carried on a bracket over its head a set of bells to give warning to other users of the track to move clear. No eyewitness accounts survive but we know of similar operations in the West Country where strings of ponies could only pass with extreme difficulty on the narrow tracks. The range and quantity of goods which could be carried by this method was obviously limited. We have seen how oxen were often employed in hauling heavy items like stone, and seaborne routes were preferable for valuable, fragile or bulky goods.

In the 18th century inland routes began to improve. As early as 1720 Emmanuel Bowen's *Britannia Depicta* shows a route over the moors via Ruswarp, Sneaton and Saltersgate to York. A new turnpike was built as far as Saltersgate in 1759, on a route further to the west than the older one. The new roads allowed more sophisticated vehicles to travel on them. A diligence commenced running to York from 1788 and was soon followed by coaches to Scarborough and Sunderland, and a mail coach to York began in 1795. All the Whitby coaches ran from the *Angel Inn* in Baxtergate. Cary's *New Itinerary* of 1798 details the three main routes leading out of Whitby at that date.

99 *Part of a shed carried on cruck trusses made of whale jaws! This was photographed in 1930, during demolition. Two pairs of jaws have already been removed (one can be seen lying on the ground to the left of the picture). The shed stood near the gasworks and the Scarborough railway viaduct, which can be seen in the background. The shed must be earlier than 1837 and probably dates from the great age of Whitby whaling in the early 19th century.*

It is said that a fine house in Spring Hill, now demolished, was built by the guard of the York mail coach out of his profits from carrying lobsters! It was known, appropriately enough, as Lobster Hall. The Royal Mail officially discouraged carriage of such goods, but the drivers and guards were under great temptation to make money on the side from the transport of high-value perishable foodstuffs such as this. Road coaches were relatively expensive and could carry few passengers, especially with the gradients to be expected on the moorland roads.

For goods and passengers from nearer Whitby there was a network of carriers' carts which developed during the early 19th century. These travelled a regular

100 *Whitby Railway Station, built in 1847 to the design of George Andrews. Following the changeover to steam haulage the decision was taken to bring the railway station closer into the town. Its predecessor had lain further back down the track, near the engine shed, and was an altogether more modest affair. Recent alterations have restored access to the northern end of the station, for many years obscured by shops.*

route from the same Whitby inn on fixed days to certain villages, carrying goods and small parcels, and from time to time a few passengers as well, usually returning the same day. In 1823, for instance, there was a choice of three carriers to Guisborough and all points on the way. You could send your goods by Thomas Johnson at the *King's Head*, John Johnson at the *White Horse*, or Robert Knaggs at the *Jolly Butcher*. Eleven other carriers departed from other inns to places such as Pickering, Staithes and York. A carrier's cart can be seen crossing Whitby bridge in a lithograph of 1835. It was almost certainly that of Thomas Hopper, based at the Old White Horse in Church Street, who set out four days a week to Staithes.

The slow pace of these carriers presented no problems to villagers or towns-people; they preferred cheapness and reliability to speed. Many country people came into Whitby on market days in any case, and someone could usually be found to carry parcels or messages, or do some small commission. Well into the 20th century farmers' wives would hawk baskets of produce around among a circle of regular urban customers; eggs, butter and cheese frequently found a private buyer without ever going to market.

For some, however, the pace of transport was too slow. The most direct inland route was via Pickering. As well as turnpiking the road some entrepreneurs attempted to build a canal to Pickering in 1793. A survey was made and the route planned, but it never reached the building stage. Instead, some forty years later almost exactly the same route was chosen for the remarkable horse-drawn Whitby & Pickering Railway.

Begun in 1833 and completed in 1836 the railway was in advance of its time in some respects – it was very early in the railway age – but in others it was outdated before it was finished. The pioneering Stockton & Darlington Railway used horse traction for some of its traffic, but none of the plans for railways under consideration by the 1830s thought of haulage other than by steam. It is true that in the early days of railways there was much more manhandling of trucks and carriages than we tend to realise, but the Whitby & Pickering Railway was something of an oddity from the beginning.

It had, on opening, no links with the rest of the embryonic railway network – connections through to York came later. The overriding problem was that caused by the stiff gradients imposed on the line. George Stephenson, the engineer, approached this by dividing the line into two levels; a lower one from Whitby to Beckhole, and a higher one from Goathland. The two were linked by a self-acting inclined plane, achieving the differences in level in a short distance. Coaches were horse-drawn to the foot of the incline and then hitched to a rope which went round a horizontal drum at the top and was fastened to trucks carrying water tanks as a counterweight. The downhill run was effected by doing the same in reverse, only the guard of the coach had some control of the speed by means of a brake.

Coaches were very similar to road coaches, only larger and heavier. Weighing some two/four tons they ran on flanged wheels on fish-bellied rails, carried on stone block sleepers. First-class coaches had names like *Premier*, *Transit* and *Lady Hilda*. In most respects they operated like road coaches, being run as individual units. Where the gradient was downhill horses were detached and the coaches ran under gravity. They carried six inside, four in front and four behind, with further passengers on top. Most had both a driver and a guard. Charles Dickens travelled by one of these in the early days of the railway. In a letter to Wilkie Collins much later he recalls the experience: 'In my time that curious railroad by the Whitby moor was so much the more curious, that you were balanced against a counter-weight of water, and that you did it like Blondin ...'.

There were also second-class or market coaches, and many goods waggons, as well as those used by the Whitby Stone Company, which ran over the same rails and paid a toll to the railway company.

An accident on the incline in December 1836 led to the change to steam haulage there via a stationary steam-engine. The railway was very useful in opening up Whitby's hinterland but as a carrier or as a company it was a failure and its passenger traffic was negligible because of its small carrying capacity. After an initial effort, running one of the very first rail excursions in the country to Ruswarp Fair in 1835, the company seems to have lost its entrepreneurial zeal. Two first-class coaches were run each day each way between Whitby and Pickering for most of the life of the horse-drawn railway. There is no surviving timetable for the second-class or market coaches. By 1845 the growing might of the larger companies was being felt. George Hudson's York & North Midland Railway acquired the line, relaid the track and introduced steam working on both sides of the incline, the first steam train coming into Whitby in 1847.

The original carriage shed had been further back along the present line but it appears that passengers in horse-drawn days had embarked in the open air. A new station, designed by G.T. Andrews, was opened in 1847 on the site of former shipyards, more accessible from the town. Suddenly the line was part of a larger network, with access to York and beyond, and passengers began to come in numbers to Whitby. Hudson busied himself with schemes to buy up the West Cliff estate and to build accommodation for the new visitors.

In 1864 another accident at the incline led to the building of a deviation line between Grosmont and Goathland via Darnholm, a little to the east, which despite having a severe gradient allowed steam working throughout. The older line and the Beckhole Incline can still be followed on foot.

Three further railway lines were to join the Whitby & Pickering in due course. These were the Esk Valley line to Middlesbrough, linking in to the old line at Grosmont (1865), a coastal line to Scarborough (1885) and a coastal line to Middlesbrough (1883). Both the latter lines had extremely steep gradients and unstable cliffs to contend with and were short-lived in consequence, though they offered wonderful views. The Scarborough and Middlesbrough lines were served by the West Cliff Station, which was linked to the Pickering and Esk Valley lines by a steep cutting running behind Prospect Hill. At the time of writing the Esk Valley line is still surviving, although much of Whitby Station is now used by the North Yorkshire Moors Railway, which runs the former Whitby & Pickering line, closed by British Rail in 1965, and run by this successful preservation society since 1973.

Eight

SPA AND SEASIDE

Until the 19th century Whitby's charms as a seaside resort were almost unknown to the outside world. Whitby was, as we have already seen, cut off and remote, access being difficult by all means but by sea, which did not encourage many visitors.

Travel was expensive and not without its hazards until well into the 18th century. Most travellers, therefore, were from among the gentry and usually had some purpose in their travels. Typical among these aims were health, the seeking out of new spas and resorts to mend real or imaginary ills, and an interest in the growing industrialisation of the country. Added to this was a taste for ruins, a fashionable interest developed by young gentlemen and their tutors among the wreckage of imperial Rome but denied to many in the 18th century because of the state of war which enveloped Europe at intervals, making travel dangerous.

The few travellers who took the trouble to seek Whitby out were those same few who have given us our early glimpses of many English towns: Leland, Camden and Speed. The last-named gives us a description of two legends which we meet again and again and which we shall look at more fully in chapter 10. These legends were that St Hilda had turned all the serpents into stone (thus accounting for ammonites) and had caused all geese flying over to fall suddenly to the ground.

Others, such as Michael Drayton and Ralph Thoresby, also commented on these phenomena; the latter, writing in his diary in 1682, was not much impressed by ammonites:

> ... these stones, several of which, and one especially of an extraordinary bigness, I brought along with me. I gathered some out of the hard black rock, cutting them out with a knife, but look upon them merely as the sport of nature ...

This description, 'sport of nature', was indicative of the total incomprehension of geology and geological time which gave rise to the legends of St Hilda. An even more unlikely explanation, however, appeared in 1798, quoting Charlton:

> This place is noted for spiral stones that have been found here, in the shape of serpents, which, by naturalists, are called cornua ammonis. They are supposed to be petrifactions formed in the earth by a sort of fermentation peculiar to the alum mines, of which there are several in the neighbourhood.

Whitby's origin as a health resort is chronicled by the very odd poem by Samuel Jones, Gent, 'in honour of Mr Andrew Long's Recovery from the Jaundice, by drinking of Whitby Spaw Waters'. Entitled 'Whitby, A Poem', it was published in 1718. Jones was a Customs Officer who died in 1732. His poem is a eulogy to Whitby, in which he could find no fault. A few lines must suffice:

> ... The Air salubrious, and the sea just by
> Shews various Objects to the Drinker's Eye;
> There Ships of sundry sorts do sweep the Main,
> And the surpriz'd Spectator entertain:
> While Whitby Abbey on the Land no less,
> With lofty Head in Prospect strives to bless;
> Pleasures so great, suppose the Waters miss,
> Who could be angry at a Joy like this?

In his poem Jones encapsulates the attractions of Whitby which in most cases still survive as attractions – sea, air, shipping, abbey, piers and fossils. Only the 'Spaw' has gone. In fact there were three: one on the shore below the West Cliff, later destroyed by the sea, another at the root of the East Pier, remembered in the Spa Ladder, and a further one, this time still surviving in its own little pavilion at the rear of Broomfield Terrace in Bagdale. People came to drink the waters for a variety of ailments and wherever there was a spa a small resort would tend to spring up, providing accommodation and medical advice. Sea-bathing became fashionable among the gentry in the later 18th and early 19th centuries, but was very limited in its influence until the railways arrived with another breed of holiday-makers.

THE SPA,

SEASON 1921,

COMMENCES MONDAY, MAY 16th.

THE ORCHESTRA

(Conductor—Mr. WALTER ALMGILL, L.R.A.M.
Double Diploma).

PLAYS TWICE DAILY

IN FLORAL PAVILION.

Vocalists Engaged for Special Gala Nights.

No. 1 THEATRE ENGAGEMENTS.

HIGH-CLASS BUFFET.

READING and LADIES' ROOM.
CAFÉ OPEN DAILY.

For Season and Period Tickets, apply Main Entrance.

Resident Manager—THOS. FALKINGBRIDGE,
Telephone 124.   The Spa, Whitby.

101   *Advertisement of 1921 for the Spa and its orchestra.*

NINETEENTH-CENTURY GROWTH

Although the new horse-powered railway to Pickering was not a financial success it did for the first time make travel to and from the interior easier and cheaper. It has already been established that it was not the 'Railway King' George Hudson himself who initiated the West Cliff development, although he was quick to see its potential and to take credit for it. A local movement

102 *The early years of the 20th century. A paddle-steamer passes Tate Hill Pier carrying passengers for a trip round the bay or perhaps to Scarborough. On the East Cliff stand the Abbey, parish church and Coastguard Cottages. Below is Henrietta Street, with its last buildings perched at crazy angles due to slippage of the cliff, ending in the Haggerlythe, on which stands a mysterious large building, of which no trace remains today. At the extreme left of the picture is the so-called Spa Ladder, giving access to the East Pier.*

had already begun, albeit on a modest scale, to build on the cliff as early as 1843, and the idea had been around since at least 1827. We must draw the conclusion that the Whitby & Pickering Railway had had some effect on this decision.

The new development, fostered by the railway, consisted of hotels and large houses. Inns and hotels had previously sufficed to accommodate the few visitors to Whitby but the large houses were intended as guest houses or to be let by the season to families, much as had been the tradition at Bath a few generations earlier.

The most marked change in the visiting population by the mid–19th century, other than its greater numbers, was its social make-up. It had become almost entirely middle-class; the appeal was moreover to the literary, artistic and professional divisions of that great class, the backbone of Victorian society. It was no accident that Tennyson, Dickens, George Eliot, Edward Burne-Jones, George du Maurier and Bram Stoker all spent holidays here. Not all visitors, of course, were of the stature of these men and women.

The *Whitby Gazette*, which commenced in 1854, was initially a mere handlist of visitors, pleasing to their vanity and helpful to them in meeting, or avoiding, persons of their acquaintance whilst on promenades down the pier.

The publisher, Ralph Horne, respectfully announces it thus, with typically Victorian effusiveness:

> … to the Inhabitants of the town, and especially those who are interested in any effort to make Whitby a place of resort for the summer season, and whose benefit will be promoted by the influx of visitors, and the number of its lodgers, that the object sought to be accomplished is one which cannot but be considered of some importance to the fashionable, and even to the ordinary visitor; from many of whom have been called forth remarks of surprise, that a town of such size and standing, possessing capabilities for a first-class watering-place, should not provide them with a local organ of the Press, by which to announce to their friends their place of location …

The very first issue, dated 6 July 1854, publishes a list of names and addresses of visitors, including a satisfactory clutch of Reverends, a doctor or two, a military title and a number of addresses containing the magical word 'Hall' or 'Park'. There is no-one famous, but all are clearly 'respectable'. It was in the interest of lodging-house keepers to circulate a list of their guests, since the respectability of one set would encourage another such set to stay.

Another feature of this paper is the railway timetable, prominent on the centre page. It was expected that most guests would arrive by train, although other conveyances, including the paddle-steamers *Hilda* and *Goliah*, also appear. It is of some interest in this connection to quote an early poem of Lewis Carroll printed in the *Whitby Gazette* supplement:

> She is gone by the Hilda,   Tho' I take the Goliah,
> She is lost unto Whitby,   I learn to my sorrow
> And her name is Matilda,   That 'It won't', says the crier,
> Which my heart it was smit by;   'Be off till to-morrow'.

The newspaper's message is quite clear; Whitby has not yet arrived as a fashionable resort, but it is setting itself out to gain the patronage of solid and respectable visitors.

Most of Whitby's new accommodation was on the West Cliff. The scale of the buildings was much greater than anything which had been built in Whitby before, consisting of terraces of four- and five-storey houses. Soon the Royal Crescent began to be developed, but remained unfinished, as we have seen. These houses were designed for letting, but many family houses were also built on no less a scale.

Esk Terrace, another row of boarding houses, overlooking the upper harbour, was a product of the 1850s. It is a long way from sea views but perhaps its proximity to the railway station was its main attraction. By the 1880s Chubb Hill was under construction, followed by Broomfield Terrace in Bagdale. Victorian buildings were rarely shy, and at the seaside the Victorians lost all restraint. Broomfield Terrace is built of white lavatorial bricks of a type much favoured at the seaside, bricks which never mellow or tone to suit their surroundings. Chubb Hill and the western end of Bagdale contain a number of ugly yet nevertheless comfortable houses occupying awkward sites on rising ground.

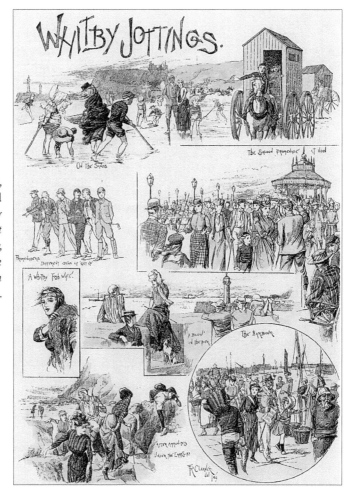

103 *'Whitby Jottings',* *from the* Illustrated London News, *October 1889. This shows what the visitors did on holiday, and contrasts with Frank Sutcliffe's photographs, which almost totally exclude them.*

Bram Stoker came to stay on the West Cliff, perhaps in Royal Crescent. His visit provided the inspiration for the beginning of *Dracula*, including the setting of the graveyard of the parish church and the shipwreck. In 1885 a Russian schooner, *Dmitry*, had come ashore in the outer harbour in a storm. Renamed *Demeter* this ship was turned into the vessel which brought Dracula to England, in the form of a large dog. In recent years Whitby has capitalised on its Dracula connection.

Stoker was not the only writer to find inspiration on holiday here. Mrs Gaskell stayed at 1 Abbey Terrace, in 1859 with her two daughters. Here she gained background information for *Sylvia's Lovers*, a tale involving the press gang and bringing in a number of recognisable portraits of Whitby people.

George du Maurier also regularly spent the summer in Whitby during the 1880s and 1890s. He and his large family, together with a succession of dogs, stayed initially at St Hilda's Terrace, outside the new zone of lodging houses. Later the family rented a house in Broomfield Terrace, but they frequently visited friends such as James Russell Lowell, the American ambassador, on the West Cliff. Whitby forms a clearly

104 *At the rear of Broomfield Terrace in Bagdale is this small circular building which antedates the houses in front of it. This is the former Victoria Spa, which was run in 1860 by John Stevenson, a druggist. Its water was compared with that of Tunbridge Wells, and season tickets could be obtained for half-a-crown.*

recognisable backdrop to a great many of du Maurier's cartoons in *Punch*.

Whitby was by no means a large resort and the area most used by visitors consisted of a mere handful of streets, so there were ample opportunities to meet old friends. Meanwhile workaday Whitby busied itself with shipbuilding, fishing and trade. The two worlds only impinged when amateur artists and photographers put local people into their pictures for the effect of their picturesque costumes and characterful faces.

For their part most of these local people were too hard at work to take much notice of the visitors. Of course they could provide some useful income when times were hard or when business was slack. It was not really until the 20th century that Whitby people, other than a few lodging-house keepers, began to take tourism seriously. Decline of other industries made them diversify their interests, and the process continues today.

ENTERTAINMENT

For entertainment in the evening there was the West Cliff Saloon, now the Spa Theatre and Pavilion, built in 1880 by Sir George Elliot. 'In the season', we are told, 'the enterprising manager engages the best musical and dramatic entertainment procurable, whilst on the promenade a selected band of professional and other musicians gives performances daily.' Not everyone was happy with the railing off of the Spa grounds and there were robust objections including direct action by local people.

In 1889 James Russell Lowell, author, poet and American Ambassador, wrote:

> ... One other amusement is the Spa, where there is a band of music bad enough to please the Shah. It is brilliantly lighted, and at night it is entertaining to sit above and watch the fashionable world laboriously diverting themselves by promenading to and fro in groups, like a village festival at the opera. The sea, of course, is as fine and irreconcilable as ever. Thank God, they can't landscape garden him.

In 1915 the Spa was bought by the Urban District Council, which built the Floral Pavilion alongside. In the 1920s there was a Municipal Orchestra under Frank

Gomez which performed at the Spa. Later, under the direction of Michael Collins, it played twice daily in the Floral Pavilion. Gomez was apparently something of a heart-throb among the young ladies.

As well as the Spa with its formal setting there was the Coliseum. Around 1919-21 Leslie Fuller's Concert Party, the Ped'lers, was in residence, offering 'a vaudeville musical melange' including Leslie Fuller himself and 'other well-known London Artists'. Another concert party which performed in Whitby, around 1913, was 'Ted Allnutts Gay Cadets'. They gave morning performances on the beach and evening shows on the Battery Parade, dressed as Pierrots.

From about the 1920s cinemas became serious contenders with live entertainment. Whitby had three: the Coliseum, which started as a theatre and music hall, the Waterloo, up a yard off Flowergate, and the Empire in Station Square, which in 1921 described itself as an 'electric theatre' and which had been purpose-built in 1914.

During the 1920s and 1930s and again after the Second World War repertory companies produced a summer season of drama at the Spa Theatre, including in the 1960s a succession of seasons with Charles Vance's company. Most of the productions were lightweight comedies and murder mysteries. The tradition continues today. In order to accommodate visitors staying for the traditional week the programme would change every Thursday, thus allowing people to see two different plays during their stay.

The Spa Pavilion provided roller-skating but most people think of it as a location for ballroom dancing. Music was by a panotrope. People danced there when the orchestra programme finished. I remember looking in through the glass roof sometime in the middle 1950s and seeing a scene of dancing in progress which looked impossibly romantic and grown-up to my childish eyes, like a Ball in Ruritania! It was probably much more tawdry in reality. In recent years the Spa, and Whitby in general, have become the playground of Goths, a broad church of interests, with black clothing as the main identifier. The Dracula connection is probably the reason for their attachment to Whitby.

What is easy to forget today is that holidays were so much more uncommon and therefore all the more exciting. Most people were saving all year for their holiday, which until 1938 might well be taken without pay, so when they reached the seaside they were determined to have a good time. Until perhaps thirty or forty years ago facilities at the seaside were far better than anything which could be had at home. One of the factors in the decline of the traditional seaside holiday has been the provision in inland towns and cities of better cinemas, theatres,

105 *The place for quiet evenings; advertisement for the Empire Electric Theatre in 1921.*

swimming pools and leisure centres. The resorts simply cannot compete, so they have in many ways returned to the simpler factors in their favour: sea air and a good location.

BOARDING HOUSES

Holiday accommodation was graded in type and price to suit the needs of the visitors. At the top end of the market were the hotels, offering all the comforts and facilities that could be desired. Some families took a whole house for the summer, or at least for an extended holiday. Then came private hotels, guesthouses, boarding houses and 'apartments', where visitors bought their own food and it was cooked for them.

The humblest of these categories included many houses which had been private, but some need had driven the occupants to make a living in one of the few ways that was permitted to respectable ladies, for it was overwhelmingly a female occupation to let rooms. In some cases it was widowhood which provided the spur; in others unmarried daughters looking after elderly parents needed to find a modest living without leaving the house. The First World War left many widows without means of support and drove them to enter the market for lodgings. Here are two examples from 1895:

West Cliff Boarding house and Private Hotel, Royal Crescent,
Unrivalled situation; uninterrupted Sea View;
near the Golf Links, and close to the Saloon, Tennis
Courts, Sands, and Bathing, and within five minutes walk of West Cliff Station.
Smoking Room; Private Sitting Rooms; Hot and Cold Baths; Excellent Cuisine ...

Mrs Storm,
4, Crescent Terrace, West Cliff.
Furnished Apartments
Uninterrupted Sea Views, close to the Saloon,
Tennis Courts, Golf Links, and the Beach.
The House is certified as possessing perfect
Sanitary Arrangements ...

By 1921 advertisements were simpler or perhaps some amenities were now taken for granted:

Esplanade Boarding House, West Cliff.
Near Beach, Spa, Piers, Tennis, Bowls, Cricket etc.
Fishing, Boating & Golf within easy walking distance of the house.
Separate Tables. Sea View ...

The Clarence Boarding House
4, Langdale Terrace
Misses Jobling, Proprietresses
Visitors will find Home Comforts combined with moderate charges.

The boarding houses and private hotels which could afford to advertise were, however, the upper end of a larger market. Many smaller establishments had only a few rooms and, if they advertised at all, took most of their business from return visits. In the official *Whitby Guide* for 1938 we find larger and medium-sized establishments taking small box adverts, mainly proclaiming electric lighting, separate tables, bath, sea view, and proximity to sporting attractions, which became important features for accommodation between the wars.

At the back of this guide-book a large number of modest boarding houses list sitting-rooms, bedrooms and whether they offer board or not. Sitting-rooms were important, since bad weather could leave visitors marooned in the house, possibly sharing public rooms with uncomfortable partners in misery.

Among those listed appears my grandmother at 2 Ocean Road, with two sitting-rooms and four bedrooms. Left a widow by the sinking of my grandfather's ship by a mine in January 1919, she made her living and paid for one daughter's education by letting rooms each summer. The house was not large but tall and narrow and food had to be carried up to rooms. A kitchen with a range and a tiny scullery had to deal with the visitors' cooking and washing up. Visitors generally arrived at the nearby West Cliff Station and had to carry bags and suitcases from there.

The war years saw a cessation in the holiday trade and afterwards things were very different. By the 1960s and 1970s there had been a profound change in the pattern of holidays. People no longer took a week in August but often took several holidays in a year, some of them out of season, and even abroad.

Caravans had long ago made their appearance, and so had holiday flats. Partly it was for cheapness, and partly it was a desire to have privacy, rather than the awkward chumminess of the boarding house lounge.

Accommodation polarised between those houses which offered bed and breakfast, and possibly an evening meal, and those which were turned over to flats or even let as whole houses. Many cottages in the town were bought up at prices out of reach of local people by people living at a distance, typically in the Leeds area, to let as a business. This situation is by no means peculiar to Whitby.

The *Whitby Official Guide*, for 1966 and 1971, shows the process well-developed. Along with accommodation for visitors, parking for cars had become important. As rail services decreased and as car ownership increased the pattern of visitors changed; the speed of change is increasing, and nowhere more so than in the problem of parking cars at the peak of the season.

TRAINS AND PADDLE-STEAMERS

Much of Whitby's new-found prosperity as a seaside resort in the 1840s was due to the railway, as we have seen. From its very earliest days the line was seen not just as a means of access, but as a scenic route in its own right. Henry Belcher produced a book in 1836 entitled *The Scenery of the Whitby and Pickering Railway* in which the visitor was shown what to look for on this journey through what had previously been a wilderness.

The new railway also opened up areas like Goathland, with its wild moorland scenery and many waterfalls, to visitors from the outside world for the first time.

In later years three more railway lines were opened through to Whitby; the Esk Valley line in 1865, the Middlesbrough line in 1883 and the Scarborough line in 1885. These last two involved massive engineering works, including cuttings and tunnels in the unstable alum shale, and steep gradients. Both were also extremely scenic, with views out over the cliffs and from high viaducts such as those at Sandsend and Staithes. A ride on these railways was very exciting as the train dived in and out of tunnels and hung far above the sea.

There was now access to intermediate points such as Sandsend and Hayburn Wyke as well as to Scarborough itself. A short-lived scheme existed in the 1890s, soon after the opening of the railway, to lay out the high exposed cliff at Peak, henceforth known as Ravenscar, as a resort. The railway was the only practicable access and that too was often impassable in winter, while the sea lay some 600 ft. below down a difficult path. Nonetheless, over 1,500 plots were laid out and some sold before the scheme finally foundered with the First World War. A visitor today among the overgrown roads and scattered houses has little inkling of what might have been.

One of the by-products of the railway was the introduction of camping coaches at various scenic positions. The first time that these were offered was in 1933. Those early camping coaches were fairly spartan in what they had to offer, but most people were happy to put up with that in return for the novelty of the experience and the beauty of their surroundings. In the 1950s there were five camping coaches at Sandsend, two near the station and three near the sea at Eastrow. Closure of the lines brought this service to an end, in 1958 on the Middlesbrough line and by 1964 elsewhere. The North Yorkshire Moors Railway now has camping coaches at Goathland.

Steamboats, and paddle-steamers in particular, are rightly associated with seaside holidays. Paddlesteamers could operate in shallow waters and many of them acted as pleasure craft in summer, while out of season reverting to another use as harbour tugs.

Tourist, an Edinburgh-London packet boat, began calling at St Ann's Staith in 1823 and by 1836 Whitby had its own paddle-steamer *Streonshalh*. By 1852 the *Scarborough* steamer was running a regular daily service to Whitby or Bridlington, at a fare of 3s. for the trip. This was the first of many such services. In 1865 the *Superb* met with an accident when she collided with the pier to avoid running down a fishing vessel that was coming in at the same time. Some of the masters of these vessels were of a rough and ready character, as were the owners. They made a profit by overloading their craft and on several occasions running them when unsafe. There were few regulations and passengers did not usually complain at gross overloading, especially when there was a holiday atmosphere.

In 1853 the Whitby and Robin Hood's Bay Steam Packet Company was formed. It owned two paddlesteamers called *Hilda* and *Esk* of 30 h.p. and 20 tons and 45 h.p. and 20 tons respectively, and ran a service to Middlesbrough, Hartlepool and Scarborough, its schedule dependent upon the weather. These vessels also acted as harbour tugs.

One vessel which seems to have been popular in Whitby was *Emu*. Built on the Tyne in 1871 of 73 tons and 30 h.p. she was bought by the Whitby Steam Tug Association in 1873. One of her first trips was to take 100 passengers to the Hartlepool Regatta in August of that year. She appears in many pictures.

When the Channel Fleet came to Scarborough in 1874 *Emu* ferried out passengers to visit the ships; her master became involved in an argument about how long he was being made to wait his turn to put passengers aboard. Consequently the Navy refused him permission to come alongside at all! In 1888 she had the indignity of becoming stranded in the most public place possible, directly in front of the Spa. *Emu* is the only vessel to be identified by name among the forty-plus ships carved into pews in the parish church, which is perhaps an indication of how she had entered local consciousness.

Other vessels such as *Cleveland* and *Cambria* followed, and the tradition came to an end with *Bilsdale,* built at Preston in 1900 of 199 tons, and capable of carrying 386 passengers. She operated from Scarborough between 1924 and 1934, when she left to be scrapped.

Looking at old photographs it seems that the essence of a Victorian or Edwardian seaside holiday involved a trip along the coast on a paddle-steamer, the passengers packed so tightly that they could not move.

WHAT THE VISITORS DID

Most visitors to Whitby in the 19th century came by railway. This pattern continued into the middle of the 20th century but gradually road transport, first motor buses and then cars, began to replace the train. As late as the early 1960s packed trains ran into Whitby in summer but within a few years the cutting back of the network and the growing availability of other transport changed the pattern.

The effect of so many visitors coming by train was that the amount of luggage that they could carry was limited and so was their mobility once they arrived. Very few would venture more than ten miles or so from their lodgings during their stay; in any case Whitby had a great variety of attractions and could satisfy most of the demands of middle-class visitors, who tended to make their own amusements.

The seaside itself was a great attraction to visitors. It had not always been so; it was made fashionable initially as a cure. People took their sea-bathing seriously, under medical advice, in the early part of the 19th century. However, during the course of the century bathing and family activities on the sand had become not only respectable but popular. Perhaps it was the Victorian creation of the idea of the family as the basic unit of society that encouraged this. In the 1890s there were bathing tents on the beach, while bathing machines plied for hire at the water's edge, many of them provided by the picturesquely named Argument family. The 1938 *Whitby Guide* states 'within certain limits 'mackintosh bathing' is permitted'. This refers to the custom of getting changed beforehand and putting outer clothes over a swimming costume to go down to the beach. It was a long time here as in other seaside resorts before the furtiveness was taken out of bathing.

If sea-bathing palled there were other activities which could be carried out on the foreshore, such as looking for crabs and starfish in the rock pools towards Upgang, or searching for fossils at Saltwick. Longer excursions, perhaps by wagonette, could be taken to Robin Hood's Bay, Runswick Bay or Staithes, where the women still wore the distinctive 'Staithes Bonnet'.

Alternatively visitors could take one of the many footpaths inland to Ruswarp and Sleights, Falling Foss, Rigg Mill or Golden Grove via Glenesk. Goathland and its many waterfalls such as Mallyan Spout or Thomasson Foss could be reached via the railway. Egton Bridge was another favourite picnic spot for visitors from Whitby.

Much seaside activity in the 19th and early 20th centuries consisted of simply promenading up and down, seeing and being seen, or listening to the many bands.

106 *A favourite holiday activity – rowing on the Esk at Ruswarp Dam. The dam itself and the mill that it served, Ruswarp flour mill, are in the right background. This mill has only recently ceased activity and is now divided into flats. The postcard is dated 1 August 1914, only a few days before the outbreak of War, but the writer mentions nothing about the momentous events unfolding, only that he had been rowing on Thursday and was going back soon 'for another four pennorth'!*

106   PUNCH, OR THE LONDON CHARIVARI   [SEPTEMBER 10, 1864.

"LOVE'S COURSE NEVER DID," YOU KNOW.

IT WAS VERY UNPLEASANT! BUT WHAT JENKYNNES HAD TO SAY TO HIS FLORA, WAS SAID UNDER THESE CIRCUMSTANCES.

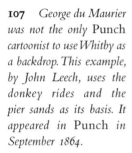

107 *George du Maurier was not the only* Punch *cartoonist to use Whitby as a backdrop. This example, by John Leech, uses the donkey rides and the pier sands as its basis. It appeared in* Punch *in September 1864.*

Those with more energetic inclinations could row on the Esk at Ruswarp Dam. At one time it was possible to bring a boat up from the harbour and pull it bodily up the mill-dam at Ruswarp, turning it into a whole day's expedition with picnic baskets. For the less adventurous the row up to Cock Mill Creek with the tide was recommended. Other sporting types could play lawn tennis, cricket or golf. The two former had courts and grounds on the West Cliff but golfing required a longer outing to Goathland. By the 1920s and '30s tennis and golf had become more popular with visitors and more facilities were provided. A new golf course had been opened at Upgang in 1895 and many tennis courts laid out, along with putting greens, in the 1920s. A trip out on a fishing boat was only recommended for the strong in 1895, 'as the experiences are decidedly novel'!

Many farms and houses still provided new milk for children and hot water for adults' tea. The Glen Esk Tea Gardens advertised 'hot water supplied to Pic-nic Parties … Swings, Tea Tables under the Apple Trees, Grass Lawn for Games, &c.' in 1895. At Saltwick there was a pleasure garden with swings etc. – the Saltwick Tea Gardens – in the same year, and for many years to come, under the Proprietress, Margaret H. Agar. It was on the undercliff and has now totally vanished.

On wet days there could be a visit to the museum in Pier Road or to the Whitby Subscription Library, which was housed on the second floor of the same building. In 1860 the subscription rate for visitors was 5s. a month for a family, or 3s. for a fortnight. Less 'worthy' books, such as novelettes, could be borrowed from one of the commercial circulating libraries. The abbey, of course, was very popular with visitors, its unconsolidated ruins dangerous but romantic.

One person who sums up the Victorian visitor to Whitby is George Eaton. A gentleman of independent means who lived in Norwich, Eaton made some 18 annual holidays in various places with his family, recording each in considerable

A GOOD-BYE TO JOLLY WHITBY.

THE BROWNS AND THEIR FAMILY DRAG THEIR LUNCHEON-BASKETS OVER THE DAM ON THE ESK FOR THE LAST TIME, ALAS!
AND FOR THE LAST TIME, BROWN SENIOR ATTEMPTS A FEEBLE FRENCH JOKE, BEGINNING "ESKER LA DAM——" AND, AS USUAL, FALLS
DOWN ON THE SLIPPERY STONES BEFORE HE CAN FINISH IT!

108 *George du Maurier and his family spent many holidays in Whitby. 'Goodbye to Jolly Whitby' records the now-impossible practice of hiring a boat in the harbour, rowing it up to Ruswarp, and hauling it bodily up the Dam in order to use the clear stretch up to Sleights for a picnic party. This appeared in September 1882.*

detail in a journal. In June and July 1883 the family came to Whitby, staying at 6 South Terrace on the West Cliff, where they rented a sitting-room and two bedrooms for the month. The holiday consisted of days on the beach or in the town, interspersed with some longer family outings to Scarborough (by paddle-steamer), to Rievaulx, and to Staithes and Runswick. Eaton also had some solo trips to Fountains Abbey, Guisborough and Roseberry Topping, and to the waterfalls at Goathland. On Sundays the family went to church, and managed to attend all the Anglican churches in the town in the course of their holiday. The length and complexity of some of the trips is remarkable, as Eaton was unusually curious and well-informed, but what is surprising is that so many places were within practical reach by public transport.

After the First World War the excursions available to visitors were lengthened by the appearance of charabancs and motor buses, run by firms such as Milburn's of Silver Street. The steep hills surrounding Whitby on all sides presented many difficulties to early motor buses, braking on the downhill run being every bit as hazardous as the uphill climb. By the 1930s another firm, Howard's Tours, was running excursions to sample the moorland and coastal scenery. The same trips, with additions, were on offer until quite recently, though to a rather different cross-section of visitors. No-one who went on one of these trips as a child can forget the excitement and sense of adventure, even if they were marred occasionally by insistent smokers or by disagreeable old ladies who disliked ventilation.

FOSSIL HUNTING

One of the obvious activities for visitors to Whitby has long been fossil hunting on the Scaur, the rocky area to the east of the East Pier, at low tide. The most productive areas are the Scaur itself, at Saltwick, and at Port Mulgrave. Here the soft shale has preserved countless ammonites, belemnites and other Jurassic fossils.

Many are pyritised and most are difficult to remove safely from the shale. However, the shale also contains many nodules of harder stone, some of which are concreted around superbly-preserved fossils. Occasionally remains of larger creatures have been found, including both plesiosaurs and ichthyosaurs, especially in the course of removing the millions of tons of shale for alum production during the 18th and 19th centuries.

Ammonites are very closely linked with Whitby in popular imagination. From early times the legend of St Hilda was invoked to explain how these strange snake-like objects came to lie in such profusion on the foreshore and it is not surprising that they were an enigma to people who had no concept of the aeons of geological time represented in the fossil record. A small industry in Whitby served to make good nature's omissions by carving heads on fossil ammonites and even providing them with jewelled eyes, in order to reconstruct them as snakes.

Whitby has no official arms but for several centuries has used the motif of three ammonites on a shield, surely an unparalleled use of fossils in a coat-of-arms. The famous china firm of Goss even made a model of the Whitby ammonite. One of the earliest references to the finding of ammonites near Whitby must be that of Camden (1551-1623): '... if you break them [stones] you find within stony serpents, wreathed up in circles, but generally without heads ...'

For those who did not wish to go to the trouble of finding specimens themselves there were a number of fossil dealers who collected and acquired popular samples. A man named Brown Marshall was active in 1824 and found at Saltwick the specimen of *teleosaurus chapmani* now in Whitby Museum. Daniel Chettleburg is listed in a directory of 1858 as a fossil dealer and his widow Jane appears in 1864, continuing the business. Jet merchants may also have sold fossils as a sideline. In any case the trade began with Whitby's rise as a seaside resort and was fostered by the curiosity value of a good specimen as a reminder of a holiday. Many ammonites were sliced in half to show their internal chambers and polished. Some were used

109 *In this* Punch *cartoon of September 1887 the joke is in the contrast between the brightly coloured visitors and the sober and dour natives. Du Maurier could never resist detail, and his backgrounds are often as interesting as the foreground.*

PUNCH, OR THE LONDON CHARIVARI. [SEPTEMBER 17, 1887.

A VIKING ON MODERN FASHION.
" WHAT DOES T'LASS WANT WI' YON BOOSTLE FOR ? IT AREN'T BIG ENOUGH TO SMOOGLE THINGS, AND SHE CAN'T STEER HERSELF WI' IT ! "

as ornaments and set in table tops or chess boards, though these must have been both uncommon and expensive.

It was left to geologists to establish that the ubiquitous ammonite varied enormously and that the various sub-species (*hildoceras, harpoceras* etc.) could be used to indicate the dating and define the relative position of the beds in which they occurred, as could various other marine shells.

As we have already seen, many larger fossil creatures were found and are recorded as far back as the early 18th century. With no background against which to place them, however, wild assertions were made that these were the bones of fossil men, perhaps even of fallen angels, cast out of heaven, or creatures drowned in the universal deluge!

In 1758 Captain William Chapman and John Wooler found a fossil crocodile in the alum shale near Whitby, which eventually found its way to the Natural History Museum. Sir George Head describes fossil remains he was shown in 1835, perhaps belonging to an ichthyosaur, in a garret of a house up an alley. A 'highly respectable tradesman' also had what was said to be a human leg, petrified, but Head saw little resemblance. Similarly, visitors of earlier times were shown 'the petrified arm and hand of a man', found on the Scaur by Dr Woodward. In about 1743 the Rev. Mr Borwick found 'a complete skeleton, or petrified bones of a man' which was broken in extracting it from the alum shale, while about 1762 what was thought to be the skeleton of a horse was found about thirty yards below ground level in Saltwick alum works.

Whitby was an exporter of fossils, sending examples to most of the significant museums in the 19th century, such as the British Museum of Natural History and the Yorkshire Museum. Dr Richard Ripley, a Whitby surgeon, handed over generous quantities of fossils to the Literary, Scientific & Natural History Society in Lancaster, his native town, between 1837 and 1843. These included 'fossils from the Lias' and the heads of *ichthyosaurus tenuirostris* and of *plesiosaurus*, and also two Whitby tokens, almost certainly those of Henry Sneaton, because of the ammonite motifs upon them.

GEOLOGY

Opinion was divided between those who (correctly) saw fossils as preserved remains of ancient animals and sea creatures and those who saw them as an enigma, resembling living things but created for other purposes, such as *lusus naturae* ('one of nature's little games') or as a result of spontaneous fermentation in the alum mines! The controversy led to the rise of geology as a science and a head-on clash with those who could only visualise the Biblical version of events and who saw everywhere the evidence of design in the world, evolution and change being anathema to them since they implied that not all was created perfect in the first place.

The full working out of this controversy lay some years in the future, but Whitby's role in the infant science of geology was assured by its rich fossil fauna. It became one of the classic locations for teaching purposes and has remained so to the present day.

One of the pioneers of those days of geology was the Rev. George Young who, with his friend John Bird, then a drawing master but later the first Curator of the Museum, published a quarto volume entitled *A Geological Survey of the Yorkshire Coast* in 1822. Bird did the illustrations, and he also printed them on his own lithographic press.

Another important figure in the middle of the century was Martin Simpson who published three geological works: *A Monograph of the Ammonites of the Yorkshire Lias* (1843), *The Fossils of the Yorkshire Lias described from Nature* (1855) and *A Guide to the Geology of the Yorkshire Coast* (1856). These established Whitby as a *locus classicus* for geologists. Unfortunately Simpson's classifications have been largely replaced in modern science by others, because he did not illustrate his type specimens. Walter White, author of *A Month in Yorkshire,* met Simpson. His kindly description reveals the latter as a complete enthusiast, totally absorbed in his work.

The Yorkshire coast was to act as

WHITBY'S
MODERN PRIVATE HOTEL
RECOMMENDED A.A. and R.A.C.

"THE MARVIC"
WEST CLIFF :: WHITBY

The " Marvic " occupies one of the finest positions on the West Cliff. It is within a few minutes of the Golf Links, the Bathing Pool, Cliff Lift, Sports Grounds and The Spa. It is in a delightfully sheltered, sunny position, yet almost on the Front. The site was deliberately chosen because of its convenience and situation. The Hotel is modern inside and outside and new in every detail.

110   The 'Marvic' Private Hotel, from a guidebook of 1938, advertised as being 'modern inside and outside and new in every detail'. Its very large windows proclaim the 1930s obsession with sun and light.

nursery for many geological talents. William Smith, Adam Sedgwick of Dent, Roderick Murchison and John Phillips are all associated with the geology of this coastline.

In the 20th century the Geological Survey has established a wider view into which the localised exposures can be fitted. The notable work of another native of Whitby, Professor J. E. Hemingway, has also been of great value, with important descriptions such as that of the Whitby area in *A Survey of Whitby and the Surrounding Area* (1958) and *Geology of the Yorkshire Coast* (1958).

Work goes on and though the last word has certainly not been said on the subject it has clearly come a very long way from the mystification and incomprehension of the 18th century.

III *A favourite viewpoint for many artists was Larpool where the river curved and a panoramic view of the harbour unfolded. This view has now been replaced by that from the high level bridge, downstream of Larpool. On the extreme left of the picture can be seen Union Mill and in the foreground the former boiling houses for whale oil. A steam-hauled train leaves for Pickering, which places the view after 1847. The steel engraving was published by S. Reed of Whitby, who produced many guide-books.*

THE REGATTA

Each August Whitby holds a Regatta, a mixture of events at sea and a carnival on land. At one time many ports and harbours held a Regatta but on the north-east coast only Whitby and Scarborough uphold the tradition.

Whitby's first Regatta was held in 1840, and the 150th anniversary was celebrated in 1990, but the event has by no means had a continuous run. There have been a number of gaps, particularly in the early years, for instance between 1853 and 1864.

It probably began with the local fishermen competing with each other in wagers. As late as 1866 we hear of a 'great Coble Race, from Staithes to Whitby' between crews from Blyth and Whitby. Whitby won easily. In the 1840s the events centred around yacht racing and an engraving of 1848 shows a noble group of yachts under full sail. In 1847 a 'Whitby Challenge Cup' was promoted by the Royal Yorkshire Yacht Club and the winner, the yacht *Hilda*, received a £50 prize.

Clearly the large yachts which dominated the early years of the Regatta did not belong to fishermen, although the crews were probably drawn from their ranks and local boatbuilders found a 'shop window' for their skills. Firms such as Falkingbridges were notable builders of yachts. By the 1930s these races were dying out in favour of other events.

Competitive rowing came in around 1872 with the formation of a Jet Works Amateur Boating Club. Three clubs still in existence and the mainstay of the Regatta today are the Scarborough Amateur Rowing Club (1874), Friendship

Amateur Rowing Club (1879) and Whitby Amateur Rowing Club (1912) which later became the Whitby Fishermen's A.R.C. One of the sights of the harbour for many years was the ancient floating boathouse of the Friendship Club. The clubs compete in a number of races run between the area of Upgang and the harbour mouth, the length depending on the age of the crew. Men and women, young and old, compete and the practising continues remorselessly between Regattas. Their boats, known as gigs, are very much more robust than river boats – they need to be given the stresses and strains of rowing at sea – and consequently considerably heavier.

Meanwhile on land the carnival element began in 1929 with fancy dress and decorated floats. This element has developed considerably and there are now air shows, car rallies and marching bands. The youth of Whitby is also involved in events like the greasy pole and motor-cycle scrambling on the beach. A fair arrives on the Sunday night and is established all down the West Pier, along with the stalls of cheapjacks of all kinds. On Monday night the whole event closes with a gigantic firework display against the dramatic background of the East Cliff.

One of the novel ideas developed for the Regatta is that many of the shops and businesses in the town co-operate in displaying a numbered card in their window. All Regatta programmes carry an individual number and if that number matches one in a shop the programme owner can claim a small prize. Never are shop windows so carefully scoured as on this occasion!

It is estimated that over 20,000 people visit Whitby over the period of the Regatta, which corresponds with the peak of the season. It is undoubtedly good for trade and its popularity does not seem to diminish. In recent years a Folk Week has been developed, to follow the Regatta. It features music in the streets and pubs, Morris and sword dancing. More recent events include the visits of the Australian-built replica *Endeavour*, which drew immense crowds and looked very well moored at Dock End.

Tourism Today

Most British seaside resorts saw an enormous boom in the post-war years when prosperity began to return after a decade of belt-tightening, before cheap air fares and sunshine began to draw off holiday-makers to continental and particularly Spanish resorts. The flight of former visitors overseas has served to cover up another trend which has grown up at the same time – the taking of second or subsidiary holidays out of season and a tendency towards short breaks. This is a very different pattern to cope with than the traditional high-season week or fortnight.

Relatively few visitors come to Whitby now by train. The journey is too complicated and there is no direct link to the south or west; York is still as much the key to a large pool of potential visitors as it was in Hudson's day, while Leeds has always regarded Whitby as its special resort. A vast increase in the use of private cars means that Whitby's limited parking is stretched to the limit and beyond, especially during Regatta and Folk Weeks. The North Promenade and the Abbey

Plain are usually packed to capacity during the summer, although recent changes to the latter, moving parking further back to the far side of the Abbey, seem to have profoundly affected the visitor pattern.

Another big change is in the field of accommodation. There are still traditional guesthouses offering the traditional facilities to weekly visitors but increasingly there has been a move to self catering holiday flats and cottages. In the case of the latter many are owned by non-resident proprietors from West Yorkshire and, although this situation is by no means particular to Whitby, it has a deleterious effect on the out-of-season social life of the town. In the 1980s and 1990s the tendency to 'encourage' workless people from elsewhere to occupy surplus seaside accommodation, to the benefit of unscrupulous landlords, had some effect on the town, though perhaps not as much as on less resilient resorts.

The last twenty years or so have also seen a great increase in caravan sites, chalets and campsites, mostly just outside the boundaries of the town. At Saltwick the existing site at the top of the cliff has grown considerably, while Hawsker, Sandsend and Upgang have also experienced developments. These cannot but be unsightly, especially in the high and dramatic positions afforded by the coastal scenery, but all planners can do is attempt to lessen their impact and density. The very existence of caravan parks indicates a considerable need for affordable accommodation at the seaside, and ignoring it will not cause it to go away.

A glance at the holiday brochures produced by Scarborough Borough Council Department of Tourism and Amenities for Scarborough, Whitby and Filey (one borough since 1974) shows that while offers of evening entertainment are intended to woo younger visitors used to the facilities of foreign resorts it is still the same basic holiday as was enjoyed in Victorian times. The same attractions – sea, beaches, moors, scenery, history and seasonal events – have been repackaged, but remain much the same. Of course it is a winning combination and if Whitby has problems they are probably the same ones, to a much lesser degree, felt by all seaside resorts.

In recent years the areas devoted to amusements in Whitby have been growing. I use the term loosely, for a large section of Pier Road has long been devoted to funfairs and coin-operated games of various sorts. The growth has not been in this area, but in something more insidious. In an increasing proportion of Church Street, for instance, ordinary shops have been driven out in favour of shops selling gifts, sweets etc. intended solely for tourists, and very seasonal in character as a consequence. These frippery productions rarely add anything to Whitby's reputation and indeed serve to disguise its true character, for many visitors will judge the town on what they see between the Church Stairs and the Bridge. Of course not all is bad and some useful and desirable businesses and attractions have resulted.

One hopes that the lesson has been learnt that it is not possible to compete with Mediterranean resorts on their own terms. Whitby can be very sunny in June or August but it can also be cold and damp with a raw sea mist. What it has to offer is a solid and lasting charm, great character and a sense of a rich history.

Nine

WHITBY, LITERARY
AND CULTURAL

After the Dissolution of the Monasteries, Whitby was cut off from the cultural and intellectual climate of its times, except insofar as these were reflected by well-travelled people such as members of the Cholmley family. It was a plain sort of place, concerned first and foremost with making a living. Only during the 18th century and more particularly the early 19th did it awake to the new interests in literature and science. The truth is that these followed prosperity and the establishment of a middle class with the time to devote to such pursuits.

Cultural changes of this kind took time to evolve. The first library appeared in the late 18th century, a Botanic Garden in 1812, the Literary & Philosophical Society in 1823, and various magazines of a literary nature in 1825 and the following years.

It was quite a small group of intelligent people with the time or the inclination to look outwards who patronised many of the earlier ventures. Indeed, we keep coming up against the same names again and again. In 1833 the *Whitby Repository* lists 'The Whitby Talents', a group of ten people to whom the town was indebted for their various contributions. Only their initials are given, but they can readily be identified. One of them, 'GY', is clearly the Rev. Dr Young, the minister of the Cliff Street Chapel, one figure who was extremely influential in the cultural community of Whitby in the first half of the 19th century. The Literary & Philosophical Society still survives broadly in the way it was set up by him and his fellow enthusiasts nearly two hundred years ago.

Another important figure of those days is Dr Richard Ripley. He was born in Wray, Lancs., the son of a stone-mason, and at the age of 18 was apprenticed to a surgeon and druggist. After a further year or so in London hospitals he took on a post in Steyning, Sussex. In 1812 he heard of a situation going as partner to Dr Nichols in Whitby, and spent the remainder of his life there. His brother John joined him in his medical practice, and both were heavily involved in the establishment of the Literary & Philosophical Society and all manner of other cultural activities, as well as serving the Dispensary with distinction. For most of his life he kept a journal, which makes most interesting reading.

A subscription theatre began in 1784, putting on dramatic productions on a regular basis for the first time. A subscription newsroom was established in 1814 but no local newspaper was published until 1854 and even then in its early stages this only recorded the arrival of visitors to the newly popular resort.

To an extent it was the resort aspect of the town from the 1840s that encouraged many writers to visit: Mrs Gaskell, for instance, Charles Dickens, and Bram Stoker. Many who came for a holiday were captivated by the place and kept on coming back year after year. We have already come across Lowell and du Maurier, prime examples of those whom Whitby drew.

The same factors which attracted writers also attracted painters to this coast, and, later on, photographers. Many professional scenic photographers included Whitby in their itinerary because of its 'quaintness'. Most of these have now been forgotten but Frank Sutcliffe, who spent most of his life here, is now receiving the recognition he deserves. It was the spending power of visitors, in any case, which made Whitby an attractive proposition to painters and photographers alike.

LITERARY CONNECTIONS

Whitby's greatest claim to literary fame is without a doubt Caedmon, a simple servant of the seventh-century Anglian monastery who was miraculously given the power of spontaneous poetry, according to the historian Bede. He is usually honoured as the first English poet.

The refounded abbey which stood between the 11th and 16th centuries produced no famous writer or historian. Post-Conquest Benedictine monks were rarely noted for these gifts in any case.

We have already seen the work of the early 18th-century poet Samuel Jones, which is more interesting for what he said and when he said it than for how well he said it. No-one would seriously argue the literary merits of his verse. Nor for that matter can any more be said for the work of the barber-poet John Twistleton, who wrote a poem in honour of Whitby in about 1765:

> What a place is Whitby grown,
> Once but a poor fisher town ...

> It was the war, I say, by which
> This place became so vastly rich
> Our transport ships, by wind and tide
> Have made our masters swell with pride ...

To find literary personages of any stature we have to look at the 19th and 20th centuries, and while there is no shortage of writers many of them are of purely local significance and very few are household names. While it is tempting to pick out the work of Mary Linskill and Storm Jameson I will dwell on just three writers: Mrs Gaskell, Bram Stoker and Leo Walmsley. None of them was a native, though Leo Walmsley certainly spent his formative years in the area. Those who want to know more about other local writers are directed to the three excellent books on the subject listed in the bibliography.

Mrs Gaskell came to Whitby for a holiday with her two daughters in 1859 and stayed at 1 Abbey Terrace. Whilst there she gathered information on the press gang and the riot which took place in 1793, which she used as the background to *Sylvia's Lovers*. Much of this information apparently she gained from Mr John Corner and a Mrs Huntrods of Whitby, as well as by consulting Young's *History*. Her story was woven from many local threads, such as the whaling industry, and a number of her characters are based on local people, such as the Sanders brothers, who had a shop and sailcloth manufactory as well as running a bank. Whitby appears in the story as 'Monkshaven'. In 1864 George du Maurier was asked to illustrate the current edition of this book. Ironically, at that date he had no acquaintance with Whitby, although later it was to become one of his favourite places.

A few years ago Bram Stoker was largely forgotten. His classic horror story *Dracula*, though still in print, was little considered and in Whitby hardly anyone had heard of it. However, a remake of the film and the recognition that vampires are good for tourism led to the opening of 'The Dracula Experience' in 1986 on Marine Parade, occupying the former Dorans' premises which had started out in 1814 as the subscription newsroom.

Bram Stoker (1847-1912) was born in Dublin and made his career as a theatre manager and critic. In 1890 a visit to Whitby gave him the setting he wanted for the arrival in England of the vampire count. The beauty of the setting contrasted nicely with the evil about to be unleashed, while the reputation of the Yorkshire coast as dangerous for shipping gave him the shipwreck. Indeed, a Russian schooner, the *Dmitry* of Narva, had been run ashore and dismasted on Collier Hope in 1885. Frank Sutcliffe took a photograph of it. This ship almost certainly inspired the literary version, the *Demeter* of Varna, which Stoker used to bring Dracula to England, complete with his boxes of Transylvanian earth. The book itself appeared in 1897.

Leo Walmsley (1892-1966) was brought up in Robin Hood's Bay, the son of an artist who relied on the patronage of summer visitors to make a precarious living. Several of Leo's novels are set in 'Bramblewick', a thinly disguised Robin Hood's Bay, while nearby Whitby appears as 'Burnharbour'. *Three Fevers* (1932), *Foreigners* (1935), and *Sally Lunn* (1937) are set in Bramblewick as are several of his less-known novels such as *Master Mariner* and parts of his autobiographical works.

Captain Cook

Captain James Cook is probably the most famous of Whitby's adopted sons. He was born in 1728 at Marton in Cleveland, where his father was a farm labourer. Soon the family moved to near Great Ayton and young James' promise was noticed by his father's landlord, who helped to get him to school in Great Ayton. After school he helped his father for a while and then went to work at Staithes, in the shop of William Sanderson.

It was probably here that he gained his taste for the sea, for within a short time he found that shop work was not for him. Mr Sanderson introduced him to John Walker, a Quaker friend of his, who owned a number of ships employed in the coal trade. Cook became Walker's apprentice and sailed first on the collier *Freelove* of 450 tons. Later he went on *Three Brothers*, another collier, then *Mary* and *Friendship*, working his way up from 'servant' to mate.

When winter drew in, the colliers were laid up in harbour until spring. The men lived ashore and the apprentices, who had nowhere else to go, lodged wherever they could in their master's house. Cook, with his fellow apprentices, lodged in John Walker's house in Grape Lane, probably in the attics. While some probably took the opportunity for as much idleness as they could get away with, the more studious would be improving their prospects with reading and navigation.

John Walker, like most 18th-century Quakers, was a plain man who avoided show and fashion in possessions, but treated his employees well. Years later, when Cook had moved on, the two men kept up a friendship.

In 1755 James Cook took another turn in his career. Instead of taking a command with one of Walker's ships, he left to join the Navy. His subsequent career, and his three voyages of discovery, are outside the scope of this book. His Whitby connections were maintained by the use of four Whitby-built ships for his voyages, renamed for their service in the Navy as *Endeavour*, *Resolution*, *Adventure* and *Discovery*, and he both visited and wrote to his old master from time to time.

There is a charming story that, when Cook returned to see John Walker in 1772, the elderly housekeeper, Mary Prowd, had been told to treat him with respect and call him 'Captain' but, faced by the man she had befriended as a young apprentice, she instead embraced him and said, 'Oh honey James how glad I's to see thee'!

In view of James Cook's enlightened attitudes, unlike so many of his contemporaries, in dealing with the peoples of the Pacific, it is a tragedy that through a misunderstanding he was killed at Hawaii in 1779. The last word on his appearance and character must go to David Samwell, the Surgeon who sailed with him on *Resolution*:

> He was a modest man, and rather bashful; of an agreeable lively conversation, sensible and intelligent. In temper he was somewhat hasty, but of a disposition the most friendly, benevolent, and humane. His person was above six feet high; and, though a good looking man, he was plain both in dress and appearance. His face was full of expression; his nose extremely well shaped; his eyes which were small, and of a brown cast, were quick and piercing; his eyebrows prominent, which gave his countenance altogether an air of austerity.

John Walker's house in Grape Lane is now an elegantly laid out museum devoted to the life and voyages of Captain James Cook.

HISTORIANS

It is apparent from these pages what a debt any modern historian of Whitby owes to predecessors in the field. Whitby has been well served by its historians, and what this book attempts to do is offer new interpretations and fitting subjects rather than introduce much new factual material.

The earliest historian of the town is Lionel Charlton (1722–88) whose *History of the Town and Abbey* was published in 1779. He came from Hexham in about 1748 and made his living as a teacher of mathematics as well as by carrying on the business of land-surveyor. His school was held in the old tollbooth or town hall (the predecessor to the present one) and many of his pupils became quite distinguished in later life. Among these were William Watkins, whom we will meet in his literary capacity, and Francis Gibson, who became Collector of Customs, playwright and mapmaker. School teaching was one of the few openings in those days for a man of intelligence but of limited means.

Charlton's erudition and skill in Latin led Mr Cholmley, the owner of the Abbey House and much of the town, to give him access to the abbey chartulary, in which was contained much of the evidence for Whitby in the Middle Ages. This became the basis for his book and although it is extremely heavy going for the modern reader, it also put down on paper for the first time much of more general historical interest. As Young wrote:

> (he) … was greatly subservient to the interests of literature, by awakening the attention of the people of Whitby to the history and antiquities of the town and neighbourhood, by exploding fables long received, and bringing to light important facts that had remained in obscurity …

The Rev. George Young (1777–1848) was born near Edinburgh of a fairly poor family. Lacking a left hand at birth he could not work on the land like his family and in consequence was given a much better education than he might otherwise have had. After four years at the University of Edinburgh, graduating M.A., he embarked upon a career in the ministry of the Presbyterian church.

He came to Whitby as minister of the chapel in Cliff Lane in 1806 and stayed here until his death in 1848. Is it unreasonable to see the particular duties of his chapel as being insufficiently demanding for someone of his clearly enormous energy and intellect? That is not to suggest that he in any way neglected his pastoral duties; indeed he took them very seriously. There can be no doubt that he brought to Whitby a period of culture and scientific interest which it had never had before and which was never to flourish so strongly again.

Until 1826 he lived in a cottage opposite his chapel; in that year he married Margaret Hunter and they went to live at 1 New Buildings (now St Hilda's Terrace) where they spent the rest of their lives.

Young's literary and historical output was very large. In 1814 he published *A Catalogue of the Plants in the Botanic Gardens* at Whitby, arranged according to the Linnaean System and followed this in 1817 with his two-volume *History of Whitby and Streoneshalh Abbey* which ran to 954 pages. In 1822 came *A Geological Survey of the Yorkshire Coast*, co-written and illustrated by his friend the artist John Bird. Two years later came *A Picture of Whitby and its Environs* which he heavily revised for its second edition in 1840. In 1836 he published *The Life and Voyages of Captain James Cook* and two years later *Scriptural Geology* as his contribution to the growing debate on the subject. In addition there were a number of minor works including printed sermons – one on 'The Downfall of Napoleon'! – and he was a frequent contributor to local magazines.

One of his most important actions was to stimulate the creation of the Whitby Literary & Philosophical Society, still going strong after nearly two hundred years. Young himself was one of its joint secretaries from its inception in 1823 until his death. This is typical of the man who preferred to stand a little in the shadow and to work largely unseen.

Young was a man of his times, if an exceptional one. His wide interests and spirit of scientific investigation characterise the early 19th-century intellect. In spite of his great abilities he remained a modest man, though he was recognised by the American college of Oxford, Ohio, with the degree of Doctor of Divinity in 1838. His historical writings suffer from the wordiness, and some of the preoccupations, of his age, but of all the books on Whitby it is his that one turns to for the authoritative version and the most rigorously established facts. He belonged to a generation poised between the Age of Reason and the Victorian age, and partook of both influences in equal measure.

Another great name in Whitby history is that of Canon J.C. Atkinson, Vicar of Danby (1814-1900). He was born in Essex, though of Yorkshire descent, and after studying at Cambridge he was ordained. In 1847 Viscount Downe, the patron, presented him to the living of Danby, then a very remote and old-fashioned place.

Atkinson is best remembered for his *Forty Years in a Moorland Parish*, first published in 1891, in which he records the life and lore of his adopted home. If this were all his published work, it would still be a significant contribution, but he also produced many other pieces of work, such as the translating and editing of the two large volumes of the *Whitby Chartulary* for the Surtees Society in 1878-79, *Cleveland Ancient and Modern* which appeared in 1874, *A Handbook to Ancient Whitby and its Abbey*, of 1882, and *Memorials of Old Whitby*, published in 1894.

Besides all these local works Atkinson was recognised as an authority on monastic cartularies and edited several others, such as those of Rievaulx and Furness. In all things his work was characterised by patience and great attention to detail; his weakness was that typically Victorian vice of prolixity and it has to be said that his writings incline not only to verbosity but also to a heavy style.

His other great interest was in prehistory and he investigated many of the ancient burial mounds which survive in such numbers on the moorlands of Cleveland. By the standards of his day, which were not very high, he was a competent archaeologist who wrote up virtually all of his excavations for posterity, mostly in the *Gentleman's Magazine*. In this he compares very favourably with a number of others who worked in the same geographical area.

Among these other diggers, searchers after the unwritten history of another age, were James Ruddock of Pickering, who worked as agent in the area for Thomas Bateman, the Derbyshire antiquary. Ruddock excavated over two hundred barrows on the North York Moors from 1849 till 1858.

Another, very shadowy, figure is that of Samuel Anderson of Whitby, active in the 1850s, who carried out an unknown number of excavations and who sold his collections to Joseph Mayer of Liverpool. Among his finds were the Viking age treasures from Lilla Howe.

We shall consider the work of Percy Shaw Jeffrey in the next chapter. Other important Whitby historians have been R.T. Gaskin, whose *The Old Seaport of Whitby* was published posthumously in 1909, and Richard Weatherill, a member of the talented artistic family, whose *The Ancient Port of Whitby and its Shipping*, published in 1908, is still required reading for anyone wishing to study Whitby's rich maritime history.

The writing of history goes on; most recent is Rosalyn Barker's *The Book of Whitby*, published in 1989, followed by the first edition of this work in 1993, and the second in 2004. New facts do emerge, but principally it is the interpretation which moves on from generation to generation, as well of course as particular hobby-horses, which can be identified most easily in retrospect.

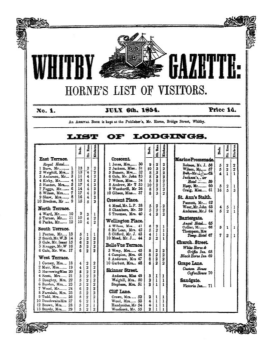

112 *Front cover of the first edition of the* Whitby Gazette, *issued by Ralph Horne on 6 July 1854. The Gazette was not a newspaper at first, but a list of visitors and their lodgings. A supplement issued with early editions contained literary attempts by readers.*

PUBLICATIONS

Whitby's first printing press was set up by Charles Plummer, printer and draper, at the Bridge End in 1770. His was a curious combination of occupations, but Ralph Horne, a later printer, also combined his printing with paper-hanging. In the *Universal British Directory* of 1798 Caleb Webster is the only recorded printer. Probably one or two printers could provide for all local needs at this period, and much of their work is likely to have consisted of advertisements and broadsheets.

Prosperity brought with it a taste, however, for literature and in many parts of the country the early 19th century saw the development of literary magazines of a quite localised kind, issued in weekly or monthly parts. Few were a financial success and few survived for more than a limited period. In Whitby the absence of a local newspaper at that period, when many were starting up, led to a demand for local news as well as literary and historical magazines.

The *Whitby Repository* was the earliest of the three main magazines and it also survived the longest. Beginning in 1825 it ran in six annual volumes to 1830; a new series of three volumes went up to 1833 and there was an attempt to revive it in 1866, but only two volumes came out. These are of some interest, however, because they contain a number of earlier engravings reissued. Two other magazines appeared in the same year and probably killed each other off, as there was only a limited market for them. They certainly saw each other as rivals. The *Whitby Magazine* ran to three annual volumes between 1827 and 1829, while the *Whitby Panorama* only ran to two, in 1827 and 1828. All carried an element of local news.

The *Whitby Spy*, in 30 parts, and *Anomaliae* were two other purely literary productions published by William Watkins in 1784 and 1797-98 respectively. Watkins was a pupil of Charlton, the historian. Watkins it was who secured for posterity, in the *Whitby Spy*, Twistleton's poem quoted above. Or did he write it as a pastiche? It is hard to decide.

Young's *History of Whitby* was printed in 1817 by the firm of Clark & Medd, whose printing-house was in Bridge Street. His 1840 edition of the *Picture of Whitby* came from the firm of Horne and Richardson, who may have succeeded Clark & Medd. Another important Whitby printer appears with the publication of F.K. Robinson's *Whitby, its Abbey and the Principal Parts of the Neighbourhood* in 1860.

Silvester Reed, whose printing-house was in the Old Market Place, was active from the 1850s until about 1880. His *Reed's Guide to Whitby,* with an essay on sea-bathing, was in its 12th edition by *c.*1870. Another of his productions was *Sketches of Whitby, its Scenery and Other Attractions.* Kirby & Son, most of whose work was in the field of broadsheets, also produced a guide-book in 1849, entitled *The Stranger's and Visitant's Guide to Whitby.*

Horne's were to have the longest connection with printing and publishing, but we will see more of them in the context of newspapers.

In more recent years the local publishers Caedmon, run by Cordelia and the late Tom Stamp, have maintained a most impressive record in reprinting important texts such as Young's *History,* Gaskin's *The Old Seaport of Whitby* and a number of books on Cook and Scoresby, thus performing a great service to local history.

Artists and Photographers

Whitby, occupying a picturesque section of the coastline, has attracted a number of important artists and photographers. Of the former J.M.W. Turner is probably the best known, while of the latter, it was a home-grown talent, that of Frank Sutcliffe, which captured the most memorable images of the town and district. In both media there were many others to whom we should be grateful for preserving for future generations something of Whitby's special flavour.

It is not done to criticise the work of Turner, that master of the watercolour, but his treatment of the East Cliff in his famous view of Whitby in 1824 in the Tate Gallery is one of the least lifelike of any I have seen – 'like a slice of fruit cake' says English, with justice. It is, of course, hardly Turner's fault if others followed his view slavishly, especially the engravers, but his vertical cliff and stumpy abbey appear again and again. Other talented artists were more permanently associated with the town. Francis Nicholson (1753-1844) was born in Pickering but moved to Whitby in about 1781, married, and stayed here until about 1792. He appears, however, in the *Universal British Directory* for 1798 as 'Landscape Artist' in Whitby still, although his career took him on via Knaresborough, Ripon and Weybridge to London. He also worked in Scarborough, where he experimented with a means of producing multiple watercolours of the same scene, by using a soft-ground etching and blacklead to copy the drawing. In this he was only following many engravers in trying to meet the insatiable demand for repeated views of the same scene.

We have already met George Chambers, Henry Redmore and the notable Weatherill family in an earlier chapter and I do not intend to repeat what I have said there. H.B. Carter (1803-68) was born in Scarborough and initially, like many others, served at sea but later made painting his full-time occupation. He also taught pupils at his home in York Place, Scarborough. His technique often involved a very simple palette of olive green, brown and grey for his sea pictures, and he would frequently create highlights to his waves by scraping the surface of the paper with a knife.

Atkinson Grimshaw (1836-93) is usually associated with Leeds but after he had a house built near Scarborough he produced many harbour scenes, including several of Whitby.

Lesser known are some of the illustrators. John Bird was at one time Curator of the Literary & Philosophical Society Museum but also a talented artist. He collaborated with Dr Young in the production of an important early work on the fossils of the coast. Many of his drawings were later engraved. Francis Pickernell is better known as the resident engineer of Whitby harbour but in his busy and

113 *The name 'WEATHERILL' is carved in handsome capitals into the parapet at the end of the East Pier. Could this be George the artist or his son Richard, both of whom would have frequented this spot?*

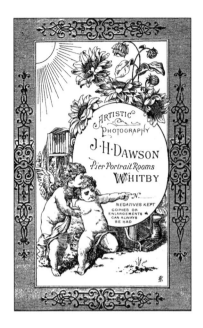

114 & 115 *Two decoratively printed reverses of cartes-de-visite portraits by Whitby studio portrait photographer J. H. Dawson, dating from the late 19th century.*

useful career he also found time to make several attractive drawings which were also later engraved. They are mainly views of the successive bridges and piers and were perhaps a working record of some of his achievements, or even views to show how some of his proposals would appear if carried out.

Among more recent artists and illustrators are J.R. Bagshawe, A.T. Pile and J. Freeman. Bagshawe (1870-1909) is best known for his charming little illustrations to a series of articles for *The Field* and *Yachting Monthly* which were later gathered into book form as *The Wooden Ships of Whitby* in 1933. In *Buildings of Old Whitby* are gathered the works of another artist, Albert Pile, who recorded the destruction of many picturesque areas of the town in the late 1950s and early 1960s. John Freeman runs an art shop in the Market Place as a sideline to more creative work in pen and ink of harbour and shore scenes.

Although they are not strictly connected with Whitby itself we cannot pass on from the subject of artists without a glance at the so-called 'Staithes Group' of artists. J.R. Bagshawe was one of this very loose group of some thirty artists, the best known of whom were undoubtedly Harold and Laura Knight. They exhibit little in common in terms of style but all the artists of the group, which existed between about 1880 and 1910, derived some of their inspiration from the scenery and working lives of the people of Staithes. Just ten miles up the coast, Staithes at that time, much more so than at present, was a strange, picturesque and immensely inward-looking little fishing harbour, where everyone except this distinctive group of incomers was related. No doubt many of the artists sought to sell their work to the multitude of summer visitors, like Leo Walmsley's father who was at work in a similar fashion at Robin Hood's Bay at the turn of the century.

It was not only artists who relied for a living on the visitors. Many of the photographers, particularly in the days when equipment was heavy and bulky, relied on the desire of the visitor to take home a memento of their visit without the trouble involved. Of course, the summer trade was all too brief and the creative work had to be supplemented by out-of-season portrait work.

Whitby's best-known photographer is undoubtedly Frank Sutcliffe. In recent years his work has met with the recognition which it deserves and not only is there a commercial gallery in Flowergate devoted to his images but four books have been published on him. There was a time when he was little known outside the town and even within it was more familiar as a studio portrait artist. Many of my family photographs bear his studio stamp. Sutcliffe snatched moments from the everyday business in order to catch fleeting effects of light and shade, or to make ordinary scenes extraordinary in some way.

There is a story that Sutcliffe was hurrying to the bridge with his equipment to take photographs on the east side of the town. Here he met a fellow photographer, a well-known pictorial specialist called Hadley, similarly burdened down with his equipment, who advised: 'There is nothing worth doing over there; I've just been.' Sutcliffe, whose complete output, more or less, was taken within the confines of the town, was suitably abashed!

Much of Frank Sutcliffe's work was concerned with the ordinary people of Whitby and since he was around in both winter and summer he was able to capture the town in all its moods. Among his practical but less creative work was the photographing of all the plates for Dr English's huge two-volume book on Whitby prints.

Born in 1853 in Leeds, the son of an artist and lithographer, Frank became interested in photography while working as a clerk. His family made many visits to Whitby for seaside holidays and eventually came to live at Ewe Cote Hall in 1871, less than a year before Frank's father died.

Frank Sutcliffe photographed John Ruskin at Brantwood in 1872 and his work was admired by the great man; however, he made an unsuccessful and unhappy beginning as a professional photographer at Tunbridge Wells, but on returning to Whitby things worked out better.

His first studio was a vacant jet shop in Waterloo Yard, Flowergate, but in 1893 he moved to a better studio at 12 Skinner Street. An advertisement of 1895 declares that

> the increase of F.M.S's business and consequent demands on the space at command in his old studio … necessitated the erection of New Premises, which he has had built on the most approved principles at 12, Skinner Street. The studio, which is on the first floor, is one of the Largest and Best Lighted in England.

On his retirement in 1923 Frank Sutcliffe took on the curatorship of the Museum, overseeing its move from Pier Road to Pannett Park, with all the complications associated with such a move.

It is instructive to compare Sutcliffe's photographs with the Whitby cartoons of George du Maurier, with whom he overlapped. While du Maurier liked to use Whitby characters as a foil to his middle-class visitors, it is the latter who predominate. Sutcliffe, in comparison, shows almost no visitors. Was this deliberate, or was he simply too busy in summer taking their studio portraits to photograph them in more casual mode?

Thomas Watson of Lythe also deserves an honourable mention, for his scenic pictures of the coast. Although much less 'artistic' than Sutcliffe, his work catches many lost moments, such as life on the Mulgrave Estate or the rebuilding of Lythe church in 1910-11.

One of the earliest studio photographers was W. Stonehouse who was in Church Street in 1848 and had the Pier Portrait Rooms in 1866. J. Waller was at 7 The Pier from 1867-70 and was succeeded by J.H. Dawson, who moved his studio to the Khyber Pass in 1890. Dorans, who started in Henrietta Street in 1889, were long a familiar landmark with their studio on Marine Parade. Many local family photographs carry the ornate and distinctive carte-de-visite designs of these photographers on their reverses.

NEWSPAPERS

As we have seen already, the *Whitby Gazette* was founded in 1854 and still continues, despite several changes of format. In its early days it was mainly a broadsheet listing visitors and their lodgings and consequently appeared only in summer. Soon extra sheets were added, containing literary efforts, and gradually news as such made its appearance.

By 1858 the *Whitby Gazette and Horne's General Advertising Medium* was published weekly on Saturdays and cost one penny. Its circulation was about 3,000 and it consisted of four pages; local advertising on the front page, a summary of news from the London papers on the two centre pages, and local news, births, marriages and deaths on the last page, together with market news and a list of visitors.

The publisher was Ralph Horne, who came to Whitby at the age of eight in 1813-14 to live with his grandmother. He was apprenticed to the firm of Clark & Medd, printers, in Bridge Street in 1818. Later, after a period in York, he returned to set up his own business in Bridge Street, or perhaps to take over from his ex-employer, in 1827. His first venture was the *Whitby Magazine* and by 1832 he was in partnership with John Richardson. The *Gazette* began in 1854 and Horne took his son into partnership in 1857. Further premises in Grape Lane were acquired for the printing works.

For a time from about 1864 there was a rival – the *Whitby Times*, published on a Friday, presumably to scoop the news, by George Lockey in Baxtergate. By 1879 the rival paper was published by Alfred Porter at 53 Baxtergate.

The *Whitby Times* came to an end in 1912 but the *Whitby Gazette* continued and remained in family ownership until quite recently. On 31 March 1978 the last issue in broadsheet form produced from hot metal appeared and since then it has been published in tabloid form on offset litho, and now is based on a trading estate and no longer in Grape Lane.

Hornes also acted as general printers, publishing among other things an irregular guide-book to Whitby which has run to 73 editions. They also had a shop adjacent to the printing works in Bridge Street for very many years, selling china and glassware, as well as printed goods. They also maintained a Circulating Library, as did Holmans, at a small charge per volume.

THEATRES

Whitby's first theatre was in the Paddock on the west side of Cliff Lane, next to Mr Hunter's house, and is recorded as early as 1763. Few provincial towns acquired a theatre any earlier because of licensing problems and most made do with temporary premises to house visiting companies of actors.

In 1784 a new theatre was built in Scate Lane by subscription, with 12 shareholders. It could hold 500 people, and performances were held there in the winter months. It was here on 2 December 1799 that Francis Gibson, Collector of Customs for Whitby, but something of a polymath, put on his play *Streanshall Abbey, or, The Danish Invasion,* a play whose patriotic sentiments were much appreciated at the time. A copy of the script, dated 1800, is in the Literary & Philosophical Society's Library. His fellow pupil from Charlton's school, William Watkins, wrote another play entitled *The Fall of Carthage,* performed in Whitby in 1801. A new play entitled *Whitby Lasses, or A New Way to Get Rid of a Wife* was performed there in February 1794.

Most Georgian theatres formed circuits, the actors often travelling between them on foot and putting on a season of plays before moving on to the next engagement. The Whitby theatre was visited by Strickland's company between 1784 and 1793, but between 1793 and 1818 it was taken over by Butler's company, who

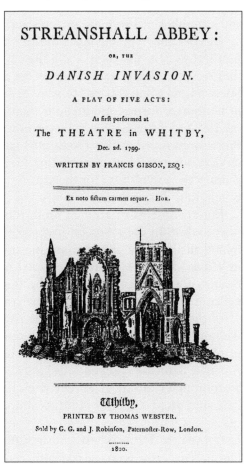

STREANSHALL ABBEY:

OR, THE

DANISH INVASION.

A PLAY OF FIVE ACTS:

As first performed at

The THEATRE in WHITBY,

Dec. 2d. 1799.

WRITTEN BY FRANCIS GIBSON, ESQ:

Ex noto fictum carmen sequar. Hor.

Whitby,

PRINTED BY THOMAS WEBSTER.

Sold by G. G. and J. Robinson, Paternoster-Row, London.

....
1800.

116 Title-page of Francis Gibson's play Streanshall Abbey, or, the Danish Invasion, *first performed at Whitby Theatre in 1799. The woodcut of the Abbey is by Thomas Bewick.*

served theatres in Beverley, Harrogate, Kendal, Northallerton, Richmond and Ulverston. A very good sequence of playbills preserved by the Literary & Philosophical Society covers the period between 1779 and the end of Butler's regime.

An illuminating addition to playbills in 1793 was intended to reassure any seamen who might choose to patronise the theatre about the intentions of the Press Gang:

> Capt. Shorland pledges his word of honour that no seamen whatever shall be molested by his people on Playnights from the hour of four in the Afternoon to Twelve at night; after which time the indulgence ceases.

While no pictures survive of its interior we may well guess that it resembled other surviving theatres of the same period, such as Richmond, Kendal or Lancaster. Thomas Thwaites, who died in 1828, had been the scene painter at Whitby theatre, and a number of surviving pictures and prints are based on his backdrops.

As a building type, Georgian theatres have been decimated by fire. Unfortunately in Whitby's case also there was a fire on 25 July 1823 which totally destroyed the theatre, which stood at what is now the junction of Brunswick Street and Newton Street. Houses built on its site were given the name Shakespeare Terrace, perhaps in honour of former productions there. George Chambers painted the scene of the fire and an engraving subsequently appeared in the *Whitby Repository*. After this a large room at the *Freemasons' Tavern* was from time to time pressed into service, but it too was destroyed by fire in 1853, and in any case during the 19th century the town's taste for theatre seems to have diminished, perhaps in the face of religious disapproval.

Entertainments of a much more robust kind were also held in Whitby from time to time. In the 1780s, for instance, Gustavus Katerfelto, a Prussian quack who toured the country giving conjuring shows and lecturing on science, performed in Whitby Town Hall. Here he raised his daughter to the ceiling, apparently by means of an immense magnet. The Rev. James Woodforde, who had seen him perform at Norwich, thought his behaviour 'exceedingly ungenteel'.

In the late 19th century dramatic performances were put on at the Spa, along with musical entertainments, and in more recent times the Spa has provided seasons of plays, though generally of a very slight description, suiting summer visitors. Amateur dramatic competitions have also been held here. Perhaps the strength of Scarborough's theatre in recent years has drawn away the audiences that might have supported a serious resident company in Whitby.

LITERARY & PHILOSOPHICAL SOCIETY

During the early years of the 19th century there was a nationwide movement towards the founding of literary and scientific institutions. They appear under a number of names, of which 'Mechanics' Institute' is probably the most common. Their aim was usually, though not universally, to provide a means of education for young artisans, both in order to help them improve themselves and to 'civilise' this large section of the population into more intellectual pursuits. It is no coincidence that societies and institutions of this kind began to make their appearance just after the riots and unrest of 1819-20.

Newcastle was early with its Literary & Philosophical Society, which was begun in 1793, but the Leeds society originated in 1819 and York and Hull gained kindred bodies in 1822. Those societies which titled themselves 'Literary & Philosophical', though having a scientific bent, particularly in their early years, may have aimed for a higher stratum of society than the mechanics' institutes. When the Whitby Society was founded in 1823 it was almost universally composed of 'respectable' persons. Of course Whitby had few of the type of young 'mechanics' who swarmed in the streets of Manchester, Leeds or Bradford. Early 19th-century Whitby was a town with a much larger middle class and this it was which made up most of the early membership.

Most of these societies included in their functions a museum, a specialist library, lectures and scientific demonstrations. With the exception of the last of these, the Whitby Society, one of the least changed of all those that sprang up more than a century and a half ago, still maintains these functions.

If the 1820s were a time of scientific and literary endeavour, then the years that followed exposed the new societies to chill winds. Cholera, a trade depression and a growing renaissance in the church were all contributory factors. While the church in Whitby never opposed its literary institution, it was a different picture elsewhere. In Bradford the new society was strangled at birth by pronouncements from the pulpit, which characterised such groups as impolitic in raising the expectations of the humbler classes beyond their station in life and being, by virtue presumably of interest in science, irreligious!

The question of geology, of course, raised great controversy between those who saw evidence for a grand design behind things such as fossils, and those which could envisage vast aeons of change and evolution in prehistory. Religion and science were thus set at each others' throats, though later on both recognised the untenable nature of their extreme positions and reached an uneasy accommodation.

Whitby's Literary & Philosophical Society survived the vicissitudes of the 1830s and 1840s and survives today. One relic of its 19th-century past is the way that lectures and 'conversaziones' are still held in the afternoon, as though no-one of any consequence needs to work!

The main purpose of the society was, and is, to run a museum, as we shall see.

MUSEUM, ART GALLERY AND LIBRARY

With the founding of the Whitby Literary & Philosophical Society in 1823 it was a foregone conclusion that a museum would follow. All over the country this was happening, usually with the intention that scientific material would be collected as a basis for lectures and self-help education. In Whitby's case the idea was planted in a circular which probably emanated from the Rev. Young in November 1822. It said:

… the facilities offered for establishing a Museum in Whitby, are such as few places enjoy, especially in the Fossil department. Whitby is the chief town of a district abounding with Petrifactions, and containing not a few interesting Antiquities …

The result, as we have seen, was the founding of the society, one of the principal purposes of which was to create and maintain a museum. Two rooms were rented above shops in Baxtergate, one for the museum and one for the council room, and John Bird was appointed unpaid curator with William Corbishley as sub-curator, at the salary of four guineas per year.

By September 1823 the museum was open to the public, although in the first year only 300 visitors came. However, the society was well satisfied. Acquisitions began to come in, such as the superb 'Fossil Crocodile, or Teleosaurus Chapmani, found in the alum shale at Saltwick by Brown Marshall. The most perfect specimen known', which was purchased for seven pounds and still forms one of the museum's most prized exhibits.

Soon ambitious plans were laid to join forces with the subscription library and a new company formed to provide a warm bathing establishment and to acquire premises on the Quay (later known as Pier Road). Subscriptions soon totalled £2,200 and a local architect, John Bolton, was appointed. The new shared building was ready by 3 January 1827. It still stands, though now used for other purposes, and is a dignified three-storey building of stone. The ground floor was occupied by the Bath Company, the first floor by the subscription library, and the museum had the top floor.

An early visitor, in 1835, was Sir George Head.

I afterwards visited the museum, wherein the specimens are imperfectly arranged, and the exhibition is altogether on a small scale; though it contains probably the very best specimen of antediluvian remains at present in England. Of the enormous skeleton of the ichthyosaurus almost every bone is perfect …

The museum remained where it was until 1931, as we shall see. In 1860 arrangements were as follows:

Strangers can inspect the museum by the payment of 1s. each; or 'in parties of more than two' at 6d. each, on application at the Baths. Members and subscribers have the privilege of introducing their friends and families free; and the rules for admission also state that 'the museum shall be open to the public on the first Monday in each month from 11 to 1, by ticket from any member or subscriber'.

Apart from local and geological items the museum collected curiosities from all over the world, as a result of its maritime connections. The museum was:

much indebted to captains of ships and other seafaring friends (for) insects from the Brazils and curiosities from New Zealand and Van Dieman's Land. Thus the characteristic generosity of the British seaman has been exemplified in the captains belonging to this port, and it may fairly be presumed that our seamen, who visit every quarter of the globe, will continue to augment our collections from year to year.

Increasingly the collections outgrew the building, which was proving to be unsuitable for other reasons as well. The Society was paralysed by indecision for a number of years but eventually stirred into action by the Marquis of Normanby, who suggested joining up with the new art gallery to be built on a site bounded by Bagdale and Chubb Hill, to house the collections of the late Alderman Pannett.

The new museum was opened in 1931 and, with a few alterations such as a better roof, remains much the same today, although major additions were put in place in 2004. The whole arrangement is a rare survival of the Age of Reason into the early 21st century, despite the vastly different external circumstances.

Alderman Pannett's gift was associated with the public park that bears his name. Pannett was a lawyer and a county councillor. Hearing that the land on the Chubb Hill estate was to be put down to speculative building, he purchased it with a view to making it into a park to contain 'a public museum ... for the reception and preservation of my water colour drawings, works of art, objects of natural history and other things ...'.

He died in 1920 and his Trustees

117 *Dr Merryweather's 'Tempest Prognosticator', invented in 1850, in Whitby Museum. A leech in each bottle responded to the approach of an electrical storm by climbing up the neck of the bottle and dislodging a small piece of whalebone, thus ringing the bell! George Merryweather lectured to the Whitby Literary & Philosophical Society on his invention for nearly three hours in 1851. It did not make his fortune.*

duly created the park and art gallery, which was opened in 1928. As his bequest was to the town it is administered by the town council. Since the Literary & Philosophical Society's museum adjoins the art gallery and effectively forms part of the same building, the two need to work closely together. Many farcical situations have naturally arisen over the years.

Alderman Pannett's collection includes works by Turner, de Wint, Cox, Varley and Constable, as well as paintings by many of the local artists discussed earlier and members of the 'Staithes Group'. The flower of the collection, to my mind, are however the 94 paintings by George Weatherill and his family.

There was a subscription library in the town as early as 1775. It was in Haggersgate, in rooms over the *Star Inn*. In 1827 it moved into the same building as the baths and museum. It was open six days a week, from 11 a.m. to 5 p.m., and

118   *A watercolour drawing of Bagdale in the 18th century, before the fall of the Abbey's great West Window in 1794. The houses on the right can still be recognised though the Bagdale Beck running in front of them is now culverted. Near the left of the picture a long low building is the Theatre in Scate Lane, destroyed by fire in 1823.*

subscribers paid half a guinea per annum, which had risen to one guinea by 1860. As a concession to visitors to the town there were also monthly or fortnightly arrangements; it is likely that most visitors availed themselves of something more lightweight in character, from Reed's or Newton's Circulating Library in the Old Market Place or Baxtergate. In 1858 there was also a Mechanics' Library in Church Street, and a number of churches possessed religious libraries.

By 1921 Horne's had two circulating libraries, mainly for visitors, one in Bridge Street and the other in Skinner Street. The place of the old Subscription Library, which closed in 1935, was taken by a new Whitby library, opened in the same year. In 1962 responsibility for its running passed to the county council, and in 1966 a new purpose-built library was opened at the foot of Bobbies Bank, to replace the old one in New Quay Road.

There were also a number of newsrooms for subscribers to newspapers. Of these the best known is the Commercial Newsroom of 1814, on Marine Parade. A tall narrow building with a tiny raised rooflight, it later became Doran's photographers premises but now serves as the home of 'The Dracula Experience'.

Ten

FOLKLORE AND CUSTOMS

FOLKLORE OF THE SEA

Whitby is very rich in folklore. That we know much about it is mainly due to one man and his books. Although Percy Shaw Jeffrey was not a native of Whitby he swiftly assimilated much of its flavour, which he distilled in three editions of his book, *Whitby Lore and Legend*.

The first edition appeared in 1919, and it was an immediate success. To my mind this is the best edition, and, although slim, it is entirely devoted to folklore. The later editions of 1923 and 1952 attempt to tell a connected history of the town, but, in doing so, jettison much that appeared in the first edition. The three editions are virtually separate books. If there is any criticism to be made it is that the author allows himself too easily to be sidetracked into pleasing but irrelevant byeways, but as a child I read the first edition again and again until I could practically recite it word for word. Some of this magic still remains with me.

The sea being such a notoriously fickle mistress it is not surprising that seamen, and fishermen in particular, are still extremely superstitious and were once even more so. Looking at the question from another point of view, when a person faces the possibility of death in their work every day, why should they not take that extra bit of care to reduce the risks by placating the gods?

Superstitions extend to the days of the week that are unlucky, the naming of unlucky animals, and whistling. On Fridays the fishing boats remain in harbour, for reasons of tradition; Friday is unlucky. Sundays were also a day of rest at one time, perhaps from religious influence, but it is usual for the boats to go out on the Sunday evening tide. So unlucky was Holy Innocents' Day or Childermass (28 December) that not only that day but the day of the week on which it fell throughout the year was once regarded as unlucky by extension.

Some animals were also considered unlucky, at least to name. Any mention of a pig could keep the fishermen from going out that day and considerable periphrasis could be needed to avoid such unlucky words. Whistling was even worse and a whistling woman the worst of all. However, it was permissible for children to whistle for a wind to bring their fathers home, and in the days of the whale fishery Whitby children would go up on the cliff and jump up and down, singing: 'Suther wind, suther An blaw mah faather heeam te mah mother'. This was called 'spelling'; that is, casting a spell.

Other superstitions surrounded such necessary gear as seaboots and nets. Seaboots should always be carried under the arm, not on the shoulder. If nets are spread out to dry across your path you should always lift them up and walk under them, never walk across them.

These superstitions are not of course unique to Whitby. They are common to the fishing community generally and in particular to the East Coast and Baltic areas, but their survival is patchy. It was remarked in 1885 that Staithes was deeply imbued with such superstitions; Staithes was a very close-knit and inter-related community and probably more than most it kept old ideas alive. Whitby may have thrown off some of these ideas earlier, but of course some survive and as it is usually incomers who note their survival, not natives, recording is a matter of chance.

Fishermen came into contact with all sorts of unusual sea creatures which they sometimes brought ashore for a nine days wonder, such as basking-sharks. Seals were at one time common on these shores. It is said that they became accustomed to the appearance of women on the Scaur, gathering bait, so that men who wished to hunt them dressed in women's clothes in order to get close enough to catch them. One story I particularly like relates to Skinningrove, a few miles to the north under the foot of Boulby Cliff, the highest sea-cliff in England. This story goes back to the 16th century, and is delightful as much for its language as for its content:

> Ould men, that would be loath to have theer credytes crackt by a tale of a stale date, reporte confidentlye that sixty yeares since, or perhaps eighty or more, a Sea man was taken by the fishers of that towne, whome duringe many weekes they kepte in an oulde house, giveing him rawe fishe to eate, for all other foode he refused. In steede of voyce, he skreaked, and shewed a curteous acceptance of such as flocked farre and neere to visyte him; fayre maydes were welcomest guestes to his harbour, whome he would behould with a very earneste countenance, as if his phlegmaticke breste had bin touched with a sparke of love. One daye, when the good demeanure of this newe gueste had made his hoastes secure of his aboade with theme, he privily stoale out of doores, and ere he could be overtaken recovered the sea, where into he plonged himself; yet, as one that would not unmanerly depart without takinge his leave, from his mydle upwards he raysed his shoulders often above the waves, and, makinge signes of acknowledging his good entertainment to such as beheld him on the shoare, as they interpreted yt, after a pretty while he dived downe and appeared no more.

Another story relates to the abbey bells. At the Dissolution, one version goes, the lead and bells of the abbey were removed and put into a ship for transport to London. This ship did not get very far with its sacrilegious load, for it struck the Black Nab at Saltwick and foundered. The other version says that it was a freebooter who heard the bells from out at sea and stole them, only to meet the same fate. Both versions agree that the bells remain there to this day and that they are still rung, by supernatural hands. Unfortunately for these picturesque ideas, it seems unlikely that the abbey had more than one bell; the central tower was a lantern, not a bell tower, and the only place for a bell was in one of the turrets. At the Dissolution it was most common for precious metals to be melted down into ingots on the site for ease of carriage, so it is unlikely that bells would be carried away complete.

FOLKLORE OF THE TOWN

Whitby's isolation led to a distinctive culture which in early days it probably shared with the moorland communities in its vicinity. As time went on, however, the town became rather more urbane and sophisticated, particularly from the mid-18th century, and had less in common with the villages.

A 'hob' was quite a common element of unhired help on a farm. Tradition is uncertain whether hobs, like fairies, were small or human-sized. However, it was not unusual for people to retire to bed having left certain jobs undone and to wake in the morning with the job completed by unseen hands. In such cases it was customary to repay the help with a jug of cream or the like. The hob, however, seems to have had a deep-rooted dislike of clothes and if some were left for him he would depart in a high dudgeon, never to work there again.

Worse was the hob who took a dislike to the farm people; such a one was the famous Hob of Farndale, who eventually drove the farm people to 'flit' (to move house) only to find that Hob was sitting on their possessions on the cart! Some hobs lived in caves, known as 'Hob-Holes'. The frequency of these around the district is a strong indication of the former large population of these creatures. Hob Thrush of Runswick lived in a cave on the beach, to which mothers brought children suffering from the whooping-cough. Their set phrase or charm was; 'Hob-hole Hob! My bairn's gotten t'kin cough: Tak't off – tak't off!'

Some customs no doubt died out before others. A belief in witchcraft, or at least uncertainty about denying its existence, prevailed at all levels of society in the early 17th century, led by no less an authority than the king himself – King James I. Dorothy Cooke of Whitby was accused in 1678 of bewitching a child to death, one of the few cases to come to the church courts, but that the prevailing belief was widespread is evident from the use of 'witch posts' in houses and from the large number of stories that have come down to us from that dark and fearful age.

'Witch posts' are timber posts usually supporting the smoke-hood of the fireplace in vernacular buildings. Near the top they have a carved cross and occasionally a date. No ancient name survives for them but it is believed that they are intended to keep witches at bay. One can be seen in a re-erected building from Rosedale at the Ryedale Folk Museum while another, detached, post from Egton is in Whitby Museum.

Numerous witches are known by name and by their area of activity. Probably these were crazed old women who from time to time responded to the taunts or blows of their neighbours by issuing curses. In the recent past there were very many diseases with a rapid onset and for which there was no known cure, so once in a while these curses may seem to have come true. It may be that these old women actually believed themselves to have powers, which could have been helpful in extracting bribes and 'protection money' from anxious neighbours.

An Aislaby butcher and grazier called Richard Wawne, who was in dispute with two local women, alleged that one of them had approached him when he was at Whitby market 'and bad [sic] an ill death light on him and his goods, cursing him with many such like expressions', immediately after which one of his already depleted herd of cattle died.

Although witchcraft was officially denied from the mid–18th century its powers were still seen as very real in country districts. A manuscript book kept by George Calvert of Kirkby Moorside in the early 19th century lists 21 witches of note at one time or another in different villages, and in the late 19th century Canon Atkinson was shown many houses in the Danby area in which witches had once lived.

Other anti-witch precautions included the use of rowan twigs and perforated stones which were hung inside stables and shippons. This, it was believed, would prevent witches from riding the horses (hence the description 'hag ridden') or ill-wishing the cows so that their milk dried up or would not turn into butter. Witches had the power of assuming the form of animals; hares seem to have been very popular. This made their nefarious activities around other people's houses less obvious. A fossil belemnite was a good alternative to a perforated stone, its projectile-like shape suggesting that it had been fired by some supernatural agency, which gave it potency.

A similar idea no doubt lay behind the prophylactic use of prehistoric flint arrowheads, found in large quantities on the Moors. Known as 'awf-shots', these were believed to have been fired at cattle by elves, causing them to gad or bolt. The sort of activity which we now know is caused by parasites was then put down to supernatural agencies. In order to counteract the effects, the cattle had to be made to drink water in which one of these arrowheads had been dipped.

Witches were not alone in creating the perplexities of life for poor country folk. The world was full of strange forces and sometimes in order to counteract them it was necessary to consult a 'white' witch or a wise man. Molly Milburn of Danby apparently worked for both sides. Whipped for afflicting a herd of cattle with the scab, she was also famous for her love charms worked on skin with a silk thread and for 'wonderful cures … never heard on afore her daye'.

Consultations with a white witch or wise man may have been quite a normal feature of rural life; after all there was almost nothing then of the panoply of state advice which exists today. Sometimes the consultation led to the purchase of a talisman, known as a 'sigill', a cast leaden object which would provide protection or good luck to the person who carried it. A curious splintwork charm in Whitby Museum may have been used as a wise man's candle-holder; its complexity, like so many other bits of paraphernalia, such as crystal balls and cabalistic writings, was intended to overawe the client.

Sometimes protection of a more practical variety would result. Wise men possessed a power over animals and particularly impressive was the use of an 'Irish Stick'. This was used to nullify the effect of the bite of an adder, by being drawn in a circle around the wound. Whitby Museum has one of these sticks, formerly used in Danbydale. Other such sticks had power over the snake itself; when a circle was drawn around the snake it was incapable of moving. One of the Lady Hilda's acts was to hurl the snakes which frequented her monastery site over the cliff and turn them into stone. Charlton records the story thus:

> ... the common people, ever since the time of Hilda, have believed that these [ammonites] were all originally real snakes, which abounded in the skroggs and rocks within the harbour ... when Hilda and her Nuns first came from Hartlepool to reside at Streanshalh, and that, being filled with terror thereat, she prayed to God that he would cause them all to crawl down over the cliff, and be converted into stones. Hence, on account of this supposed miracle, they are to this day vulgarly called St Hilda's stones, having the appearance of snakes rolled up in coils, but without their heads ...

St Hilda having thus removed their heads, the good people of Whitby obligingly carved heads back on many specimens, because they sold better to visitors.

Another of St Hilda's acts was to cause all geese which flew across the site of the monastery to fall down. This has been explained as seabirds diving over the cliffs to their nests, but this legend is not so ready of explanation as is the other one.

The only Roman road to come near Whitby also figures in local legend. 'Wade's Causeway', which crosses the Moors and is still spectacularly visible on Wheeldale Moor, is said to have been built by two giants, Wade and his wife Bell. Wade laid the causeway while his wife carried the stones. The same firm also built both Mulgrave and Pickering castles at the same time, but had only one hammer, which they threw to each other as required across the intervening miles. Bell carried stones in her apron and from time to time they spilled out, leaving the familiar cairns on the Moors. Wade is said to be buried either at East Barnby or Goldsborough, both of which have a 'Wade's Stone' to mark the site of his grave.

Certainly the most unusual of Whitby's customs is that of the Horngarth or 'Penny Hedge'. This is a structure of twigs, erected on the foreshore of the Upper Harbour in the area known as Abraham's Bosom, on the morning of the Eve of Ascension Day. It is supposed to be able to withstand the force of three tides. When the Penny Hedge has been completed, a horn is blown and one of the participants shouts the traditional cry: 'Out on you! Out on you! Out on you!'

Though there have been gaps in its performance, when the tides were wrong or when the day clashed with the feast of St John of Beverley, the ceremony has been maintained for many centuries, and seems to have originated in the 12th century or before. Although unusual it represents a form of service for tenure of lands. The lands in question were in Dunsley, Sneaton, Ugglebarnby and Ruswarp, amongst others. Most of the tenants bought out the right centuries ago, but the

Allatson's former property of Harton House Farm remains the object of the service for their successors. In 1981 it was announced that the ceremony would no longer be performed, but after public pressure it was reinstituted in the following year!

A picturesque story once popular told of how three gentlemen hunting a wild boar in Eskdale had chased it as far as the hermitage which stood there. The hermit allowed the boar in but the hounds were kept outside. In their rage at being baulked of their prey the huntsmen killed the hermit and ever after they and their successors had to perform the ceremony of the Penny Hedge as a penance. The names and details of the story do not square with known historical facts and it seems most likely that the story was made up later to explain the ceremony. The Penny Hedge has no practical use and does not seem to have had one for many centuries; attempts to explain it away as a sort of deer fence do not seem to have any merit.

Many of Whitby's other customs and delicacies are concerned with the calendar, a succession of festivals and saints' days each with their own special customs helping to break the monotony of unremitting work and a sparse diet.

GHOSTS AND SPECTRES

It is no wonder that a town with as much individual character and atmosphere as Whitby should have acquired such a motley assemblage of ghosts and spectres. The hard lives and the untimely deaths of so many of its inhabitants in the past form a perfect compost in which to grow legends and tall stories.

We have seen to what extent the Lady Hilda has entered into the folklore of the town. In the 18th century she was even believed to appear at a certain time of the year in one of the upper windows of the abbey. Unfortunately it is the wrong abbey, the one St Hilda knew now lying many feet underground. Charlton recorded the story first:

> At a particular time of the year (namely in the summer months) at ten or eleven in the forenoon, the sunbeams fall in the inside of the northern part of the choir, and 'tis then that the spectators, who stand on the west side of Whitby Churchyard, so as just to see the north side of the abbey past the north end of Whitby Church, imagine they perceive, in one of the highest windows there, the resemblance of a woman dressed in a shroud. Though we are certain this is only a reflection caused by the splendour of the sunbeams, yet fame reports it, and it is constantly believed among the vulgar to be the appearance of the Lady Hilda in her shroud, or rather in a glorified state.

I have sought in vain to see this vision. Perhaps it is the ambiguity of the instructions or perhaps, as English suggests, that the fall of the tower and other parts of the structure since Charlton wrote, have altered the play of light on the ruins and robbed us of this spectacle.

Shaw Jeffrey enumerates several ghosts of a more conventional kind, if any ghost can be said to be conventional. One of these, who carries his head under his arm, haunts Fitz Steps between Prospect Hill and Ruswarp. His name is not recorded, nor anything of his story. The path is an ancient pannier track and the steps lead down on to the Fitts (hence the name) where the river ran before the railway came. It has no atmosphere of evil today, but then I should not like to walk it alone at night!

Another haunted path was that through the woods from Hawsker to Cock Mill, where a clapping gate hung at the point where it opened on to the Rigg. This gate clapped to-and-fro, swung by ghostly hands. Cock Mill itself had an evil reputation, perhaps deliberately put about at the time of the French Wars to keep the press gang at bay. These woods are said to have provided sanctuary for returning seamen who wanted to avoid impressment.

Several houses in the town had the reputation of being haunted. One, on a site opposite the present Roman Catholic church at the end of Baxtergate, was pulled down and its stone and details used to build a row of smaller houses. The reason was that great crowds of people gathered in gardens opposite to watch the activities of a ghost which moved around the upper floors at night, to a point where life became intolerable for the occupants. Young records of another house in Baxtergate that it had 'stood long empty, as it had obtained the character of being visited by ghosts; it is now frequented by spirits of another kind, having been converted into an inn.'

It has been claimed that the building in question is *The Olde Ship Launch*, more recently the *Old Smugglers*, but on no very clear grounds.

Whitby has its full complement of ghostly hearses and mourning coaches which appear to the living, according to the *Whitby Repository* of 1828. The same magazine records a local belief in 1831 that:

> ... whenever a seaman of Whitby is buried, on the night following the funeral a bargheist coach, drawn by six coal-black horses, with two out-riders clad in black, and sometimes bearing blazing torches ... and sometimes without either driver or horses, starts from a particular part of Green Lane ... till it reaches the Churchyard, where it stops. A long train of mourners encircle the grave thrice, and then, re-entering the coach, accompanied by the recent dead, they drive thundering and rattling down the Church steps, along Haggerlyth, and, plunging headlong over the cliff, are lost to view ...

It seems that the poor seamen of Whitby thus gained the grandiose funeral, albeit in reverse order, which they had been denied by poverty. The word 'bargheist' and its variants are widely used in the area for anything supernatural. All the details agree with what we shall see were the customs of gentry funerals in the previous century; perhaps the people who had witnessed these were so impressed by their awful solemnity that they took the description into their own folklore.

Wafts were regarded as even more awful and frightening. A 'waft' was a doppelganger or double. To meet your own waft was a sure sign of impending death. The only course of action open to one, as Norway points out in a story of a Guisborough man visiting Whitby, is to address it boldly: 'What's thou doing here? Thou's after no good, I'll go bail. Get thy ways yom wi' thee, get thy ways yom'.

This form of address seems to have been effective, so if you should meet your own double in the streets of Whitby, you will know what to do.

Another custom which could lead to an unwelcome encounter of the spiritual kind was that of watching in the porch of the parish church on St Mark's Eve (24 April). It was believed that on this night the spectres of all those that were going to be buried in the churchyard that year would pass through the porch! History does not relate what was the correct thing to do in these circumstances if you saw your own spectre.

This seems once to have been a widespread belief, and Atkinson refers to an old woman of Fryup in the late 19th century whose claim to fame was that she still maintained the 'Mark's e'en watch' and so had foreknowledge of the deaths that would occur in the next year. It was common knowledge that once one began the vigil it was impossible ever to stop. In 1817 Young had not heard of any spectres actually seen in Whitby church, but it was the old Norman porch, however, to which the belief related, not the present one, and it had been removed before Young's day. This may explain the lack of sightings and, perhaps, some confusion on the part of the spectres.

FUNERALS

Death today has attracted many of the taboos which used to surround sex, and we have what seems a natural reluctance to discuss or even consider the subject. Not so our ancestors, for whom death was ever-present, with high infant mortality and a host of ailments which could be fatal, now banished by greater medical knowledge.

As a consequence death was talked about and funerals were a social occasion for the whole community. Fear of death was no less, however, and many customs were symbolic and prophylactic, designed to protect the living or to ease the future lot of the dead person. Whitby was no exception and, as in so many other ways, its isolation led to very distinctive customs.

It was fashionable in the 18th century for gentry to be buried at night. General Peregrine Lascelles, who died in March 1772, was buried by torchlight, and this was also customary for members of the Cholmley family. No doubt the combination of torches, black drapes, black horses and black-clad mourners was highly theatrical. By the early 19th century the fashion had changed; genteel people were now buried in the morning, the pall-bearers having black gloves and silk scarves if the deceased were married, white if unmarried. Female relations did not attend.

At most funerals, however, between two and four women called servers handed out wine and sugar-biscuits before the procession moved off, and then walked before it, dressed in white, with white ribbon breast-knots.

The biscuits may have taken the place of small loaves which had been handed out to mourners in previous generations. Many bakers had a regular trade in funeral biscuits. According to a correspondent to the *Gentleman's Magazine* in 1802 the mourners ate Savoy biscuits and received a paper packet containing two long Naples biscuits to take home to their families. These were in packets printed with the name of the supplier and bearing motifs such as coffins, cross-bones and hour-glasses, but later they were simply wrapped in writing paper.

Of course not all funerals were as elaborate as this, but fashions tended to percolate down the social scale and the gentry's customs of one generation became poorer people's customs of the next. Funerals, like weddings, were not stinted.

Grand funerals made use of hearses and processions of carriages. Green Lane was once known as 'the hearse road' because it was the most gradual approach to the churchyard. Many people were carried by their friends up the church stairs. This is probably why there are a series of level areas at intervals, to allow the coffin to be rested. Men carried men and women carried women, though it is possible that they did not carry the coffin the whole way. At Goathland the custom persisted until 1915, but women only took over at the church gates. The coffin was carried on crossed sticks or by folded towels passed underneath and through the handles.

Young records another custom, nearly obsolete by his day. At the funerals of unmarried women a garland of two hoops containing cut paper flowers and a paper glove with the name and age of the deceased was carried before the coffin and later hung up from the church roof. This custom was once widespread and a few such 'maiden's garlands' survive, notably a series of five from Fylingdales Old Church at Robin Hood's Bay. These include one which had ribbons attached, each one originally held by one of the friends of Jenny Keld who died about 1838, and a very elaborate example carried at the funeral of Janey Levitt in 1859. The custom is clearly a very old one.

So many customs have passed away unrecorded and with no artefactual evidence left to reconstruct them by. Before the 19th century many people were buried without coffins or grave-markers, which were too expensive. Charlton records the custom of reusing gravestones from the Abbey for burials in the churchyard up to the early 18th century, a custom stopped by the incumbent in 1736, to make sure he gained his fee, by the simple expedient of having likely stones broken up! Poor people were buried in shrouds alone, and could not expect to lie undisturbed. Graves in the churchyard were very shallow and, without markers, would be dug over again for new occupants within a few years. Consequently the churchyard became very full and a cemetery was provided at Larpool in 1862 as part of the new Victorian regime of public health, the only burials henceforth allowed in the old churchyard being those in existing vaults.

A belief long current in the north of England and recorded in Cleveland in Elizabethan times was that after death a person must make a journey barefoot across a moor covered with thorns and furze, and that if they had in life given a poor man a pair of shoes these would be given back to them for their own journey. Immediately relevant to people who lived in the shadow of the North York Moors, this idea is still preserved in the song known as the 'Lyke Wake Dirge'.

Many Whitby men have no known graves, having been lost at sea. One sailor, however, who died at the Greenland whale fishery, had his body brought back to Whitby for burial, his coffin slung in the rigging of the whaler for many weeks.

'VESSEL-CUPS'

One odd survival of an old custom in Whitby was that of 'vessel-cup'. As late as the 1940s and for 30 years before that Miss Dora Palmer of Whitby used to travel the coast from Skinningrove to Robin Hood's Bay at Christmas time. Singing the 'vessel-cup' song she carried and showed a box containing a doll representing the Christ child, decorated with sprigs of box and sometimes fruit.

Percy Shaw Jeffrey records the tradition at the beginning of the century. Carol singers would go around in the two or three weeks before Christmas with a small box containing a wax figure of the Christ child, surrounded with green sprigs of box; recognisably the same as Dora Palmer's. They would sing 'God rest ye, merry gentlemen' and, in order to acquire good luck for the house in the New Year, they must be invited to cross the threshold.

In 1811 the *Gentleman's Magazine* reviewed methods of celebrating Christmas in the North Riding of Yorkshire:

> … it is customary for a party of singers, mostly consisting of women, to begin, at the feast of St Martin, a kind of peregrination round the neighbouring villages, carrying with them a small waxen image of our Saviour adorned with box and other evergreens, and singing at the same time a hymn, which though rustic and uncouth, is nevertheless, replete with the sacred story of the Nativity. This custom is yearly continued till Christmas eve, when their feasting, or, as they usually call it 'good living' commences …

'These choristers', says Young, speaking of the early 19th century, 'are almost all of the very lowest dregs of the populace, depraved and ignorant …'!

The symbolism is a little confused; the box and doll appears to be very like a number of Catholic reliquaries in which relics of saints were preserved and shown as a mark of favour. On the other hand the 'vessel-cup' element sounds rather like a confusion with the New Year Wassail tradition, which has very little to do with Christianity. Miss Palmer was undoubtedly at the end of a very long tradition. Her box can still be seen; it is in the Museum of Childhood in Edinburgh.

There were many other customs associated with Christmas. In terms of food the most important items were Yule cakes, frumity and gingerbread. We will take a closer look at Whitby gingerbread later. Yule cakes were rich fruit cakes. In Whitby they were rectangular in shape and marked into squares so that they could be broken up into portions. Frumity, which was a glutinous dish made with creed wheat, milk and spices, was traditionally associated with Christmas Day itself. Young records that in his time over twelve tons of creed wheat was sold in Whitby market for the purpose.

119 *View from near the top of the famous '199 Steps' or 'Church Stairs', looking down towards the harbour. There are many records of repairs to these steps over the centuries and they have gradually been increased in number to their present total. Level platforms at intervals are probably for resting the coffin in the days when people were carried by hand to the grave by their friends and family. The earliest view of the steps, at that time of wood rather than stone, is in a naive painting of 1717, in Whitby Museum.*

Goose pies were made on St Stephen's Day (26 December) and given to needy neighbours by those who could afford it. The same day was also the traditional one for the sword dancers to perform, while the Plough-Stots performed on Plough Monday, the first Monday of the New Year.

At New Year it was the custom as it was generally in the north of England for the first person to cross the threshold to be a dark-haired man, often known as the 'Lucky Bird', otherwise bad luck would follow. This custom, known as 'first footing', I heartily recommend, having practised it for many years with satisfactory results.

LOCAL DELICACIES

We have already come across a number of local foodstuffs still made in the traditional way, such as kippers. Many special foods were served on particular days or at particular seasons. Several other delicacies survive from the Victorian – or is it specifically Yorkshire? – high tea, a custom which was perpetuated by hotels and guesthouses and by older people into the 1960s and 1970s. The fragility of food customs is illustrated by the disappearance of several items mentioned below in the years between editions of this book.

Kippers were certainly being produced from the 1830s in the kipper-houses at Tate Hill and later by Fortune's of Henrietta Street, who still prepare them in the traditional way. Other fish and crustacea have been sold for centuries fresh from the sea on the fish quay. Today most are sold to wholesalers but many proprietors of eating-houses and guesthouses used to buy direct from the fishermen, the remainder of the catch being sent inland, at first by pack ponies and later by railway. In Whitby cockles and mussels tend to be regarded as bait for long lines, rather than as something to eat.

At Easter special biscuits were made on a Good Friday as late as the 1870s, perforated so that they could be strung from the ceiling for future eating. On Easter Sunday there were custards to be eaten or, as we would now describe them, custard tarts. Such seasonal dishes eased the monotony of the diet and even in the poorest households there would be some attempt to follow the custom.

There were once many bakers and confectioners who supplied these traditional foods as well as pastries and cakes of a sort which were widely available in the 19th and early 20th centuries. In 1921 you would have had the choice of Edwards' Café Restaurant at 3 St Ann's Staith, James' at 2 St Ann's Staith or 10 Skinner Street, or E. Botham & Sons at 35-7 Skinner Street and 64 Baxtergate. Some of these were on old-established sites where bakers and confectioners had long traded, even if some of the names were new. I am tempted to speculate that two bakeries on St Ann's Staith may have begun as bakers of ship's biscuits.

The traditional element of these bakers was that apart from using the best ingredients they made a range of cakes and fancies with names which have now passed out of common use. Only at shops such as Botham's can you still find Japs, Turks, Ethels, Russian Slice and Ceylons, and even these seem to be slowly disappearing before an onslaught of cream cakes, more tempting to early 21st-century visitors.

As I have suggested before, these delicacies may have survived because of the serving of high teas by many hotels and guesthouses. This may also account for the taste for pork products such as ham and pork pies. It is only in recent years that Botham's have switched production of the latter from mid-afternoon to morning. Another delicious pork item was once produced by the old-established firm of Johnson's in Church Street. This was Best (or Smoked) Polony, a sort of thick sausage, eaten cold. Smoked food is an important tradition of the North East, a tradition shared with north Germany and Scandinavia.

If anyone wonders why I have spent so much time on food my rejoinder is that of all traditions food is one of the most distinctive, but also one of the most transitory. All over the world local delicacies are either being homogenised for international sale or disappearing without trace. It would repay us to record them before they are altogether lost. The fragility of food customs is illustrated by the disappearance of several of the items mentioned in the ten or so years since the first edition of this book.

GINGERBREAD

Whitby gingerbread was once famous but is now only a memory. It was of the firm kind, made of a stiff dough with ginger, coriander, treacle and peel, often impressed into wooden moulds in order to create a pattern or a picture on the surface.

Young describes Whitby gingerbread as being a Christmas dish, or one for women after childbirth, when it was eaten with cheese. Over twelve tons of it were sold each year in Whitby in his day. At an earlier time it may have been imported from London by sea, perhaps because of the availability of spices there.

Although some writers regard 'peppercakes' as being the same thing under another name, the recipe for these includes Jamaica pepper and the mixture was raised with yeast.

Ditchburns made gingerbread at their shop in Church Street from about 1868 until 1952 while in 1895 both Foster & Wright of St Ann's Staith and Beilby & Edwards next door to them offered 'noted Whitby Gingerbread' for sale.

120 *Advertisement of 1895 by one of the makers of Whitby gingerbread.*

There are no less than 14 gingerbread moulds on display in Whitby Museum. Some are of the 17th or early 18th centuries, judging by the designs or the costume depicted, and several others are dated 1876. Names carved into the moulds include Hebden and Doran, perhaps indicating the suppliers. A different and still dry kind of gingerbread, but more cake-like in consistency, is made by Bothams and travels widely, partly because it has good keeping characteristics.

QUOITS

The game of quoits is now limited to a few villages in Eskdale, but was once both more popular and more widespread. Indeed it was played throughout the Yorkshire Dales. A visitor to the hamlet of Beckhole will see on one of the very few level areas of grass a series of wooden covers protecting the quoits 'boxes'. This distinctive game has its own league, with matches in May, June and July.

A quoit is an iron ring weighing 5¼ lbs. with one side bevelled and one flat. At one time lads were taught to use quoits made from two horse-shoes fastened together by the blacksmith, graduating later to the real thing. It is thrown so as to land on or near the 'hob' or iron pin set in clay inside a wooden breastwork or 'box'. The distance from hob to hob is 11 yards.

Play is complex and skilful, with names for the various throws such as those where the quoit lands over the hob – a 'ringer' – or where it lands propped up against the hob so as to deny a ringer to an opponent – a 'gater'. Each game is a knock-out between two competitors, whose aim is to get their quoits either over the hob or nearer to it than their competitor. With several pitches a number of games can proceed simultaneously.

The iron pin or hob is set in a clay base. Quoits teams will go to great lengths to fetch the clay from the traditional spot on the Moors where it is believed to have the correct consistency.

In the 1850s a team was made up of 12 members, but the teams have decreased in size over the years, probably with the falling numbers of young people in the villages.

Simpler forms of this game were played on farms along with merrills and more conventional games, mostly distinguished by needing little in the way of equipment and capable of being played in snatched minutes of rest from the daily round of work. The complexities seem to have been introduced as a result of competitive play.

Quoits is now a village game but it was also played in Whitby. There was a quoits ground on the West Cliff, behind the Waterloo cinema. A photograph reproduced in the *Whitby Gazette* shows quoits players of the 1920s, probably at a league fixture. According to F.K. Robinson, a Quoits Club was formed in Whitby as early as 1851, with 50 members.

SWORD DANCES

The sword dance is one of a number of customs associated with the season of Christmas. It is a very ancient custom and seems during its history to have become intermingled with other customs such as the mummers' play and the plough-stots.

Young describes such events in 1817. On Plough Monday a company of young men fantastically dressed would drag a plough around the area while another six of their number would perform the sword dance. Meanwhile another group, dressed in women's clothing and called 'Madgies' or 'Madgy Pegs' (dialect words for magpies) would descend on the houses round about to beg for money. Sometimes instead of the straight sword dance a number of actors would be introduced, playing the parts of the king, the miller, the clown and the doctor. This is clearly borrowed from the mummers' and Pace-Eggers' plays. Even in Young's day the home of sword dancing was Egton Bridge.

An account of 1811 places the proper date of performing the sword dance as St Stephen's Day (Boxing Day):

> On the feast of St Stephen six youths (called sword dancers from their dancing with swords), clad in white and bedecked with ribbands, attended by a fiddler, and another youth curiously dressed, who generally has the name of Bessy, and also by one who impersonates a Doctor, begin to travel from village to village performing a rude dance called the sword dance. One of the six above mentioned acts the part of king in a kind of farce, which consists of singing and dancing, when the Bessy interferes while they are making a hexagon with their swords and is killed. These frolicks they continue till New Year's Day, when they spend their gains at the ale-house with the greatest innocence and mirth, having invited all their rustic acquaintance.

The actual dance varies. It usually consists of a circular dance to begin with, the movements increasing in complexity with the swords held together or overhead, the climax being when the swords are interwoven into a hexagon and brandished overhead by one of the dancers, the 'king', usually chosen as being the tallest or the leader of the troupe. Despite the name the swords are made with a parallel-sided blunt blade, no guard and a plain wooden handle.

Goathland was latterly the main centre for sword dancing but in recent year the Sleights sword dance has been revived and is used by a number of groups. At the Whitby Folk Week each year there are usually some sword dancers to be seen. The sword dance seems to be the northern equivalent of the morris, though distinctions and boundaries have become blurred during the revival of both.

Originally the purpose of these dances was three-fold; to entertain country people at a quiet time in the farming year, as an entertainment for and by the youth of the area, and as a means of raising a little cash for food and drink at a feast which formed the culmination of the performances. It is recorded that the Goathland troupe once marched across the moors to Whitby, preceded by a brass band and led by their 'king' on horseback, the whole company numbering one hundred!

PLOUGH-STOTS

The best known of the 'plough-stots' (are they the only surviving group?) are those from Goathland. They may, however, be taken as typical of many unorganised or semi-organised groups of young men who went around the district at the beginning of the New Year before the farming year restarted in earnest. As such they belong firmly to an agricultural tradition dependent on labour-intensive farming, which has died out in the 20th century.

As we have seen, the plough-stots were usually part of a larger group including sword dancers and players and probably represented the younger unattached men of the countryside, who mostly worked on the land. The season of Christmas and New Year gave them some leisure for these activities and some licence for begging money with a little good-natured menace. Those who did not pay up could find a furrow ploughed across their lawn or garden by the ploughmen, while the occasion was made an excuse for the teasing and kissing of the womenfolk, particularly by the 'Madgy Pegs', sometimes also known as 'Toms', who could make quite a nuisance of themselves.

In 1923, as Shaw Jeffrey tells us, the Goathland troupe engaged to perform at practically every house in the parish, no mean effort. Often the week or fortnight after Plough Monday would involve the troupe in entertaining further afield, including Whitby and Scarborough. Undoubtedly this increased their 'take' very considerably. As Brears has pointed out, such performances were a sort of formalised begging; as poverty reduced so did the customs of this type, except where they were deliberately preserved as a 'colourful' custom, the money collected now going to charity.

NOTES

In these notes books and articles are listed by author and date which can then be located in the Bibliography

Chapter 1
DOMESDAY:
Morgan, 1986
Darby & Maxwell, 1962, 101, 105, 126,
 135-6, 138
Kendall, 1932, 43
Smith, 1928

CHARTERS AND BURGAGES:
Beresford & Finberg, 1973, 189
Young, 1817
Atkinson, 1894

PARLIAMENTARY REPRESENTATION:
Young, 1840, 214-16
Robinson, 1860, 116, 320
Brears, 1987, 155
Lit. & Phil. Soc. Annual Report,
 2000, 11

**DEVELOPMENT OF THE STREET
 PATTERN:**
Gaskin, 1909, 100
Daysh, 1958, 51-77
Kendall, 1948
Charlton, 1779, 349

BUILDINGS OF THE OLD TOWN:
DoE List, 1972
N. Yorks Vernacular Archaeology Grp.,
 1993, 4-5
Whitby Gazette 22/4/94
Daysh, 1958, 51-77
Clifton-Taylor, 1984, 44-75

GEORGIAN GROWTH:
Pevsner, 1966, 395-400
White, 1995, *passim*
Clifton-Taylor, 1984, 44-75
Girouard, 1990, 110
Shaw Jeffrey, 3rd edn., 1952, 136
Wood's Map, 1828
Davidson, 1985, 171
Dunbar (ed.), 1997, 40-2
English, 1931
Cruickshank, 1985, 253-4
Daysh, 1958, 59-66

THE WEST CLIFF:
Wood's map, 1828
White, 1998, 78-93

Peacock, nd., 463-6
English, 1931
WG 21/8/87
Clifton-Taylor, 1984, 70-1
Pevsner, 1966, 398-9
ILN, 1852
Fawcett, 2011
Whitby Magazine, 1827, 306-9
Kendall, nd., 18-19

POPULATION:
Young, 1817, 515-16
Robinson, 1860, 116

YARDS, COURTS AND STEPS:
Kendall, 1948
Gaskin & Stamp, 1990
Harston, 1989
Rodway, nd.
Pile, 1979

THE PARISH CHURCH:
Woodwark, 1923
Gaskin, 1909, 370-3
Pevsner, 1966, 395
Clifton-Taylor, 1984, 48-52
Charlton, 1779, 344ff
White, 1990, 46-50
Gent, 1735, 52

OTHER CHURCHES:
English, 1931
Young, 1840
Young, 1817
Pevsner, 1966, 395-6
DoE List, 1972
Wesley, Journal, 1788
Stell, 1994, 223-4
Woodwark, nd.
White, 1998, 91

COMMERCE AND TRADE:
English, 1931
Raistrick, 1968, 326
Williamson, repr. 1967, 1344
Baines, 1823, 571-84
Rodway, nd.
Whelan, 1999, 100-3

EDUCATION:
Whitworth, 1991, 12-13, 37-8

Emmison, 1974, 76 & Pl.5b
Baines, 1823, 571-84
Young, 1817
Young, 1840
PO Directory, 1879
WG, 'Memory Lane' features
Official Guide, 1938

HEALTH CARE:
Post-Medieval Archaeology, 2003, 290
English, 1931
Wood's Map, 1828
Anon., 1897, 759-60
Rules of the Public Dispensary, 1787
Lit. & Phil. Soc. Annual Report, 2000,
 27-33
WG 16/9/77
WG 19/10/79

BOMBARDMENT!:
Mould, 1978
Shaw Jeffrey, 1923, 117-21
WG 18/12/1914
Marsay, 1999, 343-66

Chapter 2
**DEVELOPMENT OF THE HARBOUR
 AND PIERS:**
English, 1931
East, 1932, 484-97
Pickernell's Plan, 1796
Wood's Map, 1828
Pickernell's Map, 1841
Head, 1836, 279-80
Young, 1817
Young, 1840
Colvin, 1978, 634
WG 28/12/1861
WG 14/7/1944
Wooler's chart, 1740
Daysh, 1958, 247-51
East, 1932, 484-91

ENCROACHMENT ON THE HARBOUR:
Wood's Map, 1828
Pickernell's Map, 1841
Farmer, 1976, 7-10
Ayers, 1979
WG 21/5/1993, 31/12/1993
Daysh, 1958, 252

THE BRIDGE:
VCH Yorks. NR, 2, 1968, 511
Gaskin, 1909, 342-57
Northern Archaeological Associates
    excavations on behalf of Yorkshire
    Water plc, leaflet c.1999
Whitby Magazine, 1827, 363
Whitby Lit. & Phil. Ann. Rep., 1987,
    16
English, 1931
Young, 1840, 179, 180-1
Jervois, 1931, 64-5

Chapter 3
SITE OF THE EARLY MONASTERY:
Gelling, 1978, 189
Ekwall, 1960
HE, III, 24
Haverfield, 1912, 201-14
Collingwood & Wright, 1965, no.721

ROMAN ANTECEDENTS?:
Shaw Jeffrey, 1952, 17
Daysh, 1958, 54
Rigold, 1977, 70-5
Bell, 1998

EXCAVATIONS:
Peers & Radford, 1943, 27-88
Wilson, 1976, 223-9
Thomas, 1971, 42
Cramp, 1973, 112-4
Daniels, 1988, 158-210
Cramp, 1969, 21-66
HE, IV, 25
Johnson, 1993
Med. Arch., 39, 1995, 261
English Heritage Website, 2001
WG, 7/1/2000, 26/1/2001
Lit. & Phil. Ann. Rep., 2002, 56-7

THE NATURE OF THE MONASTERY:
Wilson, 1976, 228

ARCHAEOLOGICAL FINDS:
Peers & Radford, 1943, 33-4
Backhouse, 1981, 31, Pl.18
Peers & Radford, 1943, Figs. 21, 12.8
Rahtz, 1967, 72
Rahtz, 1962, 605-18
Wilson, 1964, 192-201
Lit. & Phil. Ann. Rep., 2002, 4-5

FINDS FROM BLACK HORSE YARD:
Haigh, 1875, 370
White, 1984, 33-40
White, 1988, 212-13
Battiscombe, 1956, 336-55

BEDE AND HIS HISTORY:
The Foundation:
HE, III, 24

The Synod of Whitby:
HE, III, 25
Higham, 1986, 288-9

St Hilda:
HE, III, 24

HE, IV, 23
Collingwood, 1927, 59ff

St Cuthbert; Caedmon:
Stenton, 1971, 148
Bede, Vita S.Cuth. in Farmer 1983, 34
HE, IV, 24

THE END OF THE MONASTERY:
Blair, 1959, 6
Wilson, 1976, 223
Atkinson, 1877
Simeon of Durham, LVI

Chapter 4
REFOUNDATION BY THE NORMANS:
Atkinson, 1878
Kendall, 1932, 39-48
Simeon of Durham, 1.111, 2.201-2

HISTORY OF THE ABBEY:
Kendall, 1932
Young, 1817
Clapham, 1952
Platt, 1985
L&P, Hen.VIII, 14, 576
Cal. Pat. R. 1555, 2, 257-8
L&P, Hen.VIII, 14, 683

THE ABBEY LANDS:
Atkinson, 1878, 1879
Platt, 1969, 243-4
Waites, 1961, 483-7
Waites, 1967
Le Patourel, 1973

RELATIONSHIP WITH THE TOWN:
Kendall, 1932
Young, 1817
VCH, 2, 504

THE ABBOT'S BOOK:
Atkinson, 1878
Young, 1817
Whitby Lit. & Phil. Ann. Rep. 1975

THE ABBEY BUILDINGS:
Kendall, 1932
Atkinson, 1894, 300-6
Platt, 1984, 85-6
Platt, 1985
Coppack, 1990, 41-3
Clapham, 1952

THE DECAY OF THE ABBEY:
Coppack, 1990, 142-5
Hall, 1979, 326
English, 1931
Samuel Buck's Yorkshire Sketchbook,
    1979, 326
Whitby Repository, 1832, 223
Gibson, 1792, 124
Sharpe, 1868, 94

EXCAVATION AND RESTORATION:
Gents' Mag., 1841, 87
Hood, 1950
Kendall, 1932
Coppack, 1990, 142-5
Peers & Radford, 1943, 27-88

Chapter 5
SHIPBUILDING:
Borthwick Inst., Will of Benjamin
    Coates,
Cleveland D., Mar., 1757.
Weatherill, 1908, 25-30
Young, 1817, 548-55, 600
WG files

SHIPBUILDERS:
Gaskin, 1909, 232
MacGregor, 1985, 14-22
Rodway, nd.
Stamp, 1981
Tindale, 1987, 16
Vickers, 1986, 77
Weatherill, 1908, 25-30
Whitby Magazine, 1829, 25 Jul
Will of James Moore of Lancaster,
    Lancaster City Museums
Young, 1817, 548-55, 600
Young, 1840, 204
Whitby Parish Registers
    (transcripts in Lit. & Phil. Soc. library)

PORT TRADES:
Baines, 1823
Young, 1824, 202
Young, 1817, 555-7
Lit. & Phil. Ann. Rep., 1993, 12-16
Weatherill, 1908, 27
Finch, 1976, 16
Wooler's Chart, 1740
Miller (ed.), 2002, 89-95
Northern Archaeology Associates
    leaflet c.1999
OS 60-inch map, 1852
Charlton, 1779, 366

NOTABLE WHITBY SHIPS:
MacGregor, 1985, 131
Weatherill, 1908, *passim*
WG files
Bagshawe, 1933, 1-8
Nelson, 1936, 113-18
Stammers, 1984, 304-6
WG, 29/7/1994
Baines, 2010
Ossowski, 2008

THE SHIPPING TRADE:
Morrison, 1981
Weatherill, 1908, 104
Finch, 1973
Davis, 1962, 33-5
Hughes, 1952, 201-5
East, 1932
Defoe, 1971, 532
Humble, 1972, 20-7
MacGregor, 1985, 21
Bateson, 1959, 289-325

SEAMEN & SEAMANSHIP:
Vickers, 1986, 72-3
Clowes, 1898, III, 63
Willan, 1938, 18-19
Letters of G. S. Willis, author's
    possession
Barrow, 2001, 59

EVIDENCE:
Ward Jackson, 1978, *passim*
Russett, 1996
Buchanan,1950
Credland, 1987
White, 1990, 46-50
MacGregor, 1985, 127, 168-9
MacGregor, 1984, Figs. 64-5

LIFEBOATS:
Humble, 1974
Weatherill, 1908, 402-3
Tindale, 1987, 52-67
Morris, 1989
Wilson, 1981

Chapter 6
TRADITIONS; COBLES & MULES;
    LONGLINING; HERRING:
Finch, 1976, 84-5
Miller (ed.), 2002, 89-91
March, 1973, 103ff
Archaeologia, 41, 1866, 369
Marshall & Sparham, 1987, 173-8
Simper, 1984, 33, 52
Tindale, 1987, 34ff, 79-95
Young, 1817, 820ff

KIPPERING; DEEP SEA FISHING;
    FISHMARKETS & QUAYS:
Robinson, 1989, 222-3
Brears, 1987, 114-15
Davidson, 1985, Pl.64
Daysh, 1958, 249-51
Gaskin, 1909, 205-16
Tindale, 1987, 93-5
Young, 1817, 575-6, 820ff
Young, 1840, 200

VESSELS; FISHING TODAY:
Daysh, 1958, 120-8, 251-3
Finch, 1976, 86-7
Tindale, 1987, 104-14
Walker, 1973
Wilson, 1998

Chapter 7
INTRODUCTION:
Daysh, 1958, 57-8
Raistrick, 1973, 214-15
Young, 1817, 806-19
Young, 1840, 201-6, 217-22
Binns, 1994, 86-104

JET:
Coates, 1983
Elgee, 1930, 108-19
Allason-Jones, 1996
Kendall, 1936
Muller, 1980
McMillan, 1992
Peers & Radford, 1943,
    Figs. 19, 24
Head, 1836, 288
White, 1858, 130-3, 152

ALUM:
Charlton, 1779, 359
Miller (ed.), 2002
Atkinson, 1974, 313, 319

Egan, 1989, 58-60
Marshall, 1991
Marshall, 1994
Morrison, 1981
Raistrick, 1973, 62-4, 214-15
Atkinson, 1974, 313, 319
Turton, 1938
Willan, 1938, 112-13, 118, 160
Head, 1836, 283-6
White, 1858, 137-46
Walker, 1814, Pl.XXXIV

ROMAN CEMENT:
Daysh, 1958, 17
Head, 1836, 286-7
Tindale, 1990, 20-2

IRONSTONE:
Atkinson, 1974, 325
Clarke & Soulsby, 1975
Counsell, 1981
Daysh, 1958, 12-13
Young, 1840, 221-2

BUILDING STONE:
Clifton-Taylor & Ireson, 1983, 34-5
Clifton-Taylor, 1984, 45-75
Daysh, 1958, 18, 20, 24
English, 1931

WHALING:
English, 1931
Dykes, 1980
Jackson, 1978, 11, 82
Barrow, 2001
Lidster, 1985
Lubbock, 1937
Barrow, 2001, 40
Stamp & Stamp, 1975
Walker, 1814, Pl.XVIII
Whitby Magazine, 1827, 380

TRANSPORT:
Baines, 1823
Bairstow, 1989
Belcher, 1836
Bowen, 1720
Cary, 1798
Vale, 1960, 54-5, 214-15
Breakell, 1982
White, 2006, 40–1
Hayes, 1988
Joy, 1969
Lidster, 1977
Lidster, 1983
Bell, 2008
White & White, 2017
Potter, 1906
Belcher, 1843
Shaw Jeffrey, 1952, 8-9
Young, 1817, 579-80
Daysh, 1958, 207-17

Chapter 8
EARLY VISITORS:
Atkinson, 1885, 174-5
Gaskin, 1909, 439-45
Whitworth, 1991
Shaw Jeffrey, 1919, 14-16
Charlton, 1779, 353ff

UBD, 1798, 738
Lit. & Phil. Ann. Rep. 2003, 26-7

NINETEENTHTH-CENTURY GROWTH:
Peacock, nd., 463-6
WG, 6/7/1854
ILN, 1852
Kendall, nd., 16
Whellan, 1859, 285-6

WEST CLIFF & CRESCENT:
Whitworth, 1991, 35-45
Shaw Jeffrey, 1952, 113-18
Peacock, nd., 463-6
Robinson, 1860, 207-8

ENTERTAINMENT:
WG 'Down Memory Lane' feature
Kendall, nd., 9
Horne's Guide, 73rd edn, nd.
Horne's Guide, 1895, 1921, 1939
Daysh, 1958, 147-96

BOARDING HOUSES:
Horne's Guide, 1895, 1921, 1939
Whitby Official Guide, 1938, 1966,
    1971

TRAINS & PADDLE-STEAMERS:
Belcher, 1836
Bairstow, 1989
Lidster, 1983, 29ff
Godfrey, nd.
WG 2/8/1873
Body, 1971, 185
Robinson, 1860, 196

WHAT THE VISITORS DID:
Robinson, 1860, 153-4
Horne's Guide, 1895, 1921, 1939
Daysh, 1958
White and Whitworth, 1999, 57-85

FOSSIL HUNTING:
BM Mesozoic Fossils
White's Directory, 1858
Slater's Directory, 1864
Bigland, 1812, 335-9
Head, 1836, 289-90
Browne, 1949, 2-4, 9-10
Gents. Mag. XXIX, 1759; XXX, 1760

GEOLOGY:
Young, 1817, 769ff
Young & Bird, 1822
Simpson, 1843
Simpson, 1855
Simpson, 1856
Browne, 1949, 20-3, 25-6
Hemingway, Wilson & Wright, 1958
Daysh, 1958, 1-47
Wilson, 1948, 17-52

THE REGATTA:
English, 1931
Wigglesworth, 1987, ix
Regatta Programme, 1990

TOURISM TODAY:
'Scarborough, Whitby, Filey, Holiday

92' brochure
Horne's Guide, 73rd edn.

Chapter 9
**WHITBY, LITERARY
& CULTURAL:**
Browne 1949
Whitby Repository, ns III, 1833, 129-33
Lit. & Phil. Ann. Rep., 2000, 31-2 and
    correspondence
Whellan, 1859, 301-5
Whitworth, 1991

LITERARY CONNECTIONS:
Eagle & Carnell, 1977, 287, 337
Shaw Jeffrey, 1952, 113-22
Lit. & Phil. Ann. Rep. 1990, 28
Kendall, nd.
Smales, 1867
Keighley, 1957
Whitworth, 1991, 39
Shaw, 1990, 12

CAPTAIN COOK:
Shaw Jeffrey, 1952, 93-5
Stamp & Stamp, 1981
Guidebook, The Captain Cook
    Memorial Museum, nd.
Lit. & Phil. Ann. Rep., 1981, 16-24
Lit. & Phil. Ann. Rep., 1984, 17-21
Cobbe, 1979
Cordingly, 1988

HISTORIANS:
Shaw Jeffrey, 1952, 106-7, 107-8
Young, 1817, 637-8, 869-70
Browne, 1949, 20-2
Atkinson, 1874
Atkinson, 1879
Atkinson, 1882
Atkinson, 1891
Atkinson, 1894
Marsden, 1974, 90ff
Bateman, 1861, 204ff
Gaskin, 1909
Weatherill, 1908
Barker, 1989

PUBLICATIONS:
English, 1931
Young, 1817, 637-8
UBD, 1798
Robinson, 1860, 201
Smales, 1867
Keighley, 1957
Whitby Repository, 1825-33, 1866-8
Whitby Magazine, 1827-9
Whitby Panorama, 1827-8

ARTISTS & PHOTOGRAPHERS:
Humble, 1972
Bullamore, 1976
Mallalieu, 1976
English, 1931
Bagshawe, 1933

Pile, 1979
Phillips & Sons, exhibition catalogues
    of the Staithes Group, 1976-8
Hemming, 1988, 187
Lit. & Phil. Ann. Rep., 1984, 26-7
Browne, 1949, 55-7
Eglon Shaw, 1974, 1978
Shaw, 1990
Hiley, 1979
Wilcock, 2011, 34-7

NEWSPAPERS:
English, 1931
Kendall, nd., 16
Robinson, 1860, 201
Gibson, 1987, 57
White's Directory, 1858, 622, 630
Slater's Directory, 1864, 717
PO Directory, 1879, 321
WG 31/3/1978

THEATRES:
Young, 1817, 636
Young, 1840, 252
Whitby Repository, 1867
Baines, 1823, 575
Robinson, 1860, 199
Beresford, 1968, 171n.
Cruickshank, 1985, 171
Cheyne, 2007, 18-26

**LITERARY & PHILOSOPHICAL
    SOCIETY:**
Browne, 1949
Brears & Davies, 1989, 16-18
Robinson, 1860, 155, 170-1

MUSEUM, ART GALLERY & LIBRARY:
Browne, 1949, *passim*
Whitby Magazine, 1827, 29, 225-8
Robinson, 1860, 155-61
Head, 1836, 290-1
Brears & Davies, 1989, 20, 26, 92, 97
Browne, 1949, 43f
Lit. & Phil. Ann. Rep.. 1980, 16-19
Pannett Art Gallery Catalogue, nd.
Robinson, 1860, 153-5
Young, 1817, 638-9
Horne's Guide, 1921

Chapter 10
FOLKLORE OF THE SEA:
Shaw Jeffrey, 1919, 42-8, 49-56
Shaw Jeffrey, 1923, 134-43
BM Cotton MSS

FOLKLORE OF THE TOWN:
Hartley & Ingleby, 1972, 8-10, 122-5,
    144-52
Sharpe, 1992, 10; 1996, 174
RCHM, 1987, 218
Shaw Jeffrey, 1919, 25-32
Shaw Jeffrey, 1923, 38-45, 130-6,

173-84
Atkinson, 1908, 81ff
Whitby Magazine, II, 1828
Brears, 1989, 63-4
Charlton, 1779, 32
WG 29/5/1981

GHOSTS & SPECTRES:
Shaw Jeffrey, 1919, 19-24
Shaw Jeffrey, 1923, 167-72
Norway, 1903, 139
Charlton, 1779, 32
English, 1931
Young, 1817, 883
Whitby Repository, 4, 1828
Whitby Repository, ns 1, 1831
Atkinson, 1908, 219

FUNERALS:
Shaw Jeffrey, 1952, 55, 65-70
Young, 1817, 884
Hartley & Ingleby, 1972, 125
Brears, 1987, 191-6
Brears, 1989, 196-9
Norway, 1903, 116-17
Litten, 1991

'VESSEL-CUPS':
Brears, 1989, 194
Hartley & Ingleby, 1972, pl.260
Shaw Jeffrey, 1919, 84-8
Gents. Mag. LXXXI, 1811, 423
Brears, 1987, 160, 172-8
Young, 1817, 878-9

LOCAL DELICACIES:
Brears, 1987, 114, 164, 175
Hartley & Ingleby, 1972, 126-7
Horne's Guide, 1921, 1939
Mason & Brown, 2007, 63-109

GINGERBREAD:
Young, 1817, 880
Hartley & Ingleby, 1972, 126
Brears, 1987, 175
Horne's Guide, 1895

QUOITS:
Hartley & Ingleby, 1972, 131-2
WG 19/3/82
Robinson, 1860, 200
Hartley & Ingleby, 1981, 199

SWORD DANCES:
Young, 1817, 880-1
Gents. Mag. LXXXI, 1811, 423-4
Hartley & Ingleby, 1972, 126
Shaw Jeffrey, 1919, 87-8
Shaw Jeffrey, 1923, 193-8
Sharp, nd.

PLOUGH-STOTS:
Shaw Jeffrey, 1923, 193-201
Brears, 1987, 158-60
Walker, 1814, Pl.XI

BIBLIOGRAPHY

The best sources of books on Whitby are the Local Collection of Whitby Library and the Library of the Whitby Literary & Philosophical Society, kept in the Kendall Room at Whitby Museum. The Annual Reports of the Literary & Philosophical Society over the years themselves offer a range of interesting snippets and articles. Back numbers of the *Whitby Gazette* newspaper are very valuable for all sorts of details back to the mid-19th century; before that *The Whitby Repository* and *The Gentleman's Magazine* contain much of interest. Whitby Abbey is covered by many documents in the Public Record Office; these are most readily accessible through the many Calendars, eg. Letters and Papers of Henry VIII, which are to be found in most good libraries and now increasingly online. Other public records are rather scattered; wills and probate inventories are to be found in the Borthwick Institute of Historical Research at York, which is also the Diocesan Registry. Other documents are in the North Yorkshire Record Office in Northallerton. Probate inventories for the 18th century are listed in Vickers, 1986.

Allason-Jones, L., *Roman Jet in the Yorkshire Museum* (1996)
Anon., *Rules of the Public Dispensary at Whitby Instituted in the Year 1786* (1787)
Anon., *Reed's Guide to Whitby … with an essay on sea bathing*, 12th edn., nd.
Anon., *The Stranger's and Visitant's Guide to Whitby* (1849)
Anon., *Picturesque Pocket Companion* (1850)
Atkinson, D.H., *Ralph Thoresby the Topographer; His Town and Times*, Vol. 1 (1885), 174-5
Atkinson, F., *Industrial Archaeology of North-East England*, 2 vols. (1974)
Atkinson, J.C., *Cleveland Past and Present* (1874)
Atkinson, J.C., *The Whitby Chartulary*, Surtees Society (1878-9)
Atkinson, J.C., *A Handbook to Ancient Whitby and its Abbey* (1882)
Atkinson, J.C., *Forty Years in a Moorland Parish* (1891, 1908)
Atkinson, J.C., *Memorials of Old Whitby* (1894)
Ayers, B., *Excavations at Chapel Lane Staith, 1978*, Hull Old Town Report Series, 3; East Riding Archaeologist, 5 (1979)
Backhouse, J., *The Lindisfarne Gospels* (1981)
Bagshawe, J.R., *The Wooden Ships of Whitby* (1933)
Baines, E., *History, Directory & Gazetteer of the County of York …*, Vol. 2, East & North Ridings (1823)
Baines, S., *The Yorkshire Mary Rose: the ship General Carleton of Whitby*, (2010)
Bairstow, M., *Railways around Whitby* (1989)
Bairstow, M., *Railways around Whitby, Volume 2* (1996)
Barker, R., *The Book of Whitby* (1989)
Barrow, A., *The Whaling Trade of North-East England 1750-1850* (2001)
Bassett, M.G., 'Formed Stones', Folklore and Fossils (1982)
Bateman, T., *Ten Years' Diggings in Celtic and Saxon Grave Hills* (1861, repr. 1978), 239-41
Bateson, C., *The Convict Ships 1787-1868* (1959)
Bebb, P., *Life in Regency Whitby* (2000)
Belcher, H., *Whitby & Pickering Railway. A Stranger's Guide for a Summer Day's Excursion from Scarborough to Pickering and thence by the railway to Whitby* (1843)

Belcher, H., *The Scenery of the Whitby and Pickering Railway* (1836, reprinted 1976)

Bell, G., *Whitby, Pickering & Scarborough Railway; early Victorian Guides* (2008)

Bell, T., 'A Roman Signal Station at Whitby', *Archaeological Journal*, 155, 303-22 (1823)

Beresford, J. (ed.), *The Diary of a Country Parson*, 2, 1782-1787 (1968)

Beresford, M. & Finberg, H.P.R., *English Medieval Boroughs: A Handlist* (1973)

Bigland, J., *The Beauties of England & Wales, XVI, Yorkshire* (1812)

Binns, J., 'Sir Hugh Cholmley: Whitby's Benefactor or Beneficiary?', *Northern History*, XXX, 86-104 (1994)

Blair, P.H., *Bede's Ecclesiastical History of the English Nation and its Importance Today*, Jarrow Lecture (1959)

Body, G., *British Paddle Steamers* (1971), 185

Breakell, W., *Old Pannier Tracks* (1982)

Brears, P., *Traditional Food in Yorkshire* (1987)

Brears, P., *North Country Folk Art* (1989)

Brears, P. & Davies, S., *Treasures for the People; The Story of Museums and Galleries in Yorkshire and Humberside* (1989)

Bridbury, A.R., *England and the Salt Trade in the Later Middle Ages* (1955)

British Museum (Natural History), *British Mesozoic Fossils* (1975)

Browne, H.B., *Chapters of Whitby History 1823-1946* (1946)

Browne, H.B., *The Story of Whitby Museum* (1949)

Buchannan, M., *George Weatherill: His Family and Their Art* (1950)

Bullamore, C.P., *Scarborough & Whitby Watercolourists* (1975)

Calendar of Patent Rolls 1 & 2 Philip & Mary (1555), 257-8

Cary, J., *Cary's New Itinerary* (1798)

Charlton, L., *The History of Whitby and of Whitby Abbey* (1779)

Chatfield, M., *Churches the Victorians Forgot*, 2nd edn. (1989), 151-4

Cheyne, E., *Whitby in the Limelight; a History of the Theatre in Whitby*, 2nd ed. (2007)

Clarke, B.W. & Soulsby, J., *The Story of Grosmont: Church and Village* (1975)

Clifton-Taylor, A., *Another Six English Towns* (1984)

Clowes, W.L., *The Royal Navy: A History from the Earliest Times to the Present*, III (1898), 63

Coates, B.R., 'The Living Standards of Jet Workers in Victorian Whitby', unpublished BA dissertation, University of Salford (1983)

Cobbe, H. (ed.), *Cook's Voyages and Peoples of the Pacific* (1979)

Colgrave, B. & Mynors, R.A.B. (eds.), *Bede: The Ecclesiastical History of the English People* (1969)

Collingwood, R.G. & Wright, R.P., *Roman Inscriptions of Britain* (1965), no. 721

Collingwood, W.G., *Northumbrian Crosses of the Pre-Norman Age* (1927), 59ff.

Colvin, H.M., *A Biographical Dictionary of British Architects* (1995)

Cooke, G.A., *Topographical and Statistical Description of the County of York* (1810)

Coppack, G., *English Heritage Book of Abbeys and Priories* (1990)

Cordingly, D. (ed.), *Capt. James Cook, Navigator* (1988)

Counsell, D., *A Short History of Grosmont* (1981)

Craig, R. & Jarvis, R., *Liverpool Registry of Merchant Ships*, Chetham Society, Vol. 15 (1967)

Cramp, R., 'Excavations at the Saxon Monastic Sites of Wearmouth and Jarrow, co. Durham: an Interim Report', *Medieval Archaeology*, 13 (1969), 21-66

Cramp, R., 'Anglo-Saxon Monasteries of the North', in *Scottish Archaeological Forum*, 5 (1973), 112-14

Cramp, R.J., 'Monastic Sites' in D.M. Wilson (ed.), *The Archaeology of Anglo-Saxon England* (1976), 223-9

Credland, A.G., *Henry Redmore of Hull, Marine Artist 1820-87* (1987)

Cruickshank, D., *A Guide to the Georgian Buildings of Britain and Ireland* (1985)

Daniels, R., 'The Anglo-Saxon Monastery at Church Close, Hartlepool, Cleveland', *Archaeological Journal*, 145 (1988), 158-210

Darby, H.C. & Maxwell, I. S., *The Domesday Geography of Northern England* (1962)

Davidson, C., *The World of Mary Ellen Best* (1985)

Daysh, G.H.J. (ed.), *A Survey of Whitby and the Surrounding Area* (1958)

Department of the Environment, *List of Buildings of Special Architectural or Historical Interest. Urban District of Whitby* (1972)

Dunbar, J.G. (ed.), *Sir William Burrell's Northern Tour 1758* (1997), 40-2

Dykes, J., *Yorkshire's Whaling Days* (1980)

Eagle, D. & Carnell, H., *The Oxford Literary Guide to the British Isles* (1977)

East, W.G., 'The Historical Geography of the Town, Port, and Roads of Whitby', *The Geographical Journal*, LXXX (1932), 484-97

Egan, G., 'Post-medieval Britain and Ireland in 1988', *Post-Medieval Archaeology*, 23 (1989)

Eglon Shaw, W., *Frank Meadow Sutcliffe, Photographer; A Selection of his Work* (1974)

Eglon Shaw, W., *Frank Meadow Sutcliffe; A Second Selection* (1978)

Ekwall, E., *Oxford Dictionary of English Place Names*, 4th edn (1960)

Elgee, F., *Early Man in North-East Yorkshire* (1930)

Elgee, F. & H.W., *The Archaeology of Yorkshire* (1933)

Emmison, F.G., *Archives and Local History* (1974)

English, T.H., *An Introduction to the Collecting and History of Whitby Prints* (1931)

Farmer, D.H. (ed.), 'Eddius Stephanus: Life of Wilfrid' and 'Bede: Life of St. Cuthbert' in *The Age of Bede* (1983)

Farmer, P.G., *Scarborough Harbour and Borough from the 10th to the 16th Centuries* (1976)

Farmer, P.G., *Scarborough Harbour and Borough from the 10th to the 16th Centuries* (1976)

Fawcett, W., *George Townsend Andrews of York 'The Railway Architect'* (2011)

Finch, R., *Sailing Craft of the British Isles* (1976)

Finch, R., *The Ship Painters* (1975)

Frank, P., *Yorkshire Fisherfolk* (2002)

Freeman, J.M., *W.D. Caroe: His Architectural Achievement* (1990)

Gaskin, J. & Stamp, C., *Whitby Yards* (1990)

Gaskin, R.T., *The Old Seaport of Whitby*, 1909 (repr. 1985)

Gelling, M., *Signposts to the Past; Place Names and the History of England* (1978), 189

Gent, T., *A History of Hull* (1735)

Gentleman's Magazine, The, 1809, 513

Gentleman's Magazine, The, 1811, 423-4

Gentleman's Magazine, The, 1813, 633-4

Gentleman's Magazine, The, 1830, 113

Gentleman's Magazine, The, 1841, 87

Gibson, F., *Archaeologia*, X (1792), 124

Gibson, F., *Streanshall Abbey, or, the Danish Invasion* (1800)

Gibson, J. S. W., *Local Newspapers 1750-1920; A Select Location List* (1987)

Girouard, M., *The English Town* (1990)

Girouard, M., 'Moulded by the Sea' and 'Great Days of Trade', *Country Life*, 5 May 1988, 182-4 and 12 May 1988, 138-41

Godfrey, A., *Pleasure Steamers of Old Yorkshire*, nd.

Hadfield, C., *The Canals of Yorkshire and North East England* (1973), 327-8

Haigh, D.H., 'The Monasteries of S.Hieu and S.Hild', *Yorkshire Archaeological Journal*, 3 (1875), 349-91, esp. 370-2

Hall, I., *Samuel Buck's Yorkshire Sketchbook* (1979), 326

Harston, J.G., *A Plan of the Whitby Yards* (1989)

Hartley, M. & Ingilby, J., *Life in the Moorlands of North East Yorkshire* (1972)

Hartley, M. & Ingilby, J., *Life and Traditions in the Yorkshire Dales* (1981)

Hartley, W.C.E., *Banking in Yorkshire* (1975)

Haverfield, F., 'Notes on the Roman Coast Defences of Britain, Especially in Yorkshire', *Journal of Roman Studies*, 2 (1912), 201-14

Hayes, R.H., *Old Roads & Pannierways in North East Yorkshire* (1988)

Head, (Sir) G., *A Home Tour through the Manufacturing Districts of England in the Summer of 1835* (1836, repr. 1968)

Hemming, C., *British Painters of the Coast and Sea* (1988), 187

Higham, N., *The Northern Counties to AD 1000* (1986), 288-9

Hiley, M., *Frank Meadow Sutcliffe* (1979)

Holt, R., *Whitby Past and Present*, nd.

Hood, P., *Whitby Abbey*, 5th edn. (1950)

Hoole, K., *Railway Stations of the North East* (1985), 14-15, 102

Hoole, K., *North-Eastern Branch Line Termini* (1985), 139-78, 192

Hughes, E., *North Country Life in the Eighteenth Century; The North East 1700-1750* (1952)

Hugill, J., *A Prospectus of a Plan for Establishing a Ship-Building Company at Whitby* (1831)

Humble, A.F., 'An Old Whitby Collier', *Whitby Literary & Philosophical Society Report* (1972), 20-7

Humble, A.F., *The Rowing Life-Boats of Whitby* (1974)

Jackson, G., *The British Whaling Trade* (1978)

Jervoise, E., *The Ancient Bridges of the North of England* (1931)

Johnson, M., 'The Saxon Monastery at Whitby: past, present and future', in Carver, M. (ed.), *In Search of Cult* (1993)

Jones, S.K., 'A Maritime History of the Port of Whitby, 1700-1914', University of London unpublished PhD thesis (1982)

Joy, D., *Whitby and Pickering Railway* (1969)

Keighley, M., *Whitby Writers – Writers of Whitby and District 1867-1949* (1957)

Kendall, H.P., *History of the Abbey of Whitby* (1932)

Kendall, H.P., *The Story of Whitby Jet; Its Workers from the Earliest Times* (1936)

Kendall, H.P., *The Streets of Whitby and their Associations* (1938, 2nd edn. 1948)

Kendall, H.P., *Whitby in Literature*, nd.

Le Patourel, H.E.J., *The Moated Sites of Yorkshire*, Medieval Archaeology Monograph 5 (1973)

Letters and Papers, Foreign and Domestic, of Henry VIII, vol. 14 (1539), 576, 682-3

Lidster, J.R., *The Scarborough & Whitby Railway* (1977)

Lidster, J.R., *Yorkshire Coast Lines* (1983)

Lidster, J.R., *The Whitby, Redcar and Middlesbrough Union Railway* (1994)

Litten, J., *The English Way of Death* (1991)

Long, A. & R., *A Shipping Adventure. Turnbull Scott & Company, 1872-1972* (1974)

Lubbock, B., *The Arctic Whalers* (1937)

March, E.J., *Sailing Drifters* (1969)

March, E.L., *Inshore Craft of Britain in the Days of Sail & Oar* (1970)

Marsay, M., *Bombardment! The Day the East Coast Bled* (1999)

Marsden, B.M., *The Early Barrow Diggers* (1974), 36, 46, 90, 92

Marshall, G., 'Preserving the Ravenscar Alum Works', *Industrial Heritage* 9, no. 1 (1991)

Marshall, G., *Saltwick Alum Works; an Archaeological Interpretation*, Scarborough Archaeological & Historical Society Research Report 11 (1994)

Marshall, M.W. & Sparham, L., *Fishing: the Coastal Tradition* (1987)

Mason, L. & Brown, C., *From Eccles Cake to Hawkshead Wig; a Celebration of Northern Food* (2007)

McCall, B., *Whitby: Modern Seaport* (1988)

McKee, E., *Working Boats of Britain; their Shape and Purpose* (1983)

McMillan, M., *Whitby Jet Through the Years* (1992)

Miller, I. (ed.), *Steeped in History; the Alum Industry of North-East Yorkshire* (2002)

'Monastic Arts of Northumbria, The', *Arts Council Exhibition Catalogue* (1967)

Morris, J. (ed.), *Domesday Book, Yorkshire* (1986)

Morris, J. *The Story of the Whitby Lifeboats* (1989)

Morrison, A., *Alum: North East Yorkshire's fascinating story of the first chemical industry* (1981)

Mould, D., *Remember Scarborough 1914* (1978)

Muller, H., *Jet Jewellery and Ornaments* (1980)

Nelson, P., 'Liverpool Delft Ship-Bowls', *Transactions of the Historic Society of Lancashire and Cheshire*, 8 (1936), 113-18

Nicholson, A. & Morter, P., *Prospects of England* (1989), 120-31

Norway, A.H., *Highways and Byways in Yorkshire* (1903)

Ossowski, W., *The General Carleton Shipwreck, 1785 (Wrak Statku General Carleton, 1785)* (1903)

Page, W. (ed.), *The Victoria History of the County of York North Riding*, Vol. 2 (1923)

Paget Tomlinson, E.W. & Smith, R.B., *City of Liverpool Museums: A List of the Museums' Collection of Ship Models* (1967)

Peacock, A.J., *George Hudson 1800-1871. The Railway King*, nd.

Peers, C. & Ralegh Radford, C., 'The Saxon Monastery of Whitby', *Archaeologia*, 89 (1943), 27-88

Pevsner, N., *The Buildings of England; Yorkshire, the North Riding* (1966), 387-400

Pile, A.T., *Buildings of Old Whitby* (1979)

Platt, C., *The Monastic Grange in Medieval England* (1969)

Platt, C., *The Abbeys and Priories of Medieval England* (1984)

Platt, C., *Whitby Abbey* (English Heritage guidebook) (1985)

Potter, G.W.J., *A History of the Whitby and Pickering Railway* (1906, repr. 1969)

Rahtz, P.A., 'Whitby 1958', *Yorkshire Archaeological Journal*, 160 (1962), 605-18

Rahtz, P.A., 'Whitby 1958, Site Two', *Yorkshire Archaeological Journal*, 165 (1967), 72-3

Raistrick, A., *Quakers in Science and Industry* (1968)

Raistrick, A., *Industrial Archaeology* (1972)

RCHM(E), *Houses of the North York Moors* (1987)

Reed, S., *Sketches of Whitby, its scenery and other attractions*, nd.

Rhodes, S.M., *Ravenscar; the town that never was* (1998)

Richardson, G., *T. Watson Photographer of Lythe, near Whitby, est. 1892* (1992)

Rigold, S.E., 'Litus Saxonum – the Shore forts as mission stations' in D.E. Johnston (ed.), *The Saxon Shore*, CBA Research Report, no. 18 (1977), 70-5

Robinson, F. K., *Whitby: Its Abbey and the Principal Parts of the Neighbourhood ...* (1860)

Robinson, R., *A History of the Yorkshire Coast Fishing Industry, 1780-1914* (1987)

Robinson, R.N.W., 'The Fish Trade in the Pre-Railway Era: The Yorkshire Coast 1780-1840', *Northern History*, XXV (1989), 223-34

Rodway, E., *Whitby in 1851*, nd.

Rosenfeld, S., *The Georgian Theatre of Richmond Yorkshire and its circuit: Beverley, Harrogate, Kendal, Northallerton, Ulverston and Whitby* (1984)

Runciman, W., *Collier Brigs and their Sailors* (1925), 70, 105, 110, 183, 188

Russett, A., *George Chambers 1803-1840 His Life and Work* (1996)

Sharp, C.J., *The Sword-Dances of Northern England*, pt.II, nd.

Sharpe, E., *Architectural Parallels, or the Progress of Ecclesiastical Architecture in England through the Twelfth and Thirteenth Centuries* (1868)

Sharpe, J.A., *Witchcraft in Seventeenth-Century Yorkshire: Accusations and Countermeasures*, Borthwick Papers, 81 (1992), 10

Sharpe, J.A., *Instruments of Darkness. Witchcraft in England 1550-1750* (1996), 174

Shaw, M., *Frank Meadow Sutcliffe, Photographer; A Third Selection* (1990)

Shaw, M., *Frank Meadow Sutcliffe, A Fourth Selection* (1998)

Shaw Jeffrey, P., *Whitby Lore and Legend* (1919)

Shaw Jeffrey, P., *Whitby Lore and Legend*, 2nd edn. (1923)

Shaw Jeffrey, P., *Whitby Lore and Legend*, 3rd edn. (1952)

Simeon of Durham, Rolls Series, 75, A&B, 1, 111, 296; 2, 201-2

Simper, R., *Beach Boats of Britain* (1984)

Simpson, M., *The Fossils of the Yorkshire Lias described from nature* (1855)

Smales, G., *Whitby Authors and their Publications* (1867)

Smith, A.H., *English Place-Name Society, Vol. V, Place-Names of the North Riding of Yorkshire* (1928)

Spratt, D.A. & Harrison, B. J. D. (eds.), *The North York Moors Landscape Heritage* (1989)

Stammers, M.K., 'Liverpool Delft Ship-Bowls – the Maritime Historian's View', in L.L. Lipski (ed. M. Archer), *Dated English Delftware; Tin-Glazed Earthenware 1600-1800* (1984), 304-6

Stamp, T.&C., *William Scoresby, Arctic Scientist* (1975)

Stamp, T.&C., *Captain Cook and his ships* (1981)

Starkey, D.J., *British Privateering Enterprise in the Eighteenth Century* (1990)

Stell, C., *An Inventory of Nonconformist Chapels and Meeting-Houses in the North of England* (RCHM(E)) (1994)

Stenton, F.M., *Anglo-Saxon England* (1971)

Sutcliffe, F.M., *A Quaint Picture of Whitby; the Town of Whitby, October the 28th, 1717* (1949)

Sythes, D.G., *Around Whitby* (1997)

Sythes, D.G., *Whitby; the Second Selection* (1999)

Thomas, C., *The Early Christian Archaeology of North Britain* (1971)

Tindale, J., *Fishing out of Whitby* (1987)

Tindale, J., 'Sandsend's Roman Cement', *Industrial Heritage* 8, no.3 (1990)

Turton, R.B., *The Alum Farm* (1938)

Vale, E., *The Mail Coach Men of the late Eighteenth Century* (1960)

Vickers, N., *A Yorkshire Town of the Eighteenth Century; Probate Inventories of Whitby, North Yorkshire 1700-1800* (1986)

Waites, B., *Moorland & Vale-Land Farming in North-East Yorkshire; The Monastic Contribution in the Thirteenth and Fourteenth Centuries*, Borthwick Papers No.32 (1967)

Waites, B., 'The Monastic Settlement of North-East Yorkshire', *Yorkshire Archaeological Journal*, XL (1961), 478-95

Walker, D.M., *A Talk on Ship Models* (1946)

Walker, D.M., *The Panorama of Whitby Shipping* (1960)

Walker, D.M., *Whitby Shipping* (1960)

Walker, D.M., *Whitby Fishing* (1973)

Walker, G., *The Costume of Yorkshire* (1814), repr. 1978

Ward-Jackson, C.H., *Ship Portrait Painters*, National Maritime Museum Monographs & Reports, no.35 (1978)

Waters, C., *Whitby; a Pictorial History* (1992)

Watts, J.J., 'The Age of the Mule (*c*.1875-1930)', *Whitby Literary & Philosophical Society Annual Report* (1988)

Welford, R., 'Whitby, Local Ship Assignments', *Proceedings of the Society of Antiquaries of Newcastle on Tyne*, 3rd ser., 3, 29-30

Whelan, E., 'The Corn Windmills of Scarborough and District', in Whitworth (1999)

Whitby Magazine, The, 1, 1827 to 3, 1829

Whitby Repository, The, os 1, 1825 to 6, 1830; ns 1, 1831 to 3, 1833; ns 1, 1866-7 to 2, 1867-8

White, A., 'Finds from the Anglian Monastery at Whitby', *Yorkshire Archaeological Journal*, 56 (1984), 33-40

White, A., *The Buildings of Georgian Whitby* (1995)

White, A., 'The Victorian Development of Whitby as a Seaside Resort', *The Local Historian*, Vol. 28, 2, (1998) 78-93

White, A., 'Wish you were here! The 1883 Holiday Journal of George Eaton of Norwich', in Whitworth (1999)

White, A., 'Whitby Carriers', *Whitby Literary & Philosophical Society Annual Report*, (2006), 40-1

White, A. & R. *The Whitby and Pickering Railway; the Horse-Drawn Era 1833-1847* (2017)

White, A.J., 'Copper-Alloy Combs from Britain and Frisia', *Medieval Archaeology*, 32 (1988), 212-13

White, A.J., 'Carvings of Ships in Whitby Parish Church', *Folk Life* (1990), 46-50; also published in more detail as a booklet with more illustrations; *Carvings of Ships in Whitby Parish Church* (2002)

White, W., *A Month in Yorkshire* (1858)

Whitworth, A., *Whitby as they saw it* (1991)

Whitworth, A., *A to Z of Whitby History* (2002)

Whitworth, A., *Long Live the King! George Hudson and Whitby* (2002)

Whitworth, A., *The A to Z of Whitby Yards* (2003)

Whitworth, A. (ed.), *Aspects of the Yorkshire Coast* (1999)

Whitworth, A. (ed.), *Aspects of the Yorkshire Coast 2* (2000)

Wigglesworth, N., *Victorian and Edwardian Boating from old photographs* (1987)

Wilcock, R., 'Photographers of Whitby', by *Whitby Literary & Philosophical Society Annual Report* (2011)

Willan, T.S., *The English Coasting Trade 1600-1750* (1938)

Williamson, G.C., *Trade Tokens Issued in the Seventeenth Century in England, Wales and Ireland …* (1889-91, repr. 1967)

Wilson, D.M., *Anglo-Saxon Ornamental Metalwork 700-1100 in the British Museum* (1964)

Wilson, G., *Fishing Boats of Whitby and District* (1998)

Wilson, K., *The Wreck of the Rohilla* (1981)

Wood, G.B., 'When Local Pound Notes were Best: Banking Houses of Old Whitby', *Country Life*, 20 October 1960, 910-13

Woodwark, T. H., *The Parish Church of St Mary, Whitby* (1923)

Woodwark, T. H., *The Proprietary Chapel of Saint Ninian in Whitby* (nd)

Young, G., *A History of Whitby*, 2 vols. (1817)

Young, G., *A Picture of Whitby and its Environs* (1824, 2nd edn. 1840)

Young G. & Bird, J., *A Geological Survey of the Yorkshire Coast* (1822)

INDEX

Numbers in **bold** refer to illustration page numbers.